# JEWISH LAW
## and
# THE NEW
# REPRODUCTIVE
# TECHNOLOGIES

*Edited by*

EMANUEL FELDMAN
and
JOEL B. WOLOWELSKY

KTAV PUBLISHING HOUSE, INC.
HOBOKEN, NEW JERSEY

Library of Congress Cataloging-in-Publication Data

Jewish law and the new reproductive technologies / edited by Emanuel Feldman and Joel
B. Wolowelsky.
    p.   cm.
    Includes bibliographical references.
    ISBN 0-88125-586-6
    1. Human reproduction (Jewish law)  2. Fetus—Legal status, laws, etc.
(Jewish law)  3. Human reproduction—Religious aspects—Judaism.  4. Human
reproductive technology—Religious aspects—Judaism.  I. Feldman, Emanuel,
1927–   II. Wolowelsky, Joel B.
LAW <GENERAL Jewish 1997>
296.3'66—dc21
                                               97-24080
                                                  CIP

Manufactured in the United States of America

# Table of Contents

# Introduction

EMANUEL FELDMAN and JOEL B. WOLOWELSKY

We live in an age of technological wonders and miracles. Generations past could not possibly have imagined to what extent twentieth-century man would be able to decipher the mysteries of creation and control the focus of nature.

For the most part, these advances pose few religious challenges. After all, man and woman are commanded at the dawn of creation to "fill the earth and subdue it." "Man reaching for the distant stars," wrote the late Rabbi Joseph B. Soloveitchik ("The Lonely Man of Faith," *Tradition*, 7:2, Summer 1965), "is acting in harmony with his nature which was created, willed, and directed by his Maker. It is a manifestation of obedience to rather than rebellion against God."

Nonetheless, one area of recent scientific advance confronts us with the challenge of humility. It is man, woman, and God who join together to create a new human child, says the Talmud. Now, with the advent of the New Reproductive Technologies, the doctor-scientist has joined the team, so to speak. Suddenly, man is not only controlling nature, but it creating as well.

All this presents us with challenges on philosophical as well as practical levels. More than a quarter century ago, Azriel Rosenfeld raised for the readers of *Tradition* some of these questions, and others since then have offered insights into the halakha's approach to these issues. Indeed, it is remarkable—as indicated in the *Tradition* articles collected in this volume—that the sources of old still continue to offer insights into the most contemporary of problems.

Dr. Feldman, editor of *Tradition,* is rabbi emeritus of Atlanta's Congregation Beth Jacob and editor of the Rashi translation project of the Ariel Institute in Jerusalem.

Dr. Wolowelsky, associate editor of *Tradition,* is Chairman of Advanced Placement Studies at the Yeshivah of Flatbush.

# 1

# The Rabbinic Conception of Conception: An Exercise in Fertility

EDWARD REICHMAN

The extraordinary technological advances of this century have been applied with full force to the field of science, and in particular to genetics and reproductive medicine. Man now has more control over his own reproduction than ever before in history, such that the old notion of the doctor playing God has taken on new meaning. In the ultimate form of *imitatio dei*, it now appears that just as God creates, so does man. We currently have the capability to isolate a single sperm, unite it in-vitro with an egg, and test the resultant embryo for genetic abnormalities before subsequent implantation into a human being for the completion of gestation.[1]

Although all acknowledge the value of this technology, it is not without cost. Whereas the Talmud mentions only three partners in creation (see below), the husband, the wife, and God, current reproductive practices have expanded the list of potential partners to include the sperm donor, egg donor, surrogate mothers, and soon, with the application of genetic splicing to human gametes, the partial gene donor. If our limited experience is any measure, then introducing more partners clearly introduces more complications, be they emotional, financial, legal or ethical.

Dr. Reichman, Assistant Professor in the Department of Epidemiology and Social Medicine, Division of Philosophy and History of Medicine, Albert Einstein College of Medicine, and attending physician at Montefiore Medical Center, received *semikha* from Yeshiva University's Rabbi Isaac Elchanan Theological Seminary.

To solve these ethical dilemmas, secular ethicists utilize philosophical principles, some with historical precedent, others simply products of imagination. In either case, ethicists are in no way bound to the ideas of the past. We, however, as Orthodox Jews who subscribe to the halakhic process and live by the words of *Hazal*, employ the past to solve the dilemmas of the present and future. We turn to our predecessors for both halakhic and ethical guidance.

All contemporary halakhic discussions of reproductive technology cite sources from antiquity to the renaissance to modern times. As the understanding of reproductive anatomy and physiology has changed throughout the centuries, the author of each source, depending on the historical period, assumes a unique understanding of embryology and reproductive medicine. Therefore, an awareness of the embryological theories contemporary with each author may aid our understanding of his discussion of medical or scientific ideas. Furthermore, if the context of the source is halakhic, it may enhance our appreciation of the halakhic issues with which each source is dealing. This knowledge can perhaps assist current *poskim* in their utilization of rabbinic source material for incorporation into medical halakhic responsa. I therefore submit that we pause for a moment from addressing modern halakhic dilemmas of reproductive technology and turn our eyes backward to see how our predecessors understood the conception of conception.[2]

This article discusses selected passages from Jewish literature from antiquity to modern times which explicitly address or allude to theories relating to reproduction. The sources will be discussed in their own right as well as placed in a medical historical context. Although rabbinic sources cover the gamut of issues of reproduction and heredity, three topics have been chosen for the purpose of illustration, each highlighting a different aspect of reproductive medicine. The first topic addresses the very nature of the male and female seeds, focusing largely on embryology: who contributes what to the fetus. The second section traces the history of artificial insemination, a matter of reproductive physiology, and contains sources often quoted in contemporary halakhic discussions. Therefore, the rabbinic sources in this section receive disproportionately greater treatment than the secular. The final section addresses a particular notion regarding reproductive anatomy. In each section the secular sources are discussed separately. In the first section only, in order to facilitate our objectives, the secular sources precede the Jewish.

## EMBRYOLOGY
### Secular Sources

Almost all major figures in the history of science in antiquity devoted time to the study of animal and human embryology.[3] As knowledge of anatomy[4] and physiology was limited, theories were based on simple observation and philosophical intuition. Analogies were often made to agriculture, the male seed being compared to the plant seed and the uterus to the nourishing earth.[5] The male contribution to conception was readily observable, as the male seed was emitted outside the body (more on the male seed below). The nature of the female contribution, however, was a matter of intense debate.

### Female Seed

Since the female seed was not visible to the naked eye and was not emitted externally, its very existence was a matter of conjecture. As a result, two competing theories evolved in antiquity which coexisted until pre-modern times.[6] Galen (130–200),[7] following in the footsteps of Hippocrates (4th-5th centuries B.C.E.),[8] maintained that both the male and female contributed seed. The exact identity of the female seed was in question, but he conjectured it might be located in the uterus. He also claimed that the male semen provides the material for the development of the nerves and the walls of the arteries and veins in the fetus, while the menstrual fluid is the source of the blood.[9] Aristotle, on the other hand, denied the existence of a female seed, claiming that only the male possessed seed. This seed provided the "form" and the "principle of the movement" of the fetus, while the female provided the material from which the fetus was formed, i.e., the menstrual blood.[10]

It can be argued which of these theories predominated throughout the middle ages, but the falsehood of Aristotle's theory was decisively demonstrated by William Harvey. Harvey

(1578–1657), best known for his description of the circulation of the blood, was also a pioneer in the field of embryology. While the ovum had not yet been described in his lifetime, he nonetheless postulated that all living beings must derive from eggs.[11] Aside from placing the first nail in the coffin of the theory of spontaneous generation,[12] Harvey superseded Aristotle and paved the path for Reinier De Graaf, who in 1672 first described the egg follicle.[13] The microscopic female human egg, as we now know it, was not described until 1827, when Ernst Von Baer published his classic description of the mammalian ovum.[14]

### Male Seed

There were three Greek theories regarding the origin of the sperm.[15] The encephalo-myelogenic doctrine claimed that the sperm was ultimately a derivative from the brain and traversed the spinal cord on its way to the male genital organs. The second theory, which Hippocrates advocated, was called the pangenesis doctrine and contended that the sperm was a derivative of the entire body. The sperm extracted from each limb would yield the corresponding limb in the fetus. Aristotle supported the hematogenic doctrine, claiming that the seed originated from blood, and was in fact nothing but blood in a certain state of coagulation.

Although a male seed was always acknowledged, it was not until 1677 that Antony Von Leeuwenhoek first visualized human spermatozoa under the microscope.[16]

### Preformation and Epigenesis[17]

The discovery of egg follicles by De Graaf and spermatozoa by Leeuwenhoek gave birth to two opposing theories regarding the embryological development of the fetus in utero. Some scholars maintained that the fetus formed in a stepwise fashion with the development of one organ or limb preceding the next, i.e., epigenesis. Others believed that within the seed, either male or female, there existed a minuscule, complete, preformed being that simply enlarged during the course of gestation. These so-called preformationists were split into two camps, those claiming that the preformed child was within the female egg (ovists) and those claiming it was within the male sperm (animalculists).[18]

So convinced of this belief was one animalculist that he drew a diagram of a completely formed child crouched within the confines of one human sperm. This figure became known as the homunculus.[19] It is unclear exactly when the theory of preformation was disproved, but it had its supporters up to the late nineteenth century.

## JEWISH SOURCES[20]

Equipped with the historical background, we can approach the Jewish sources throughout the ages that address embryological theories explicitly and implicitly. For the sake of clarity, the sections on male and female seed are separated, as above. Since the same sources often discuss both seeds, there will be, by necessity, limited repetition. For the repeated sources, the bibliographical information will be referenced the first time the source is mentioned.

### Female Seed

The Talmudic source which serves as the foundation of all subsequent rabbinic discussions on embryology, especially with regard to the female seed, is found in *Gemara Nidda* (30a):

> Our Rabbis taught: There are three partners in the creation of man, God, the father and the mother. The father seminates (*mazria*) the white substance, from which are derived the bones, vessels (*gidim*),[21] fingernails, brain and the white of the eye. The mother seminates (*mezara'at*) the red substance, from which are derived the skin, flesh, hair and the black of the eye.[22] God provides the spirit (*ruah*), the soul (*neshama*),[23] the beauty of the features, vision for the eyes, hearing for the ears, speech for the mouth . . . and intelligence. When the time comes for a man to depart this world, God takes back his part, leaving behind the contributions of the mother and father.

It seems clear that the rabbis, similar to Galen and in contrast to Aristotle, clearly acknowledged both a male and female seed, the female seed appearing to be identified with the menstrual blood. It is interesting to note that the list of organs that are derived from the respective seeds roughly resembles that of Galen. However, even though Galen was a contemporary of R. Yehuda ha-Nasi, the compiler of the Mishna, there is absolutely no mention of Galen, or Hippocrates, for that matter, in the entire text of the Mishna and Talmud.[24] As a result, any suggestion of cross-cultural borrowing is purely speculative.

The next source appears in the Biblical commentary of R. Moses ben Nahman. Although Ramban is known for his exceptional Talmudic scholarship, he was also a practicing physician, purportedly at Montpellier,[25] a major center of medicine in the middle ages.[26] One of the few references we have to Ramban's medical practice states that he treated a non-Jew for infertility.[27] The Ramban comments on the phrase in *Vayikra*, "*Isha ki tazria ve-yalda zahar.*" The root of the word "*tazria*" is "*zera*," or seed, hence the translation could be, "When a woman emits seed." While most Biblical commentators interpret this phrase to mean "When a woman conceives," and thereby ignore the issue of the existence of the female seed, Ramban takes this opportunity to address rabbinic theories of embryology:

> . . . Although it says "when a woman emits seed" . . . the implication is not that the fetus is made from the female seed. For even though a woman has ovaries (*beitzim*) analagous to those of the male (*beitzei zahar*) [testicles], either no seed is made there, or the seed has nothing to do with the fetus. Rather, the term "*mezara'at*" refers to the uterine blood . . . that unites with male seed. In their opinion [*Gemara Nidda* above], the fetus is created from the blood of the woman and the white [semen] of the man, and both of them are called seed . . . and likewise is the opinion of the doctors regarding conception. The Greek philosophers thought that the entire body of the fetus derives from menstrual blood, and that the man only provides . . . form to the material.

The mere fact that Ramban mentions this embryological debate reflects that it was still a topic of discussion in his time. Here Ramban accepts the contribution of a female seed and identifies that seed with uterine blood, based on the passage in the *Gemara*. He states that this is also the position of the doctors. As we know that the Ramban was himself a physician, we ascribe greater authority to his statement. Although he mentions no names of specific doctors, he may be aligning the Talmudic position with the teachings of Galen. Ramban also clearly rejects what we know to be Aristotle's position.

R. Bahya ben Asher (13th century) follows Ramban in his interpretation of the phrase in *Vayikra*, but adds a novel explanation of the term "*tazria.*" It means, he says, "When a woman gives over the *zera.*" The *zera*, he maintains, is a deposit which is given to the woman by the man for safe-keeping, as a plant seed is deposited in the ground. In both cases the matured seed is to be returned from its repository when the time is right.[28] As mentioned above, the agricultural analogy is one that has been used since antiquity.

While Ramban claimed that a woman may or may not have her own seed independent of the menstrual blood, Rambam clearly acknowledges the existence of a female seed:

> . . . between the *heder* and the *prozdor*[29] lie the two ovaries of the woman and the pathways [?fallopian tubes] wherein her seed matures.[30]

Rambam does not, however, address whether this seed has any role in conception. This issue is discussed in the following sources.

R. Shimon ben Tsemah Duran (1360–1444), Tashbets, devotes a significant section of his philosophical work, *Magen Avot,* to the anatomy and physiology of reproduction. In this citation he confronts the issue of the female seed:

> Regarding whether the female seed has a role in conception, this has been debated by Aristotle and Galen. We have explained that *Hazal* say it has no role whatsoever in conception . . . philosophers have concluded that the female seed has no role in conception . . . and they reached the same conclusion that was received by *Hazal* from the prophets and teachings of the Torah.[31]

R. Duran later identifies the menstrual blood as the contribution of the female.

In contradistinction to the above source, which acknowledges an independent female seed but gives this seed no role in conception, the following reference grants a prominent role to this seed. This passage is excerpted from the work of Meir ben Isaac Aldabi (1310–1360), the grandson of R. Asher ben Yehiel, entitled *Shevilei Emuna.*[32]

. . . and next to the uterus are the woman's two ovaries . . . and from them the female seed flows into the cavity of the uterus. When the male seed is emitted into the uterus the female seed also is emitted from the ovaries and joins with the male seed (to form the fetus).[33]

This appears to be the first Jewish source that ascribes such significance to the female ovarian seed, and thus ends our discussion of Jewish sources prior to the works of Harvey and Leeuwenhoek. (see above). In summary, all the Jewish sources espouse the doctrine of the two seeds, both male and female, yet opinions differ as to the identity and contribution of the female seed. These sources are better understood in the context of the ongoing scientific debate in the secular world regarding the existence and nature of the female seed.

We now turn to Jewish references to embryology at a time when the scientific world had recently undergone major upheaval. The sperm had been identified, the existence of a female egg was universally accepted, although the egg itself had not yet been observed, and the theories of preformation and epigenesis were prevalent.

Tobias Cohn (1652–1729),[34] a graduate of the famous University of Padua,[35] was educated in this scientific milieu. His classic work, *Ma'ase Tuvia*, covers topics including botany, cosmology, and medicine, and the following passage on embryology reflects the climate of his time. As Cohn was well educated in rabbinic as well as scientific literature, his words are of particular interest:

Aristotle, who rejected the Torah of Moses, brought a number of disappointing proofs that menstrual blood is in place of the seed, and besides this, a woman has no other seed. However, recent physicians, who accept our holy Torah, have . . . brought other proofs which contradict his disappointing proofs. . . . The first proof is that one cannot deny the existence of a female seed, for it was not for naught that a woman was created with *beitzim* and pathways that transmit seed similar to a man.

There is almost no need for the proofs brought by the great physician Harvey on the existence of a female seed. . . . The great physicians of late maintain that the purpose of the ovaries (*beitzim*) is to give rise to tiny eggs (*beitzim*), similar to fish eggs, which have been seen with the microscope.[36]

This is probably the first Hebrew source that uses the term *beitza* to describe the female egg as we understand it today. In all previous sources, the term *beitzim* refers to the ovaries or testicles interchangeably, and the female seed is called simply her *zera*. Given an understanding of the history of embryology, this observation makes perfect sense, as it is only during this period that Harvey's theory of the existence of a female egg was developed.

A more detailed physiological description of conception is found in the anatomical work of Baruch Schick (1744–1808),[37] entitled *Tiferet Adam*. Schick is perhaps best known for translating Euclid's Geometry into Hebrew for the Vilna Gaon.[38] In this excerpt, the author, after discussing the passage from *Gemara Nidda*, mentions the single egg.[39]

> . . . in the body of the woman are found the ovaries . . . the seed emitted by the man . . . induces the emission of a single egg from the ovaries . . .

The next passage alludes to another embryological theory and stems from a question entertained by R. Yaakov Emden (d. 1776) regarding whether it was possible for a virgin to conceive in the absence of conjugal relations, e.g. bathhouse insemination (more on this topic below). In this passage he invokes the theory of preformation, in particular that of the animalculists, to answer the above question in the affirmative. The references to the male and female seeds are as follows:[40]

> . . . such a thing is decidedly not in the realm of the impossible . . . as *Hazal* said, "Maybe she conceived in the bathhouse?" [*Hagiga* 14b] . . . and this is compatible with the ideas of the scientists, who describe only a limited role for the female seed in conception (. . . but it is now clear that the female seed provides no material contribution to the fetus whatsoever . . . and this does not contradict what is written in the Torah, "*Isha ki tazria ve-yalda.*" See the commentary of Ramban on this verse and you will see that it is not a contradiction.)[41] They have found through the use of the glass [microscope] and other experiments that man, like birds and fish, is created from an egg in the ovary of the woman. And in the male

seed they have seen . . . the image of a tiny human being, complete with its limbs. . . .

R. Emden goes on to explain that the preformed fetus in the male seed receives its nourishment and sustenance, including warmth and moisture, from the female seed. It is interesting to note that he accepts the notion of the homunculus (preformation) and claims that this is in consonance with the commentary of Ramban. As mentioned above, Ramban granted no role to a female seed independent of the menstrual blood. However, Ramban does maintain, based on the *Gemara* in *Nidda*, that the menstrual blood does contribute materially to the fetus. This latter notion is not compatible with the theory of preformation. In any case, R. Emden incorporates the contemporary embryological theories into his halakhic discussion.

The final selection in this section comes from the work of Pinchas Eliyahu Hurwitz (1765–1821), *Sefer haBerit.* This work is a compilation of medical and scientific theories culled from sources in many languages, and served as a valuable resource for its Jewish audience, to whom many of these ideas were otherwise inaccessible. This accounts for the book's popularity and multiple reprintings. This selection gives a balanced view of the opposing embryological theories, while at the same time incorporating the teachings of *Hazal:*

> Some scholars have written that all the features of the entire human body, complete with its limbs, are found within the egg of the woman . . . and some scholars have written that within the seed of the man is the form of a minuscule human being, for when male seed . . . are viewed under the microscope small creatures can be seen within them moving to and fro. . . . God knows the truth of this matter. However, it is known in truth that the woman also emits seed, as the verse explicitly states, "*Isha ki tazria.*" And her seed is not white, but red, as *Hazal* have said, "The mother emits the red substance."[42]

In conclusion of the discussion of the female seed, it is apparent that these sources do not reflect a consensus of opinion regarding the identity and nature of the female seed. Many of the sources, irrespective of the theories they espouse, attempt to align their positions with the words of *Hazal*, in particular the passage from *Gemara Nidda*.

## Male Seed

At this point, we will analyze a selection of Jewish sources that address theories regarding the origin and nature of the male seed. Some of these sources have already been encountered in the above section on the female seed. We begin with a passage from the Talmud, from which can be inferred the understanding of the origin of the male seed:[43]

> Levi was sitting in a bathhouse and observed a man fall and strike his head. He said, "His brains were agitated (*nitmazmez*)" . . . Abaye said, "He has lost the ability to procreate."

According to Rashi, the implication is that an injury to the brain somehow affects the male seed. This is an allusion to the encephalo-myelogenic theory of the origin of the sperm (see above).[44]

In *Sefer haBahir*, a kabbalistic work attributed to R. Nehunia ben haKana (a first century *Tanna*), the reference to the encephalo-myelogenic doctrine is more explicit: "The spinal cord, which comes from the brain, enters the male organ (*amma*) and from there comes the seed."[45]

Meir ben Isaac Aldabi (1310–1360) (see above) mentions the encephalo-myelogenic as well as the pangenesis doctrine, but does not indicate which he advocates:

> The scientists have debated. Some say the seed comes from the brain, via the spinal cord, to the . . . testicles, and there it matures and whitens. The proof to this is that pain in the spine sometimes heals with emission of seed, and also, one whose spinal cord is severed cannot procreate. However, Hippocrates maintains that the seed is an extract from all the limbs of the body.[46]

Tashbets (1361–1444) (see above) refers to the pangenesis doctrine: "We must ascertain . . . if the seed derives from the entire body or not. Behold, the ancients have said this . . .".[47] But he ultimately rejects this in favor of the hematogenic doctrine of Aristotle, which he claims *Hazal* also espoused:

> . . . and this is their intent, z"l, when they said, "The seed is inter-
> mixed" (*mebalbel zarei*). The meaning of this phrase is that from all
> the limbs there is a combined power, not that each limb yields its
> corresponding limb [pangenesis doctrine] . . . this is their opinion,
> z"l, in agreement with the opinion of the philosopher [Aristotle].[48]

In summary up to this point, Jewish sources refer to all three
theories regarding the origin of the male seed.[49] We now shift our
attention to the period following the discoveries of Leeuwenhoek
and Harvey, when the theories of epigenesis and preformation
were prevalent.

Pinchas Eliyahu Hurwitz (1765–1821), in the passage cited
above, refers to the theory of preformation and mentions the position of the animalculists as well as the ovists. In the following
citation, he invokes the position of the animalculists in a novel
interpretation of a Talmudic passage.

> . . . and they have seen with a microscope that in the seed of a man
> . . . exist tiny creatures, whose form resembles that of man, and
> that are alive and move within the drop.

> With this we see how all the words of *Hazal* are to be believed and
> how all their words are truthful and just . . . even regarding those
> matters which seem far fetched or inconceivable. . . . Our Talmud
> treats this sin [*hotza'at zera le-vatala*] harshly, equating it to murder,
> as it is written, R. Eliezer ben Yaakov said that one who emits seed
> wastefully is considered as if he killed a soul . . . and so said R.
> Yitzchak and R. Ami in tractate *Nidda*. This statement seemed so
> far fetched in the eyes of the philosophers amongst our people . . .
> who were unaware of the looking glass mentioned above [micro-
> scope]. How could it be considered murder prior to the concep-
> tion of the child . . . when the human being had not yet appeared?
> . . . the seed at this time is only fluid from the brain[50] and is still
> substance without form. . . . But now, after it has been seen with
> the aforementioned instrument that living beings in the image of
> man move to and fro within the seed, it is remarkable . . . to hear
> such a thing. Every intelligent person would judge such a sin as
> truly equivalent to murder.[51]

While most Jewish sources accepted the theory of preformation, Baruch Schick (1744–1808) (see above) stood alone, I be-

lieve, in rejecting the theory of preformation in favor of epigenesis:

> The limbs of the body are not all formed at once, rather they grow one by one like a tree. . . . Some have said that the form of a small human being is found within the egg, and there is no place for their words. Still others have said that within the male seed is found the image of a tiny living being, their proof being that when the male seed is viewed under the microscope moving objects, like worms,[52] can be observed. They therefore say that these worms are in fact little human beings . . . This assertion is also baseless. First, if they are correct, why are there so many worms [sperm]? Second, the very form of the worm attests that it is not the likeness of a man.[53]

Despite Schick's rejection of the theory of preformation, it was still perpetuated by rabbinic sources, especially with reference to the prohibition of *hotza'at zera le-vatala*.[54] This may be due, in part, to the fact that while *Sefer haBerit* was a popular, widely read work, *Tiferet Adam* was more obscure.

In summary, Jewish sources run the gamut of embryological theories regarding the origins of the male seed. As with the female seed, attempts were made to align these theories with the words of *Hazal*, including areas of Halakha. An historical understanding of the various embryological theories contemporary with each of these sources gives us a better appreciation of each author's context and scientific frame of reference.

## ARTIFICIAL INSEMINATION

Artificial insemination[55] is a common treatment for infertility. Although the procedure has grown tremendously in popularity and application over the last two decades, the concept of intentionally injecting sperm into a woman for the purpose of impregnation dates back to at least the mid eighteenth century, when John Hunter successfully inseminated a woman whose husband had a severe form of hypospadias.[56] As early as 1934, Hermann Rohleder wrote the first history of the artificial impregnation of human beings.[57] However, since the widespread application of this procedure is, as stated, only relatively recent, it is in this period that we find the proliferation of rabbinic responsa dealing with every imaginable halakhic consequence of artificial insemination.[58] But what sources could there be in the Talmud or *Rishonim* that could possibly aid in the halakhic analysis of this seemingly novel procedure? To answer this question one must mention yet another form of artificial insemination, this one more indirect in nature. There was a widely held belief dating back to antiquity that a woman could become pregnant in a bathhouse, for it was thought that when a woman bathes in a bath into which a man had previously emitted sperm, she may conceive. The following section briefly traces the history of the notion of artificial insemination in both Jewish and non-Jewish sources from antiquity to the present.

## JEWISH SOURCES

Two early references to so-called "bathhouse insemination" have served as the source for virtually all contemporary halakhic discussions of modern artificial insemination. The first case is mentioned in the *Gemara Hagiga*[59] in the course of a discussion about whether a *kohen gadol,* who is prohibited from marrying any woman who is not a virgin, may marry a pregnant woman who claims she is still virginal.[60] How could a virgin become pregnant? Shmuel attests that it is possible to have intercourse without perforating the *betulim,* but the *Gemara* entertains another possibility, that of impregnation in the bathhouse, in which case the woman, still being a virgin, would be permitted to marry a *kohen gadol.*

The second case is mentioned in the *Alphabet of Ben Sira*[61] in reference to the nature of Ben Sira's birth. This narrative work, of questionable date and authorship (some date this work from the Geonic period), details the life of Shimon Ben Sira (second century B.C.E.), the author of *Divrei Shimon Ben Sira* (The Wisdom of Ben Sira). The relevant passage appears in the first section of this work, which is a biography of Ben Sira from his conception to the age of one year. The passage, apparently omitted in many editions, describes how the prophet Yirmiyahu was simultaneously both the father and grandfather of Ben Sira. Ben Sira's mother was Yirmiyahu's daughter. Yirmiyahu was forced by evil men to perform an act of onanism in a bathhouse, and his daughter conceived from his emissions when she inadvertently entered the same bath. Ben Sira was born seven months later,[62] the product of artificial insemination.[63] The text further mentions that it is no mere coincidence that the numerical value (gematria) of the Hebrew letters of "Sira" equals that of "Yirmiyahu," thereby hinting that Ben Sira is, in fact, the son of Yirmiyahu.

Not everyone accepted the veracity of the aforementioned story of Ben Sira's birth. Solomon Ibn Verga (15th–16th century) states in his historical narrative, *Shevet Yehuda,* that Ben Sira was the grandson of Yehoshua ben Yehotzadak and makes no mention of relation to Yirmiyahu.[64] R. David Ganz, the seventeenth century chronicler, claims that this story is mere exaggeration, as "I have not found it anywhere in the Talmud, and I have not heard from my teachers that it is found in any aggada or midrash.[65]

Assuming for our discussion the veracity of the passage in the *Alphabet of Ben Sira,* some important halakhic points can be derived, which explains why it has been so extensively quoted by subsequent *Rishonim* and *Aharonim.* Ben Sira is clearly assumed to be the product of Yirmiyahu and his daughter. Whether this was known to Yirmiyahu by *ruah ha-kodesh* or whether this is because Yirmiyahu's daughter was trusted to have been a virgin is unclear. In either case, despite the fact that Ben Sira is the product of an halakhically illicit relationship, nowhere does one find aspersions cast on his lineage, and never is he referred to as a *mamzer;* the implication is that only the marital act can create the prohibition of *arayot* and label the resultant child a *mamzer.* The relevance of this case to artificial insemination with donor sperm should be obvious. Secondly, Ben Sira was known as the son of Yirmiyahu. This fact implies that a child born from artificial insemination may be considered halakhically related to the sperm donor.

One of the earliest references to the case of Ben Sira is by R. Peretz ben Eliyahu of Corbeil (c.1295) in his glosses on *Sefer Mitzvot Katan* (also referred to as *Amudei Gola*).[66] He states that a woman need not refrain from sleeping on her husband's sheets while she is a *nidda* for fear that that she might bear a child from the remnant seed on the sheet and the child would be a *ben nidda.* However, R. Peretz does warn that a married woman should not sleep on the sheets slept on by a man other than her husband. Why R. Peretz differentiates between these two cases is a matter of halakhic import, but implicit in these statements is that R. Peretz acknowledged that a woman could become pregnant in this manner. He brings proof from the case of Ben Sira. Jacob Moellin (?1360–1427) also mentions the case of Ben Sira in *Likutei Maharil*, where it appears as a statement without particular halakhic context.[67]

More elaborate treatment of this topic is found in the responsa of Rav Shimon ben Tzemah Duran,[68] to whom a question was posed about a woman who claimed to have had a virginal conception. R. Duran, who was also a physician, was asked to determine whether this was in fact possible, and, if so, what would be the halakhic ramifications. Whether this so-called bathhouse impregnation was actually feasible or simply contrived for the sake of halakhic analysis was a matter of intense debate amongst the *Aharonim*, as we shall soon see. Tashbetz was one of few *Rishonim* who addressed this topic. He concluded that it is feasible, marshalling evidence from the aforementioned passage in *Gemara Hagiga*, as well as from the case of Ben Sira. With respect to the latter, he prefaces with the disclaimer that "if we believe the apocropha," then we have proof from Ben Sira. What is particularly interesting is Tashbetz's reference in a gloss to two of his contemporaries, one an unnamed non-Jew and the other named R. Abraham Israel, both of whom claimed to have been familiar with cases of virginal women who had conceived.

The next Jewish reference to artificial insemination is not rabbinic in origin, but appears in the case studies of the famous marrano physician Amatus Lusitanus (1511–1568).[69] This discussion, like the aforementioned passage of Ben Sira, is not found in all versions of Lusitanus' classic work, the Centuria, as it was expurgated by censors.[70] Here Lusitanus invokes the notion of artificial insemination (sine concubito) to exonerate a nun with a uterine mole who was accused of impropriety. He adduces his proofs from the case of Ben Sira, as well as from other scientific sources discussed below.

Another famous Jewish physician makes mention of artificial insemination in his work,[71] but this particular work is halakhic, not medical in nature. Rabbi Isaac Lampronti (1679–1756),[72] in his magnum opus, *Pahad Yitzhak*, poses the following riddle: a child is the son of a woman who was impregnated by her father, yet he is not a *mamzer*. How is this possible?[73] He answers, "This is Ben Sira" and recounts the incident in the bathhouse, "as is written in *ketubot*." This reference is clearly not to the Talmudic tractate, as the story derives from the *Alphabet of Ben Sira*. The term "*ketubot*" is likely to be translated as "the writings," in which case it may refer to the apocrypha.[74]

We now turn to the scientific question of whether bath house impregnation is even possible. Implicit from all the above sources is that they accepted the possibility of this unique form of artificial insemination. However, few of them address the question specifically, with the exception of Tashbetz and Lusitanus, both of whom accept the possibility. One of the first to expressly deny the possibility of such an event was R. Judah Rosanes (d. 1727), who articulates his position in his glosses to the Rambam's *Mishne Torah*, entitled *Mishne leMelekh*.[75] R. Rosanes maintains that a woman can only become pregnant through the completion of the natural marital act (i.e. *gemar bia*). He brings support for this notion from Talmudic sources, and also discusses the Talmudic teaching that a woman cannot become pregnant from the first intercourse (*bia rishona*). Based on these as well as other sources, he concludes that bathhouse impregnation is impossible.

This passage from the *Mishne leMelekh* is cited widely by subsequent authorities, some with approbation,[76] others with condemnation, as we will soon see. Although a number of *Aharonim* mention the *Mishne leMelekh* approvingly, including R. Moses Schick, perhaps his most enthusiastic advocate was R. Solomon Schick. In a responsum to R. Yoseph Edinger, coincidentally a student of R. Moses Schick, R. Solomon Schick states assuredly and with no ambiguity that bathhouse impregnation could never happen. In addition to quoting R. Rosanes and R. Moses Schick as his support, he interprets the passage in *Gemara Hagiga* in a novel fashion. As the aforementioned passage follows the story of the four rabbis who entered "*pardes*" (however it is to be defined), and one of those rabbis is the same Ben Zoma of our relevant passage, and this Ben Zoma was harmed by his journey into "*pardes*," R. Schick maintains that the *Gemara* is possibly mocking him. Never, according to R. Schick, did the *Gemara* believe that bathhouse insemination could occur.[77]

Other authorities subsequent to R. Rosanes independently questioned the possibility of bathhouse impregnation. R. Yosef Hayyim (1833?–1909), author of the *Ben Ish Hai*, espouses a novel position in his work *Torah Lishma*.[78] R. Hayyim was asked whether he would allow sperm procurement from an ill man to facilitate a proper medical diagnosis. The questioner maintained that since the sperm could subsequently be used to impregnate a woman, this should mitigate the prohibition of *hashhatat zera.* R. Hayyim's contention is that "nature has changed" (*nishtane ha-teva*)[79] with respect to artificial insemination. Whereas insemination through an intermediary medium (e.g. bath house impregnation) was possible in the times of the *Tannaim,* owing to their greater bodily strength and potency of their seed, such was not the case from the time of the *Ammoraim* and onward. If it was at all possible, it would be an extremely rare occurrence, as, he maintains, was the case mentioned by Tashbetz. Therefore, as the likelihood of impregnating a woman with the remaining seed was so remote, sperm procurement would not be allowed.[80] Around the time this responsum was written, John Hunter performed the first successful artificial impregnation of a human being. However, this success was not widely publicized.[81]

Along a similar vein, a number of *Aharonim* also maintained that bathhouse impregnation was not possible in their time due to the changed nature. However, it was the changed nature of the bath, they maintained, not that of the seed, that explained why insemination was no longer possible.[82] According to this opinion, since the baths in Talmudic times were heated from below,[83] it was theoretically possible for insemination to occur, either because a man was more likely to emit seed in this kind of bath, or because this particular heat source was more conducive to the survival of the seed.[84]

While others questioned the possibility of bathhouse impregnation, R. Rosanes was always hailed as the main opponent to this notion. His position did not remain unopposed, as a number of *Aharonim* reject his contention.[85] Three different approaches were invoked in response to R. Rosanes. R. Yehonatan Eybeschutz (1690–1764) argued against R. Rosanes based on a re-analysis of the Talmudic passages that R. Rosanes cites, concluding that the latter's interpretations were incorrect, and that artificial insemination is possible.[86] R. Chaim Yoseph David Azulai (1724–1806) mentions in three separate places in his writings that bathhouse impregnation is possible because it was accepted as fact by the *Gemara,* as well as by a number of prominent *Rishonim.*[87] The third approach of refutation is scientific in nature and was taken by R. Baruch Mordechai ben Yaakov Libschitz (1810–1885). R. Rosanes had stated that conception could only be accomplished with *gemar bia.* R. Libschutz responded that with respect to bathhouse impregnation, the waters of the bath could transport the seed to the internal organs of the woman, thereby effectively accomplishing the same result as *gemar bia.*[88]

Contemporary *poskim*, in their discussions on modern therapeutic artificial insemination, refer to some of the aforementioned sources. However, as the possibility of such an occurrence, at least in the modern medical context, is an accepted fact, little space is devoted to the scientific question of feasibility.[89] More time is apportioned for the resolution of attendant halakhic dilemmas.

### Secular Sources

The notion of virginal or non-natural conception[90] dates back to antiquity and antedates Christianity.[91] Explicit reference to the phenomenon of artificial insemination, however, is found in sources from the Middle Ages. Avicenna (980–1037), in his *Canon* on medicine, and Averroes (d. 1198), in his *Colliget,* acknowledge the possibility of artificial impregnation.[92] Thomas Aquinas (d. 1274) relates that a woman became pregnant from lying in a bed into which sperm had been discharged.[93] As discussed above, R. Peretz of Corbeil (c.1295), a contemporary of Aquinas, accepted this possibility and therefore dealt with the halakhic ramifications. Amatus Lusitanus quotes Avicenna and Al-Jazzar (10th cent.)[94] as authorities who accept artificial insemination.[95]

In 1750, a pamphlet by Dr. Abraham Johnson entitled "Lucina Sine Concubito" was published in London.[96] It was submitted by Johnson to the Royal Society, the pre-eminent scientific body in England, and consists of a personal account of a patient of Johnson's, whom the latter believed had conceived by artificial insemination. In this fantastical essay, Johnson postulates the means by which this insemination was achieved. He believed, based on classical sources, that the reproductive seed derived from the western winds and was accidentally ingested by his female patient.

He claimed that he tested his theory experimentally on his housemaid, without her consent, and achieved positive results (i.e., the maid became pregnant). He therefore submitted his results to the Royal Society with suggestions for wider applications of his technique.

While the belief in artificial insemination persisted into the twentieth century,[97] like the Jewish sources above, it was not without its detractors. Paolo Zacchias (1584–1659), physician to Pope Innocent X and prominent medical legal writer,[98] rejected the possibility, as did the great scientist Albrecht Haller (1708–1777).[99]

In conclusion, since the possibility of bathhouse insemination is difficult to disprove, whether it has or can actually occur remains a mystery.[100]

## THE TWO PATHWAYS *(SHNEI SHVILIN)*

Rabbinic sources throughout the ages have discussed the intricate details of male reproductive anatomy, as they directly relate to the definition of a halakhically infertile man (i.e. *petzua daka* and *kerut shafkha*).[101] In the context of one such discussion, the *Gemara* in *Bekhorot* (44b) makes a statement that seems somewhat puzzling today. The *Gemara* states that there are two pathways in the male genital organ, one for urine and one for seed,[102] and that these two pathways are separated by a fine membrane the width of a garlic peel whose integrity is necessary for fertility. Should this membrane rupture and allow communication between the two channels, the man may be rendered halakhically infertile *(petzua daka)* and consequently may be forbidden to marry.

The existence of these two pathways in the male organ was an accepted fact amongst *Rishonim* and early *Aharonim,* and many halakhic discussions revolved around cases where one or the other pathway was perforated, especially in cases of hypospadias (i.e. when the opening of the urethra is not at the tip, but at varying points along the shaft).[103] In the latter case it was unclear whether the existing opening was only for the urine, which could easily be ascertained, or whether it was also for seed, which was halakhically difficult to determine given the prohibition of *hotza'at zera le-vatala.* The following section highlights some of the sources, both Jewish and secular, that have addressed this unique anatomical notion.

## JEWISH SOURCES

R. Shimon ben Tzemah (1361–1444) mentions the notion of the two pathways in his philosophical work, *Magen Avot.*[104]

> . . . for the organs of reproduction in the man are two, the *ever* and the *beitzim* [testicles] . . . and *Hazal* added the *hutei beitzim*[105] . . . should any of these three organs be damaged a man will be rendered infertile . . . and *Hazal* have written extensively on these topics, based on their *kabbala*, and have understood matters that scientists have not . . . and in the Canon [of Avicenna][106] it states that there are three pathways, one for urine, one for seed and one for [other] fluids . . . but this does not appear to be so according to *Hazal* [who say there are two] . . . all this is based on the true *kabbala*, which the scientists have not acquired . . . and since the wisdom of our sages has been lost through the exiles we must labor (to restore it) . . . and one should not err and say that *Hazal* were not expert in the sciences. . . .

Most *poskim* have understood the passage in *Gemara Bekhorot* to mean that there are two pathways extending all the way to the tip of the *ever,* and such was clearly the opinion of R. Moses Sofer in considering the suggestion of physicians to repair a hypospadias.[107] R. Yisroel Yehoshua Trunk (1820–1893), however, interpreted the *Gemara* differently. He understood that the two pathways for urine and seed refer to the internal anatomy, but not that they extended into the *ever.* It is a mistake to think this, he maintained, as both the urine and seed traverse one path in the *ever.*

The Hazon Ish, R. Avraham Yeshayahu Karelitz (1878–1953), apparently agreed with the anatomical observation of R. Trunk, but did not accept his interpretation of the *Gemara:*

> In the *Gemara* it states that there were two pathways, one for the urine and one for the seed . . . in this matter the nature has changed (*nishtanu ha-teva'im*)[108] as today there is only one pathway in the *ever.*[109]

The Hazon Ish also claimed, based on his discussion with physicians, that the *ever* is subject to variation, be it a function of time or of geographical location.[110] R. Yoseph Hayyim mentions a number of such anatomical variants that were found in the city of Baghdad.[111]

## SECULAR SOURCES

The notion of there being more than one pathway in the *ever* was prevalent in the middle ages, especially in the Arab world,[112] but does not appear to have clear roots in antiquity. Galen, a contemporary of R. Yehuda haNasi, states unequivocally that there is one path for both urine and semen,[113] and Hippocrates, to the best of my knowledge, makes no mention of the two path theory. Avicenna (980–1037), as quoted by R. Duran above, claimed there were three canals in the *ever,* and Mondino (d. 1326), the Italian anatomist, described a separate canal for the sperm.[114] These ideas permeated the works of the renaissance artist and anatomist Leonardo DaVinci (1452–1519), who drew two distinct passages in his anatomical drawings.[115]

Andreas Vesalius (1514–1564) is credited with rectifying the Arab beliefs and clarifying, by anatomical dissection, that there is only one pathway in the *ever.*[116] He also postulates how the Arabs came to their conclusion.[117] Interestingly, he cites an actual case of a young man from Padua who had two passages at the tip of the ever, one for semen and one for urine.[118]

The susceptibility of the urethra to anatomical variation, and in particular to duplication, has been recorded in medical case records.[119] Frank Netter, in his contemporary classic, *The CIBA Collection of Medical Illustrations,* draws accessory urethral channels as an example of congenital variations.[120]

## NOTES

1. For a remarkable account of the application of this technology, see Jiaen Liu, et. al., "Birth After Preimplantation Diagnosis of the Cystic Fibrosis F508 Mutation by Polymerase Chain Reaction in Human Embryos Resulting From Introcytoplasmic Sperm Injection With Epididymal Sperm," *Journal of the American Medical Association* 272:23 (Dec., 1994), 1858–60.

2. See E. Reichman, "The Halachic Definition of Death in Light of Medical History," *Torah U-Madda,* 4, (1994), 148–74. The same methodological approach was applied to the determination of death.

3. For an overview of the history of embryology, see J. Needham, *A History of Embryology* (New York, 1959); Howard Adelmann, "A Brief Sketch of the History of Embryology before Fabricius" in his trans. of *The Embryological Treatises of Hieronymous Fabricius of Aquapendente* (Ithaca, 1967), I, 36–70. For references to embryology in Jewish sources, see Samuel Kottek, "Embryology in Talmudic and Midrashic Literature," *Journal of the History of Biology* 14:2 (Fall, 1981), 299–315; David I. Macht, "Embryology and Obstetrics in Ancient Hebrew Literature," *Johns Hopkins Hospital Bulletin* 22, 242 (May, 1911), 1–8; W.M. Feldman, "Ancient Jewish Eugenics," *Medical Leaves* 2 (1939), 28–37; D. Shapiro, *Obstetrique des Anciens Hebreus* (Paris, 1904); W.M. Feldman, *The Jewish Child* (London, 1917), 120–44; H.J. Zimmels, *Magicians, Theologians and Doctors*, 62–64; Needham, op. cit., 77–82; Julius Preuss, *Biblical and Talmudic Medicine* (New York, 1978), 41–138; Ron Barkai, *Les Infortunes De Dinah: Le Livre De La Generation-La Gynecologie Juive au Moyen Age* (Paris, 1991). (I thank Mr. Tzvi Erenyi for bringing this latter book to my attention.)

4. There are no clearly documented human dissections from the time of Rashi, although scattered references to autopsies and dissections appear in the thirteenth and fourteenth centuries. Mundinus (1270–1326) is recognized to have been the first to incorporate human anatomical dissection into the medical curriculum. See, for example, C.D. O'Malley, Andreas Vesalius of Brussels (Berkeley, 1964), 1–20; Ludwig Edelstein, "The History of Anatomy in Antiquity," in *Ancient Medicine* (Baltimore, 1967), 247–302; Charles Singer, *A Short History of Anatomy and Physiology from the Greek to Harvey* (New York, 1957); Mary Niven Alston, "The Attitude of the Church Towards Dissection Before 1500," *Bulletin of the History of Medicine* 16:3 (October, 1944), 221–38; Nancy Sirasi, *Taddeo Alderotti and His Pupils* (Princeton, 1981), 66–69.

5. Hippocrates, in his essay, "The Seed and the Nature of the Child," devotes a lengthy section to agriculture. He says, "You will find that from beginning to end the process of growth in plants and humans is exactly the same." (G.E.R. Lloyd, ed., *Hippocratic Writings* (New York, 1978), 341). See also A.J. Brock (trans.), *Galen On the Natural Faculties* (London, 1916), p. 19.

6. See Joseph Needham, *A History of Embryology* (New York, 1959), for extensive discussion of ancient theories of embryology. The most complete account of pre-Aristotelian theories of sexual generation is by Erna Lesky in *Die Zeugungs und Vererbungslehre der Antike und ihre Nachwirkung* (Mainz, 1950). This work is widely quoted. See also the classic work by Monica Green, *The Transmission of Ancient Theories of Female Physiology and Disease Through the Early Middle Ages*, Doctoral Dissertation, Princeton University, 1985, and Sarah George, *Human Conception and Fetal Growth: A Study in the Development of Greek Thought From Presocrates through Aristotle*, Doctoral Dissertation, University of Pennsylvania, 1982.

7. Galen discusses his theories of generation in many places. See, for example, Margaret Talmadge May, trans., *Galen: On the Usefulness of the Parts of the Body* (Ithica, 1968), vol 2, 620–54. See also Anthony Preus, "Galen's Criticism of Aristotle's Conception Theory," *Journal of the History of Biology*, 10:1 (Spring, 1977), pp. 65–85.

8. Modern scholarship has revealed that the hippocratic corpus is not the work of one author. For ideas of conception see, for example, G.E.R. Lloyd, ed, *Hippocratic Writings* (New York, 1978), pp. 317–46, chapter entitled "The Seed and the Nature of the Child."

9. Preus, op. cit., p. 83. See also Needham, op. cit., p. 78 who cites a similar idea from Hippocrates.

10. See A.L. Peck, (trans.) *Aristotle: Generation of Animals* (Cambridge, 1942), pp. 71, 100–101 note a, 109–12.

11. *Exercitationes de Generatione Animalium* (Amsterdam, 1651), later translated and annotated by Gweneth Whitteridge, Disputations Touching the Generation of Animals (Oxford, 1981).

12. The belief in spontaneous generation in Jewish and secular sources merits its own article. A passage in *Gemara Shabbat* 107b seems to indicate that the Rabbis believed that lice could spontaneously generate. This passage, as well as others that conflict with our current understanding of science, have been the subject of many a heated discussion. Francesco Redi (1620–97) was the first to scientifically study spontaneous generation, and he dealt the theory its first major blow in his work, *Esperienze Intorno Alla Generazione Deg'lisetti* (Florence, 1668). Louis Pasteur (1833–93) laid the theory to rest. For treatment of this topic in Jewish sources see Isaac Lampronti, *Pahad Yitzhak* (Bnei Brak, 1980), s.v. *Tzeda haAsura*; Arye Carmel, ed., Eliyahu Dessler, *Mikhtav meEliyahu* (Jerusalem, 1984), vol. 4, 355, note 4; Arye Carmel and Yehuda Levi, *"R'ot haEnayim bi-kviut ha-halakha,"* HaMaayan 23:1 (*Tishrei*, 1983), pp. 64–9; David Ruderman, "Contemporary Science and Jewish Law in the Eyes of Isaac Lampronti of Ferrara and Some of His Contemporaries, *Jewish History*, 6:1–2 (1992), pp. 211–24.

13. See his *De Mulierum Organis Generationi Inservientibus Tractatus Novus* (Leyden, 1672).

14. *De Ovi Mammalium et Hominis Genesi* (Leipzig, 1827).

15. See Pieter Willem Van Der Horst, "Sarah's Seminal Emmission: Hebrews 11:11 in the Light of Ancient Embryology," in *Greeks, Romans and Christians: Essays in Honor of Abraham J. Malherbe*, edited by David Balch et al. (Minneapolis, 1990), pp. 287–302. I thank Dr. Shnayer Leiman for directing me to this source, which places a number of Rabbinic sources into the context of Greco-Roman theories of embryology. Horst provides a nice summary of these three theories. See also Sarah George, op. cit.

16. A.W. Meyer, "The Discovery and Earliest Representation of Spermatozoa," *Bulletin of the Institute of the History Of Medicine* 6:2 (February, 1938), pp. 89–110.

17. Needham, op. cit., pp. 205–11; A Du Bois, "The Development of the Theory of Heredity," *CIBA Symposia* 1:8 (November,1939), pp. 235–46.

18. According to the theory of preformation, either Adam or Eve, depending on whether one is an ovulist or animalculist, contained the preformed bodies of all the people that would populate the earth. Within each preformed seed must exist the preformed seed of the next generation, and so on.

19. Regarding the origins of this depiction and its initial false attribution to Leeuwenhoek, see A.W. Meyer, op. cit.

20. See David Feldman, *Marital Relations, Birth Control and Abortion in Jewish Law* (New York,1974), esp. chaps. 6 and 7, for his excellent treatment of these topics. Some of the sources from this section derive from this book.

21. The term *gidim* can mean either blood vessels or nerves and has been used interchangeably in rabbinic literature. The clarification of Hebrew medical terms, especially in the Middle Ages, has plagued many a doctor and historian throughout history. The confusion stemmed from differing etymologies of medical terms, ranging from Latin to Greek and later Arabic, as well as the fact that these terms were not easily rendered into Hebrew. Some terms were transliterated, others translated and often entirely new words were devised. This confusion led many Jewish physicians to include a glossary of medical terms in their books. On Hebrew terminology see, for example, Juan Jose Barcia Goyanes, "Medieval Hebrew Anatomical Names," *Koroth* 8:11–12 (1985), pp. 192–201; A.S. Yahuda, "Medical and Anatomical Terms in the Pentateuch in Light of Egyptian Medical Papyri," *Journal of the History of Medicine* 2:4 (Autumn, 1947), pp. 549–73. Multiple articles have appeared over the years in the Journal *HaRofe haIvri* on the topic of Hebrew medical terminology.

22. It is interesting that blood is not mentioned as one of the contributions of the female seed, especially since this seed, according to the *Gemara,* is itself comprised of blood. For a discussion about this discrepancy, see *She'iltot deRav Ahai Gaon,* She'ilta 56 and commentaries of R. Isaiah Berlin (*She'ilat Shalom*) and R. Naftali Tzvi Yehuda Berlin (*Ha'amek Sh'aila*) on this passage. I thank Dr. Maier Halberstam for directing me to this source.

23. The terms *ruah, nefesh* and *neshama* are all abstract and difficult to define. They are often used interchangeably. See Samuel S. Kottek, "The Seat of the Soul: Contribution to the History of Jewish Medieval Psycho-physiology," *Cliomedica* 13:3–4 (1978), pp. 219–46.

24. Rabbinic sources of the Middle Ages and beyond clearly knew of Galen. In addition, Galen himself was at least peripherally familiar with Jews and Jewish medicine. See Reichman, op. cit, esp. p. 166, n. 6.

25. We know of Ramban's medical practice primarily from the responsa of his student, R. Shlomo Ibn Aderet (Rashba). Responsa numbers 177, 413 and 825 discuss the Ramban's use of an astrological figure of a lion to cure a kidney ailment. The Rashba discusses the halakhic issues involved in using astrological figures. See also R. H.Y.D. Azulai, *Shem haGedolim Ma'arekhet Gedolim*, s.v. Ramban, and David Margalit, *Hakhmei Yisrael KeRofim* (Jeruslaem, 1972), pp. 128–35.

Medical historians have mentioned that Ramban practiced in Montepellier. See Isaac Alteras, "Jewish Physicians in Southern France during the 13th and 14th Centuries," JQR 68 (1977–78), p. 218. No Jewish sources that I have found corroborate this claim.

26. On the University at Montepellier in the Middle Ages see Sonoma Cooper, "The Medical School of Montepellier in the Fourteenth Century," *Annals of Medical History*, new series 2 (1930), pp. 164–95; *CIBA Symposia* 2:1 (April, 1940), entire issue devoted to Montepellier.

Regarding the Jewish presence at Montepellier see Luis Garcia-Ballester, "Dietetic and Pharmacological Therapy: A Dilemma Among Fourteenth Century Jewish Practitioners in the Montepellier Area," *Clio Medica* 22 (1991), pp. 23–37; Joseph Shatzmiller, "Etudiants Juifs a la Faculte de Medicine de Montepellier Dernier Quart du XIV Siecle," *Jewish History* 6:1–2 (1992), pp. 243–55.

27. Rashba, responsum 120, also quoted in R. Yosef Karo, *Bedek ha-Bayit* on Y.D. 154.

28. Commentary on *Vayikra*, 12:2.

29. These terms derive from the *Mishna* in *Nidda* 2:5 and have been the source of much discussion regarding their anatomical identification.

30. *Hilkhot Issurei Bia* 5:4.

31. 40a.

32. This book is a compilation of theories in philosophy, theology, psychology and medicine. The material was culled from the existing literature of that time, as stated by Aldabi in his introduction, but unfortunately there are no references, for which Aldabi apologizes. This book was first printed in 1518 in Riva di Trento, but because of its immense popularity it has been reprinted many times over the centuries, the last time being in Jerusalem, 1990.

33. *Shevilei Emuna* (Jerusalem, 1990), pp. 177–8.

34. For biographical information on Tuvia Cohn see his introduction to *Ma'ase Tuvia*. See also Dr. D.A. Friedman, *Tobias Cohn* (Tel Aviv, 1940); *Encyclopaedia Judaica* (Jerusalem, ), s.v. Cohn, Tobias.

35. On the Jews of the University of Padua see, for example, Cecil

Roth, "The Medieval University and the Jew," *Menora Journal* 9:2 (1930), pp. 128–41; Jacob Shatzky, "On Jewish Medieval Students of Padua," *Journal of History of Medicine* 5 (1950), pp. 444–47; Cecil Roth, "The Qualification of Jewish Physicians in the Middle Ages," *Speculum* 28 (1953), pp. 834–43; David B. Ruderman, "The Impact of Science on Jewish Culture and Society in Venice (with Special Reference to Jewish Graduates of Padua's Medical School) in *Gli Ebrei e Venezia* (Venice, 1983), pp. 417–48.

36. (Cracow, 1908), 118. Note his mention of the microscope, which was first designed in the late 17th century.

37. Note that this author has been variously referred to as Baruch of Shklov, Baruch Shklover or Baruch Schick, the latter name under which he is listed in *Encyclopaedia Judaica*. For biographical information see David Fishman, "Science, Enlightenment, and Rabbinic Culture in Belorussian Jewry, 1772–1804," Ph.D. dissertation, Harvard University, 1985; ibid., "A Polish Rabbi Meets the Berlin Haskalah: The Case of R. Baruch Schick," *AJS Review* 12:1(Spring, 1987), pp. 95–121; Noach Shapiro, "*R. Baruch Schick mi-Shklov,*" *HaRofe haIvri* 34:1–2 (1961), pp. 230–35; David Margalit, "*Dr. Barukh Schick veSifro 'Tiferet Adam,' *" *Koroth* 6:1–2 (August, 1972), pp. 5–7. There is debate in the above sources as to whether Baruch Schick was a physician. See also Israel Zinberg, *A History of Jewish Literature: The German-Polish Cultural Center* (New York, 1975), pp. 271–74.

38. Hague, 1780. In the introduction to this book appears the oft quoted notion, in the name of the Vilna Gaon, that scientific knowledge is needed for the study of Torah.

39. *Tiferet Adam* (Berlin, 1777), 3. This book was printed together with *Amudei Shamayim*, an astronomical work by the same author. As this latter work appears first in the combined volume, the book is often referenced by its name only.

40. This is a loose translation from *Iggeret Bikoret* (Zhitomer, 1868), 25b.

41. Parentheses are in original text.

42. *Sefer haBerit* (Jerusalem, 1990), vol. 1, chap. 2, p. 240.

43. *Hullin* 45b.

44. loc. cit. s.v. *she-eno molid.*

45. *Sefer haBahir* has also been referred to as *Midrash R. Nehunia ben haKana*. Ramban refers to it by this title in his biblical commentary. This citation is from chapter 51 and is quoted by Moshe Perlman in his *Midrash haRefua* (Tel Aviv, 1926), p. 23.

46. *Shevilei Emuna* (Jerusalem,1990), *netiv* 4, p. 211.

47. *Magen Avot* 38b. Tashbets mentions some of the proofs to this doctrine. These proofs make fascinating reading and reflect the medi-

eval understanding of heredity, particularly the inheritance of acquired characteristics. The concept of heredity in *Hazal* is another topic that merits medical/historical analysis.

48. Ibid., 39a.

49. The encephalo-myelogenic doctrine was also mentioned by R. Yehiel Mikhel Epstein in his halakhic work *Arukh haShulhan*, E.H., 23:3.

50. This is a reference to the encephalo-myelogenic doctrine.

51. *Sefer haBerit* (Jerusalem, 1990), *ma'amar* 16, chapter 3, pp. 232–3.

52. Many scientists of that time referred to sperm as seminal worms. See for example, William Cullen, (trans.), *Albrecht Haller, First Lines of Physiology* (Edinburgh, 1786), p. 205.

53. *Tiferet Adam* (Berlin, 1777), pp. 3b-4a. Other arguments against the preformationists are cited in Needham, op. cit., p. 210.

It appears from the last sentence of this citation that Schick may himself have viewed the sperm under the microscope. There is debate amongst historians whether Schick had a laboratory where he performed medical experimentation. See Shapiro, op. cit., pp. 234–5; Israel Zimberg, op. cit., p. 282.

It is also interesting that this entire passage is strikingly similar to the writings of Albrecht Haller, whose works were very popular in the scientific world at the time Schick was writing. Compare the passage below with the one by Schick:

> To the father some have attributed everything; chiefly since the seminal worms, now so well known, were first observed in the male seed by the help of the microscope. . . . But in these animals there is a proportion wanting betwixt their number and that of the fetuses; they are also not to be constantly observed throughout the tribes of animals. (from Cullen, op. cit., pp. 205–6)

A broader comparison between *Tiferet Adam* and the works of Haller may yield interesting results.

54. R. Yosef Hayyim ben Eliyahu, *Rav Pe'alim*, vol. 3, E.H. 2; R. Yehiel Mikhel Epstein, *Arukh haShulhan*, E.H. 23:1; R. Eliezer Waldenberg, *Tzitz Eliezer*, vol. 9, 51.

55. A number of authors have previously written on this topic from an historical perspective. See H.J. Zimmels, *Magicians, Theologians and Doctors* (London, 1952); Immanuel Jacobovits, *Jewish Medical Ethics* (New York, 1959), pp. 244–50. This essay treats the topic more comprehensively.

56. John Hunter (1728–1793) was a prominent scientist and comparative anatomist who is known for his self-experimentation with venereal disease. His original manuscripts, detailing his application of artificial insemination, are currently housed at the Hunterian Museum in Lon-

don, where one can also see on display thousands of human and animal anatomical specimens which Hunter collected during his lifetime.

57. *Test Tube Babies* (New York, 1934).

58. See, for example, Fred Rosner, *Modern Medicine and Jewish Law,* 2nd ed. (New York, 1991), pp. 85–100; Abraham Steinberg, *Encyclopedia Hilkhatit Refuit* (Jerusalem, 1988), pp. 148–61. For a bibliography of responsa on this topic, see R. Yaakov Weinberg and R. Maier Zichal, *"Hazra'a Melakhutit,"* Assia 55 (December, 1994), pp. 75–89.

59. 14b–15a. Some have construed this passage to be a sarcastic allusion to the Christian doctrine of immaculate conception. See R. Yehoshua Boymel, *Emek Halakha,* 1:68; Jacobowits, op. cit., p. 359, n. 31. Preuss, op. cit., p. 477, claims that this cannot be, as the doctrine of immaculate conception was not yet known at the time of Ben Zoma (1st century C.E.). Preuss' historical interpretation however, is disputable.

60. See *Tosafot,* loc. cit., s.v. *betula.* Whether it is only claimed or actually verified that the woman is a virgin is a matter of discussion.

61. The text is based on an Oxford manuscipt, which was published in A.M. Haberman, *Hadashim Gam Yeshanim* (Jerusalem, 1976), pp. 125–7.

62. See Pieter W. Van Der Horst, "Seven Months' Children in Jewish and Christian Literature from Antiquity," in his *Essays on the Jewish World in Early Christianity* (Gottington, 1990), pp. 233–47. (I thank Dr. Shnayer Leiman for this reference.) Van Der Horst does not include Ben Sira in his list.

There is a notion in *Hazal* that babies born in the seventh and ninth months are viable, whereas those born in the eighth month are not (see, for example, T.B. *Shabbat* 135a and *Yevamot* 80a). This was a prevalent notion in antiquity and the Middle Ages and is another example of a topic where a medical historical analysis may shed light on Rabbinic sources. This issue has been previously addressed. See Neria Gutal, *"Ben Shemona: Pesher Shitat Hazal beNogea leVladot Benei Shemona,"* Assia 55–56 (1989), pp. 97–111; Dr. Rosemary Reiss and Dr. Avner Ash, *"Ben Shemona Mekorot Klasi'im LeEmuna Amamit,"* ibid., pp. 112–17. See also Ron Barkai, "A Medieval Hebrew Treatise on Obstetrics," *Medical History* 33 (1988), pp. 96–119, esp. pp. 101–104. For further information on the secular sources see Ann Ellis Hanson, "The Eight Months' Child and the Etiquette of Birth: Obsit Omen!", *Bulletin of the History of Medicine* 61 (1987), pp. 589–602; Sarah George, op. cit., pp. 204–33.

63. The text also mentions that the *Ammoraim* Rav Zeira and Rav Pappa were also born by artificial insemination, but unlike Ben Sira, the identity of their fathers was unknown. Yechiel Halperin in his *Seder ha-Dorot* (Jerusalem, 1988), section 2, 118, quotes *Sefer Yuhsin* by Abraham Zacuto, who, in turn, cites this notion from *Sefer Kabbalat haHasid.* Hal-

perin then cites the original source of this idea from the alphabet of Ben Sira and subsequently refutes the belief that R. Zeira and R. Pappa were products of artificial insemination. He does not, however, assail the belief that Ben Sira was a product of artificial insemination.

64. (Pietrikov, 1904), introduction.

65. *Tzemah David*, section 1, *eleph revi'i*, 448. See also *Tzitz Eliezer*, vol. 9, no. 51, gate 4, chap. 1, letter *tet*.

66. This reference is mentioned by the *Bayit Hadash* (R.Y. Sirkes 1561–1640) in Y.D. 195 (s.v. *ve-lo*) as appearing in the "*Hagahat Semak Yashan*" of R. Peretz. The glosses of R. Peretz first appeared in the printed text of *Sefer Mitzvot Katan* in the mid 1500's and all subsequent editions invariably contained these glosses. I consulted the 1556 Cremona edition and could not find this particular gloss. It seems that this gloss remained in manuscript form and was never printed, hence the term "*yashan*" of the Bah likely refers to an old manuscript edition. This fact is further evidenced by the comment of R. Chaim Y.D. Azulai (*Birkei Yoseph* E.H. 1:14) that after much effort he was finally able to locate this particular gloss of R. Peretz in an old manuscript.

A passage similar to that of R. Peretz appears in the *Shiltei haGiborim* on *Rif* (T.B. *Shavuot* 2a) attributed to an author referred to by his acronym, *HR"M*. Rav Eliezer Waldenberg (*Tzitz Eliezer* vol. 9, no. 51, gate 4, chap. 1, letter *het*) has postulated that this may be a misprint, and the text should actually read *HR"P*, an acronym for HaRav Rabbenu Peretz.

67. *Sefer Maharil*, Shlomo Spitzer, ed. (Jerusalem, 1989), pp. 611–12.

68. Vol. 3, no. 263.

69. On Lusitanus, see essays in Harry Friedenwald, *The Jews and Medicine* (Baltimore, 1944), vol. 1, pp. 332–90. The section relevant to our discussion is on page 386. Preuss (op. cit., 464) also quotes Lusitanus in discussing the *Gemara Hagiga*.

70. Friedenwald, op. cit., p. 363, n. 98.

71. See the work of another famous Jewish physician, Tobias Cohn (1652–1729), who mentions artificial insemination in his *Ma'ase Tuvia* (Cracow, 1908), section 3, 118b.

72. Although known for his halakhic expertise, Lampronti was a prominant Italian physician and a graduate of the University of Padua. See Abdelkader Modena and Edgardo Morpugo, *Medici E Chirurghi Ebrei Dottorati E Licenziati Nell'Universita Di Padova dal 1617 al 1816* (Bologna, 1967), pp. 55–57. These authors mention that Lampronti consulted the famous physician Morgagni for assistance with his difficult medical cases. Saul Jarcho elaborates on these consultations in his article, "Dr. Isac Lampronti of Ferrara," *Koroth* 8:11–12 (1985), pp. 203–6. For a discussion on the interface between science and Halakha in the work of Lampronti see David B. Ruderman, "Contemporary Science and Jewish

Law in the eyes of Isaac Lampronti of Ferrara and Some of his Contemporaries," *Jewish History* 6:1–2 (1992), pp. 211–24.

73. *Pahad Yitzhak* (Bnei Brak, 1980), s.v. *Ben Bito.* David Margalit does not mention this passage in his essay, "*Erkhim Refui'im she-bi-Encyclopedia haHilkhatit Pahad Yitzhak LeR.Y. Lampronti,*" *Koroth* 2:1–2 (April, 1958), pp. 38–61.

74. Although the *Wisdom of Ben Sira* is included in the works of the apocrypha, the *Alphabet of Ben Sira* is not.

See R. Yehoshua Boymel, *Emek Halakha,* no. 68, regarding the citation of R. Lampronti:

. . . even though he did not cite his source for this, still his words are believed, and this *tzaddik* is free from iniquity.

R. Boymel apparently thought the word "*ketuvim*" to be a generic reference, not a reference to a specific work or body of works.

75. *Hilkhot Ishut,* 15:4. See also *Mishne leMelekh* on *Hil. Issurei Bia* 17:15, where R. Rosanes discusses these matters in great detail and states that the passage of Ben Zoma in *Hagiga* is not considered halakhic.

76. See, for example, Malakhi ben Yakov HaKohen (d. 1785–1790), *Yad Malakhi* (Berlin, 1857), *kelalei Ha-dinim* no. 247; R. Moshe Schick, known as Maharam Schick, *Taryag Mitzvot* no.1.

77. *Teshuvot Rashban,* E.H. no. 8.

78. (Jerusalem, 1976), no. 481. R. Hayyim wrote these responsa under a pseudonym.

79. The concept of "*nishtane hateva*" has been invoked many times in Rabbinic literature. See, for example, *Tosafot* in T.B. *Avoda Zara* 24b, s.v. *Para; Tosafot* in T.B. *Hullin* 47a, s.v. *kol;* E.H. 156:4 in the *Rema.* For comprehensive treatment of this topic see N.M. Gutal, *Sefer Hishtanut HaT'vaim B'halakha* (Jerusalem, 1995). Two areas where authorities often discuss this principle are *Hil. Terefot* and *metzitza* in *mila.* See also later in this article regarding the two pathways of the male genital organ.

80. R. Hayyim cites other reasons for forbidding sperm procurement in this case, such as that some seed might spill in the process of collection, or, even if they collect all the seed, it might not all be used for the purpose of insemination. These concerns have been voiced by current *poskim* in their discussions on artificial insemination.

81. See Rohleder, op. cit.

82. R. Yaakov Reischer, *Iyyun Yaakov* (Wilhelmsdorf, 1725), on *Gemara Hagiga* 14b. See also R. Pinchas Horowitz, *Pitha Zuta al Hil. Nidda uTevilla* (London, 1958), 195:7, who explains the position of R. Reischer. Both of these sources question why Rambam omits the case of Ben Zoma from his code.

83. See O.H. 230:3 and *Mishna Berura,* loc. cit.

84. R. Yekutiel Greenwald, in his *Kol Bo Al Avelut* (New York, 1947), pp. 305–6, n. 8, states that the majority of *poskim* hold that bathhouse insemination could never happen. However, if it was ascertainable that such an event had occured, the parents and children would be obligated to mourn for each other. Another halakhic question unique to a child born from bathhouse insemination is whether such a child could have his *mila* performed on Shabbat. See R. Moshe Bunim Pirutinsky, *Sefer haBerit* (New York, 1973), 9, who states, based on the interpretation of R. Hananel to the *Gemara Hagiga*, that since such a birth is considered miraculous, and not by natural methods of conception, the *mila* could not be performed on Shabbat.

85. Many *Aharonim* still maintained the possibility of bathhouse impregnation without specifically addressing the *Mishne leMelekh*. See R. Yaakov Emden, *Iggeret Bikkoret* (Zhitomer, 1868) and *Sheilat Ya'avets*, vol. 2, no. 97. Emden also discusses artificial insemination in his unpublished commentary on Tractate *Hagiga, Kolon Shel Sofrim,* Oxford manuscript Neubauer #516 (Ms. Michael #326), p. 28. Here he states that bathhouse insemination is not possible since nature has changed. However, since the manuscript is in poor condition, it is unclear whether this is Emden's own opinion or a citation.

86. *Benei Ahuva* (Jerusalem, 1965), on *Rambam, Hil. Ishut* chap. 15.

87. *Birkei Yosef,* E.H. 1:14; *Yair Ozen, ma'arekhet* 1 no. 93; *P'takh Enayim* on *Gemara Hagiga* 14b. See also R. Y.S. Nathanson, *Shai laMore,* Glosses on E.H. 1;6; ibid., *Responsum Shoel uMeshiv,* Vol. 3, section 3, nos. 34 and 132 (end); R. Eliezer Fleckles, *Teshuva me Ahava,* Y.D. no. 195.

88. *Berit Yaakov* (Warsaw, 1876), E.H. no. 4. The author employs the same logic with respect to R. Peretz's pronouncement about a woman becoming pregnant from seed remaining on the sheets. Here, too, he maintains that a woman may use the sheets for internally cleaning herself, thereby bringing the seed into close proximity with the uterus.

89. See R. Shalom Mordechai Shvadron (1835–1911), *She'elot uTeshuvot Maharsham* (New York, 1962), vol. 3, no. 268, who was asked whether it was permissible to undergo artificial insemination.

90. For the material on artificial insemination in medieval times, I have relied on secondary sources, primarily Preuss. The primary sources are in Arabic and Latin and, for the most part, remain untranslated into English.

91. See Robert Graves, *The Greek Myths* (Baltimore, 1955), 51 for descriptions of non-natural methods of conception. I thank Dr. Louis Feldman for this reference.

92. Preuss, 464.

93. Ibid. Preuss provides no reference for this statement.

94. On this author see Gerrit Bos, "Ibn Al-Jazzar on Women's Dis-

eases and Their Treatment," *Medical History*, 37 (1993), 296–312. In personal communication, Dr. Bos says he is unaware of any reference to artificial insemination in the extant works of Al-Jazzar.

95. Preuss, 464.

96. This work was reprinted and appended to Hermann Rohleder, *Test Tube Babies* (New York, 1934).

97. Preuss, 464, cites Stern, who stated that the belief in bathhouse insemination was still prevalent in Turkey at that time, i.e., early 20th century. See also George Gould and Walter Pyle, *Medical Curiosities* (New York, 1896), 42–45, who state that the possibility of bathhouse insemination was still being debated. They also relate an extraordinary, if not fantastical, story from the civil war of how a woman, struck in the abdomen with a bullet that previously hit the testicle of a soldier, gave birth, after 278 days, to an eight pound boy.

98. On Zacchias and other medical legal writers see Bernard Ficarro, "History of Legal Medicine," *Legal Medicine Annual* (1979).

99. Both Zacchias and Haller are mentioned in Preuss, op. cit., 464.

100. Although I have been unable to find any contemporary medical references to bathhouse insemination, I have found an interesting case which attests to the viability of the human sperm. See Douwe A.A. Verkuyl, "Oral Conception: Impregnation Via the Proximal Gastrointestinal Tract in a Patient with an Aplastic Vagina," *British Journal of Obstetrics and Gynaecology*, 95 (Sept., 1988), pp. 933–4.

101. See E.H. 5.

102. See also *Rashi* on T.B. *Yevamot* 75b, s.v. *guvta*.

103. See *Otzar haPoskim* (Jerusalem, 1962), E.H. 5, no. 25 and Abraham Tzvi Hirsch Eisenstadt, *Pithei Teshuva*, E.H. 5, no. 5 for a series of halakhic queries regarding both acquired and congenital variants of the male genitalia.

104. 37b. A loose translation of the passage follows.

105. It is a matter of debate as to the halakhic definition of *hutei habetzim*. For our purposes we can assume it refers to the vas deferens.

106. Avicenna (980–1037), known in Hebrew sources as Ibn Sina, was a Persian physician of great reknown. His main work, *The Canon*, was considered the authoritative work on medicine for many centuries, and is quoted extensively by Rabbinic sources. The only extant Hebrew medical incunabula is a copy of Avicenna's *Canon* (Naples, 1491). Many Hebrew manuscripts of Avicenna were found in the Cairo Geniza. See Haskell D. Isaacs, *Medical and Para-Medical Manuscripts in the Cambridge Genizah Collections* (Cambridge, 1994).

It appears that the printer of *She'elot uTeshuvot Havot Ya'ir* (reprinted, Jerusalem, 1973), by R. Yair Bacharch, was not familiar with the work of Avicenna, as I believe there is a misprint in responsum no. 234. In this responsum, addressing the permissibility of using *Talmudic* remedies for medical treatment, R. Bachrach discusses a particular theory of medical therapeutics. R. Bachrach claims that he found support for this theory in, as it appears in the printed adition, "*Sefer haKinyan leEven Pina.*" I have found no bibliographical reference to such a work, and, given the medical context of the statement, believe the proper reading should be "*Sefer haKanon leIbn Sina.*"

107. R. Moshe Sofer, *Teshuvot Hatam Sofer* (Vienna, 1882) vol. 6, no. 64, s.v. *akh ma.*

108. See the position of R. Yosef Hayyim above in section on artificial insemination.

109. *Hazon Ish* (Bnei Brak, 1991) E.H. 12, no. 7.

110. Ibid. See *Tzitz Eliezer,* vol. 10. no. 25, chap. 24. These two sources deal with the halakhic aspects of prostate surgery, which can involve intentional ligation of the vas deferens. The issue discussed is whether such a procedure renders the patient a *kerut shafkha.* On this topic, see the important responsa of R. Moses Feinstein, E.H., vol. 4, nos. 28 and 29.

On the effect and importance of geographical location in the Talmud as compared to classical sources, see Stephen Newmyer, "The Concept of Climate and National Superiority in the Talmud and its Classical Parallels," Transactions and Studies of the College of Physicians of Philadelphia, series 5, vol. 5, no.1 (March, 1983), 1–12. On the concept of climatology in general, see Genevieve Miller, "Airs, Waters and Places in History," *Journal of the History of Medicine,* vol. 17 (Jan., 1962), pp. 129–140.

The notion of climatic changes in time and place has been employed to explain the concept of "*nishtane ha-teva.*"

111. *Rav Pe'alim,* vol. 3, E.H., no.12.

112. Preuss, op. cit., 110; *Magen Avot,* cited in the text above; Cecil Roth, ed., *Encyclopedia Judaica,* 2 (Jerusalem), 932.

113. Margaret Talmadge May, ed., *Galen: On the Usefullness of the Parts of the Body* (Ithica, 1968), 660.

114. J. Playfair McMurrich, *Leonardo Da Vinci the Anatomist* (Baltimore, 1930), 202.

115. Ibid., 180; Charles D. O'Malley and J.B. de C.M. Saunders, *Leonardo on the Human Body* (New York, 1983), pp. 460–3.

116. See C.D. O'Malley, *Andreas Vesalius of Brussels* (Berkeley, 1964), 358. The appendix contains a selection of translations from Vesalius' famous work, *De Humani Corporis Fabrica* (Basel, 1543).

117. Preuss, op. cit., 110.

118. C.D. O'Malley, et. al., trans., *William Harvey: Lectures on the Whole of Anatomy* (Berkeley, 1961), 142, n. 509. Harvey followed Vesalius and confirmed that there was only one path in the *ever.*

119. See George Gould and Walter Pyle, *Anomalies and Curiosities of Medicine* (New York, 1896), 317. They also quote the case studies of Fabricius Hildanus (1560–1624), Marcellus Donatus (1538–1602) and others, including Vesalius.

120. *Reproductive System*, vol. 2 (New York, 1988), 31. Here, however, the accessory urethra ends in a blind pouch and does not carry either sperm or urine.

# 2

# *Generation, Gestation, and Judaism*

## Azriel Rosenfeld

Host motherhood—the transplantation of a fetus to a womb other than that of its biological mother—is a subject that has begun to receive considerable attention during the past few years. As techniques for performing such transplants become available, they may be expected to have significant social and economic impact. An unwilling mother will no longer be faced with a choice between aborting the fetus or carrying it to term, if a willing host mother can be found. Adoption of an unborn child will become possible, and an adopting mother will be able to give birth to her adopted child. On the economic side, interspecies host motherhood can provide a means of temporarily storing valuable animal fetuses, using host mothers of a species which is easier to care for and transport.

This article considers the status of human host motherhood in Jewish law: Is transplantation of a fetus from one mother to another permissible? Which of the mothers is regarded as having given birth—the biological mother, the host mother, neither, or both? Who are the legal parents of the child?[1]

It should be stressed that the case of host motherhood is not the same as that of artificial insemination. Many authorities hold that artificial insemination by a donor other than the husband is prohibited; but host motherhood does not involve fertilization of a woman by a man other than her husband. In fact, even those

Dr. Rosenfeld is director of the Institute for Advanced Computer Studies, Center for Automation Research, at the University of Maryland.

who prohibit artificial insemination of a woman by her husband should permit host motherhood, since the child was conceived as a result of normal coitus. If a woman's ovum is fertilized in vitro (by a donor or her husband), and the resulting fetus is then implanted in her own womb, the objections raised against artificial insemination would presumably still apply; but here we are concerned with the case where another couple's child, conceived in the ordinary way, is transplanted into her womb.[2]

## PERMISSIBILITY

The question of whether host motherhood is permissible has two aspects: Is the biological mother allowed to give up her child? Is the host mother allowed to accept it?

If we assume that fetus transplantation techniques have been perfected to the point where the fetus survives in the great majority of cases, there would seem to be no reason to prohibit a woman's transferring her child to a host mother; the laws governing abortion should not apply here, since the child will almost certainly survive. Surely if there is danger to either mother or child in allowing the biological mother's pregnancy to go to term, we would permit a safe transplantation operation. The issue here, it should be pointed out, has nothing to do with the question of whether the biological parents are allowed to give up their child for adoption; even if we permit a host mother to carry the child, she may in some cases have to return it after she has given birth to it, while in other cases it may become available for adoption.

The situation is less straightforward as regards whether the host mother is allowed to accept the child. We would certainly not encourage this if she were unmarried; and at first glance, there is a serious objection to it if she is married:

> We have learned: A man may not marry a woman who is pregnant by another man, or who is nursing another man's child; and if he married her, he must divorce her and may never take her back. So R. Meir; but the sages say: He must divorce her, and when his time comes to remarry [i.e., after the child is weaned], he may remarry [her] (*Yevamot* 36b) . . . [Why?] Because she may become pregnant from him [after she has given birth to the other man's child], and her milk will dry up, so that he [the child] will die. If

so, is it not the same with his own child [i.e., why are we not concerned that she may become pregnant while nursing their own
child]? She would feed his own child eggs and milk [so that it
would survive even if her milk dried up]. Can she not feed her
child [by another man] eggs and milk? Her husband will not give
them to her. Can she not demand them of the heirs [of the child's
father]? Abbaye said: A woman is embarrassed to come to court,
even if her child may die (*Yevamot* 42a–b).

Our Rabbis have taught: If a nursing woman's husband died
within 24 months [i.e., before the child is weaned], she may not
become betrothed or married until after 24 months. So R. Meir,
but R. Yehudah permits it after 18 months . . . Rav and Shemuel
both say: She must wait 24 months . . . (*Ketuvot* 60a–b).

Our sages decreed that a man may not marry or betroth a woman
who is pregnant by another man, or who is nursing another man's
child, until the child is 24 months old . . . whether she is a widow,
a divorcee, or has strayed . . . If he transgressed and married a
pregnant or nursing woman within this time . . . he must divorce
her (*Shulhan Arukh, Even Ha-Ezer* 13:11–12).

If our sages were concerned about a pregnant or nursing
woman marrying a man who is not the child's father, should we
not certainly prohibit a married woman's becoming a host
mother, where the child is neither hers nor her husband's?
On closer examination, however, it appears that the prohibition applies only to marrying a woman who is *already* pregnant or
nursing. If a woman has sexual relations with another man after
she is married, we may at most require her to separate from her
husband for three months, when this will make it possible to determine the fatherhood of her child; but she does not have to
leave her husband:

If two men betrothed two women, and at the time that they entered the marriage canopy they were interchanged . . . we separate
them [from their husbands] for three months, since they may be
pregnant (*Mishnah Yevamot* 33b).

If a married woman was raped, and had not previously had sexual relations with her husband, she must wait [90 days] (*Shulhan
Arukh, Even Ha-Ezer* 13:6).

Only if one comes to marry [a woman who is nursing another man's child] in the first place is it prohibited; but if a married man's wife is raped, and becomes pregnant and gives birth, our sages did not abrogate the husband's rights on account of the child . . . It is nowhere mentioned that if a married woman is raped, he [her husband] should have to wait 24 months . . . If someone rapes another man's wife, once the pregnancy is apparent, she is permitted to her husband even while pregnant, and *a fortiori* while nursing; this is clear and needs no justification . . . We prohibit a woman who is pregnant by another man or nursing another man's child only when he marries her against the prohibition, but not when he had been permitted to marry her . . . The decree was only against marriage, but not when she is already married to him . . . (Authorities quoted in *Otzar Ha-Poskim* on *Even Ha-Ezer* 13:11, para. 68).

Thus if a married woman has become a host mother, Jewish law would probably require her to abstain from sexual relations with her husband for 90 days, in order to insure that the child is not his [i.e., that she has not miscarried the implanted fetus and become pregnant by her husband]; but he would certainly not have to divorce her or separate from her for 24 months.

The possibility remains, though, that we might prohibit a married woman from becoming a host mother to begin with; the sources quoted above refer to cases where a married woman has already become pregnant with someone else's child, but this does not imply that she is allowed to undertake such a pregnancy in the first place, even if no adultery is involved. However, note that the Talmud's prohibition against marrying a pregnant or nursing woman is based primarily on the fear that the nursing child may be weaned prematurely and die; thus if we were to prohibit a married woman's becoming a host mother, by the same reasoning, we would have to prohibit her becoming a wet nurse, which the Talmud certainly did not forbid:

These are the tasks which a woman must perform for her husband: . . . and she must nurse her child (*Mishnah Ketuvot* 5:6).

Why did they say "her child?" Because she need not nurse another woman's child, as we have learned: A man cannot force his wife to nurse another woman's child, nor can a woman force her husband to allow her to nurse another woman's child (*Yerushalmi ad loc*).

If she wishes to nurse another woman's child along with her child, her husband can prevent her; he can even prevent it in the case of her child by another man [after 24 months] (*Shulhan Arukh Even Ha-Ezer* 80:14).

Clearly these sources imply that, if both husband and wife agree, the wife is permitted to act as a wet nurse; we are not concerned about the possibility that since the child is not her own, she may wean it prematurely and it may die:

Some recent authorities have written that in cases where it is permitted to give a child to a wet nurse, it must be given to an unmarried wet nurse, not to a married one; for since in the Talmud the reason given that she [a woman nursing another man's child] may not marry is that she may become pregnant and her milk may dry up, then if the wet nurse is married this concern applies also to her. This is reasonable; but we have not found that the codifiers say so. On the contrary, in early responsa we find that a child was given to a married wet nurse, and the authorities did not raise this objection, and it therefore appears that one need not be particular about this. For in the Talmud they asked why we do not, for the same reason, prohibit any nursing woman to have sexual relations with her husband, lest she become pregnant and her milk be spoiled, harming the child; and they answered that the case of a father and mother is different, since if the milk is spoiled, they will feed the child milk and eggs, for parents normally have compassion on their children—whereas if she marries another man, he will not have compassion on a child that is not his, and will not give her milk and eggs, and she will have to demand them from her first husband's heirs, but will be embarrassed to make a claim against them, so that meanwhile the child will be in danger . . . But in the case of a wet nurse who has been hired, and is collecting wages for her nursing, and presumably hired herself out to nurse with her husband's consent (since if he does not consent, he can prevent her, as it says in ch. 80), then since they are collecting wages, both [she and her husband] will be concerned for the welfare of the child, and if the milk is spoiled, she will not be embarrassed to demand money from those who hired her, and her husband himself will use any available means [to save the child], since he is collecting wages, and they are like a father and mother to the child (*Arukh Ha-Shulhan, Even Ha-Ezer* 13:24).

If the authorities permitted a married woman to act as a wet nurse, it seems reasonable to conclude that, had the case arisen, they would also have permitted her to act as a host mother. The prohibition against marriage to a woman who is pregnant by another man is based on the fact that she will have to nurse the child; if we allow a married woman to nurse another couple's child, we should certainly allow her to become pregnant with another couple's child. At most, she and her husband would probably be required to abstain from sexual relations for 90 days before and after the implantation of the fetus, in order to insure that she was not already pregnant by her husband or has not miscarried the fetus and then become pregnant by her husband, so that the parentage of the child will not be in doubt.

## STATUS OF THE MOTHERS

Whether or not we permit host motherhood, cases of it will surely arise, and it will then become necessary to decide such questions as whether either mother is regarded as having given birth. (The related question of which parents have fulfilled the commandment to procreate presumably depends on the status of the child, which will be discussed in the next section.)

As regards the biological mother, the situation seems straightforward. If the fetus is removed from her[3] within 40 days after conception, she should not be regarded as having given birth, but after 40 days she should be so regarded:

> If a woman miscarries on the 40th day, she need not be concerned about [having given birth to a child]; but on the 41st day, she must [be concerned about] a male child, and a female child, and menstruation. R. Yishmael says: On the 41st day, she must [be concerned about] a male child and menstruation; on the 81st day, about a male child and a female child and menstruation—for a male is completed on the 41st day, and a female on the 81st. But the sages say: Both the formation of a male and of a female take 41 days (*Mishnah Niddah* 30A).

Presumably, the same criterion would apply in connection with the laws of the firstborn, if this is the biological mother's first child.

The case of the host mother is more difficult. True, she has given birth to a fully formed child; but it is not a child which she herself conceived. On the other hand, it is possible that her case is analogous to that of the women whose children were conceived before the Torah was given (i.e., before the inception of Jewish law); and we have learned that these women were in fact regarded as having given birth:

> "[If a woman conceives] and gives birth" (Lev. 12:2) excludes a woman who gave birth before the Revelation. Or perhaps I should exclude one who became pregnant before the Revelation and gave birth after the Revelation? It therefore says "or if she gives birth to a female" (*ibid.* 5)—the matter depends only on birth (*Sifra ad loc*).

Similarly, if a pregnant woman becomes a proselyte, when her child is born she is certainly regarded as having given birth, even though she was not Jewish when she conceived, and in fact, her child must be redeemed as a first-born (*Mishnah Bekhorot* 46a); thus it is possible that a host mother too is regarded as having given birth, even though she has not conceived.

In cases where the fetus is transplanted after the 40th day, however, a serious objection to this conclusion can be raised. Once a child has emerged from the womb, it is regarded as born even if it goes back inside:

> Once its head has come out, this constitutes birth. Have we not already learned this—"Once it has put its head out, even if it puts it back in, it is as though born?" And if you say that [the Mishnah just quoted] tells us about animals, while [our Mishnah] tells us about humans . . . have we not already learned the latter too—"If it came out normally, as soon as most of its head has emerged [it is regarded as born]"? (*Bekhorot* 46a; the implication is that in humans too, once the head has emerged, the child is regarded as born even though it re-enters the womb).

When the child later re-emerges (which might not be until the following day), this is not regarded as a second birth; we consider the birth to have taken place at the first emergence. Perhaps in our case too, once the child has been born to its biological mother, even though it re-enters the womb (of its host mother), only the first birth counts. The situation is different from that of a proselyte mother, where there was no prior birth. On the other hand, if the transplantation is performed within 40 days of con-

ception, then since no birth took place when the child was removed from the biological mother, we can regard the host
mother as having given birth.[4]


## STATUS OF THE CHILD

A more fundamental question is that of the child's status. If the
transplantation is performed after the 40th day, there seems little
doubt that we would regard the biological parents as the child's
legal parents, since the child became "completed" while still in
the biological mother's body, and she is regarded as having given
birth to it; in this case the host mother can be thought of as
merely playing the role of an incubator. If it is performed within
40 days, however, is it possible that we might regard the host
mother—who has given birth to it—as the legal mother of the
child?[5]

That a fetus less than 40 days old is not legally regarded as a
child does seem to make it plausible that, if a transplantation is
performed within this period, the connection between the biological parents and the child might thereafter be ignored. The Talmud regards such a fetus as "mere water" (*Yevamot* 69b), and
holds that even its sex is not yet determined:

> We have learned: For the first three days [after coitus], a man
> should pray that [the seed] should not rot; between three and forty
> [days], he should pray that it become a male; between forty days
> and three months, he should pray that it not become an abortion;
> between three and six months, he should pray that it not be still-
> born; between six and nine [months] he should pray that it come
> out safely (*Berakhot* 60a).

The case of a pregnant woman who becomes a proselyte can
also be regarded, at first glance, as supporting this possibility. For
example, we have seen that when she gives birth, her child must
be redeemed as a firstborn, even though she was not Jewish when
she conceived him. Similarly, an ordinary proselyte is regarded as
having no relatives; but a child born to such a woman is regarded
as related to his mother (see, e.g., *Yerushalmi Yevamot* 11:2). Perhaps in our case too, even though the host mother was not the

child's legal mother at the time of conception, she becomes its legal mother by virtue of giving birth to it?

On closer examination, however, it would appear that we have no real support for such a view. As regards the case of the pregnant proselyte, although her child is legally hers in many respects, it is not regarded as a born Jew, but rather as a proselyte, in spite of the fact that it was *born* to a Jewish mother:

> A child can be a proselyte according to Biblical law [not merely rabbinically], when a pregnant woman becomes a proselyte; as it says (*Yevamot* 78a): If a pregnant non-Jewish woman becomes a proselyte, her son does not require immersion [since he was part of his mother's body at the time of her immersion] (Tosafot *Ketuvot*, 11a s.v. *matbilin;* see also Tosafot *Yevamot* 47b, s.v. *matbilin* and Keren Orah *ad loc*).

Thus even here, in determining the status of the child, we follow the conception, not the birth. Indeed, if a married couple become proselytes at the same time, they must separate for three months, in order to make it certain whether children born to them afterwards were conceived before or after their conversion (*Yevamot* 42a), even though the children will in any event be *born* after the conversion. In our case too, the fact that the host mother is the one who gives birth to the child does not mean that its legal status is not determined at the time of conception.

True, the Talmud does not regard a fetus less than 40 days old as being a "completed" child; but this need not imply that its identity is not yet established. In fact, the Talmud's view is that the soul enters the fetus immediately upon conception:

> Antoninus asked Rabbi [Judah the Prince]: When is the soul put into a man, from the time of "remembrance" [i.e., conception] or from the time of formation? He replied: From the time of formation. He asked him: Can a piece of meat stay three days without salt and not spoil? Rather, from the time of "remembrance." Rabbi said: This thing Antoninus taught me (*Sanhedrin* 91b).

There is no contradiction to this in the Talmud's belief that the sex of a child is not fixed for 40 days; the Halakhah seems to recognize the possibility of an individual's sex legally changing (see Midrash Tanhuma on Gen. 30:22: "R. Huna said in the name of R. Yose . . . Even up to the moment when she sits on the birth stool, he may pray that she give birth to a male child; for it is not difficult for the Holy One, Blessed be He, to make females into males and males into females.") If a child has a soul from the moment of conception, it is reasonable to conclude that its identity and heredity are also fixed at that time; no matter how early it is removed from its biological mother's body, she is still its legal mother.

We are told that in the days to come "Women will be able to give birth every day, as it says (Jer. 31:7) 'Pregnant and parturient, all together' " (*Shabbat* 30b). Let us hope that, as host motherhood brings this vision closer to reality, we are also approaching the time spoken of by the prophet, when "I will bring them from the northland, and gather them from the corners of the earth; blind and lame among them, pregnant and parturient, all together—a great multitude shall return."

## NOTES

1. Regarding animal host motherhood, another question arises: What if the host mother is of a non-kosher species and the fetus is of a kosher species, or vice versa?

2. Cases more closely related to that of artificial insemination would arise if it were possible to transplant sex organs. What is the legal status of a child if its mother has an ovary transplant, or its father has a testicle transplant? Are such transplants permissible?

3. We assume here that the fetus is removed through the birth canal; if it is removed by Caesarean, the mother is not regarded as having given birth in any case.

4. In animals, however, the Talmud is in doubt whether a host mother can ever be regarded as having given birth, at least in connection with the laws of the firstborn (*Hulin* 70a): "If one stuck two wombs together, and it went out of one and into the other, what [is the law]? Does it excuse its own [mother from being subject again to the law of the firstborn], but not one that is not its own, or perhaps it even excuses one that is not its own?"

5. Presumably, if this were the case, the child would have no legal father.

# 3

# In Vitro Fertilization: Questions of Maternal Identity and Conversion

## J. DAVID BLEICH

The question of maternal identity in situations involving a host mother as well as the issue of maternal identity in instances of in vitro fertilization have been addressed in this column on two separate occasions.[1] In vitro techniques are employed when it is not possible for a woman to become pregnant by natural means because of her inability to produce viable ova, because of a blockage of the fallopian tubes, because the husband suffers from an inability to produce a sufficient number of sperm or because pregnancy has not occurred in utero for other, sometimes unknown, physiological reasons. When normal ovulation does occur an ovum or, more commonly, a multiple number of ova are removed from the ovaries. The ova are then fertilized in a petri dish by sperm ejaculated by the husband and, after undergoing a number of cell divisions, the developing zygote is inserted into the uterus of the woman from whom the ovum was removed. If, however, the woman cannot produce viable ova an ovum, or a multiple number of ova, may be donated by a relative or stranger, fertilized by means of an in vitro procedure and inserted into the

J. David Bleich is a *Rosh Yeshiva* and the *Rosh Kollel Le-Hora'ah* at the Rabbi Isaac Elchanan Theological Seminary, Professor of Jewish Law at the Benjamin N. Cardozo School of Law and Herbert and Florence Tenzer Professor of Law and Ethics at Yeshiva University.

46

uterus of the otherwise infertile woman and carried to term. When the fertility problem arises from the woman's inability to sustain a pregnancy for the full period of gestation the fertilized zygote may be implanted in the uterus of another woman, i.e., a host mother, who will carry the fetus to term. In each of these cases there is some question with regard to whether the genetic mother or the gestational mother is regarded as the child's mother for matters in which such a relationship is significant in Jewish law, e.g., consanguinity, inheritance, laws of mourning, etc.

Although there is a minority view that regards the donor mother as the sole mother of a child born of in vitro fertilization,[2] the consensus of rabbinic opinion is that a maternal-filial relationship is generated between the gestational mother and the child, despite the absence of any genetic relationship, by virtue of parturition alone.[3] Whether or not the genetic mother, i.e., the woman who produced the ovum from which the child was conceived, is also a mother from the vantage point of Jewish law is a more complex question. The question of whether the baby may, in effect, have two halakhic mothers must be regarded as yet open.[4]

## I. ABSENCE OF A MATERNAL RELATIONSHIP

R. Eliezer Waldenberg, *Tzitz Eli'ezer*, XV, no. 45,[5] has advanced the novel view that, in the eyes of Halakhah, a child born of in vitro fertilization has neither a father nor a mother even if the biological mother and the gestational mother are one and the same, as is the case in the majority of instances in which in vitro procedures are employed. Rabbi Waldenberg's arguments, which are not based upon cited precedents or analogy to other halakhic provisions, are three in number: 1) Fertilization in the course of an in vitro procedure occurs in an "unnatural" manner through the intermediacy of a "third power" extraneous to the father or mother, i.e., the petri dish. 2) Conception occurs in a manner "that has no relationship to genealogy." 3) In natural reproduction the ovum remains "attached" to the body and is fertilized therein. Maternal identity is consequent solely upon fertilization that occurs while the ovum is yet attached to the mother's body. Thus, upon "severance" and removal of the ovum from the mother's body any genealogical relationship between the ovum and the mother is destroyed.

To this writer, those arguments appear to be without substance. In response to the first argument it must be stated that the petri dish is not a "third power" and in no way contributes biologically or chemically to the fertilization process. It is simply a convenient receptacle designed to provide a hospitable environment in which fertilization may occur.[6] Rabbi Waldenberg's second argument, if indeed he intended to present it as an independent argument, is entirely conclusory. In order to demonstrate that no maternal relationship exists some evidence or argument must be presented that would serve to demonstrate that genealogical relationships are generated solely in utero. Rabbi Waldenberg provides no such demonstration. Whatever cogency the third argument may have is lost if it is recognized that parturition, in and of itself, establishes a maternal relationship.

In the early days of in vitro fertilization a position similar to that advanced by Rabbi Waldenberg was presented by R. Judah Gershuni in the Tishri 5739 issue of *Or ha-Mizrah*.[7] Rabbi Gershuni's argument is based upon a statement of *Divrei Malki'el*, IV, no. 107. There is a significant disagreement among rabbinic authorities with regard to whether a paternal relationship may occur as a result of artificial insemination or whether such a relationship can arise only as the result of a sexual act.[8] *Divrei Malki'el* expresses tentative support for the latter position but does so on the basis of the novel view that "once the semen has been emitted and has warmth only because of the ministration of the physician and his skill with the pipette or due to the heat of the bath" a baby born as a result of that process is not regarded as the son of the donor. Although *Divrei Malki'el* stands virtually alone in developing this argument[9] and himself concludes that a child born of artificial insemination is indeed the child of the donor, Rabbi Gershuni observes that a fertilized zygote sustained in a petri dish by means of "artificial nutrition and blood serum" should not be regarded by Jewish law as the child of either parent. The earlier presented rebuttal of Rabbi Waldenberg's argument applies with equal force to that advanced by Rabbi Gershuni. Moreover, any cogency the argument may have with regard to establishment of a paternal relationship notwithstanding, if parturition, in and of itself, serves to establish a maternal relationship, the sources of antecedent nutrition of the fetus are totally irrelevant.

## II. PARTURITION AS A DETERMINANT

The view that the maternal relationship is predicated upon parturition is based upon the statement of the Gemara, *Yevamot* 97b, to the effect that a fraternal relationship exists between male twins born to a woman who converts to Judaism during the course of her pregnancy. Since a proselyte is regarded as a "newly born child" and all halakhic relationships with existing blood relatives are severed upon conversion, the relationship of the child to its mother, and through her to its twin sibling, cannot be regarded as having arisen at the moment of conception.[10] From the vantage point of Halakhah, the situation of a pregnant convert is analogous to that of a woman who receives an ovum into her uterus that has been fertilized outside of her body. Upon conversion, all relationships with relatives, including her own fetus, are severed. Accordingly, the status of her fetus at the moment of conversion is precisely identical to that of a fetus that is abruptly thrust into her uterus, i.e., a fetus that has not been conceived within her body.[11] Clearly then, since a maternal relationship is recognized by Jewish law in the case of a pregnant convert, it must be the process of parturition that, at least in such instances, establishes the maternal relationships.[12] If so, it follows that the site in which fertilization occurs or the provenance of the ovum is irrelevant;[13] parturition, in and of itself, establishes a mother-child relationship.[14] This principle is also reflected in the observation of *Tosafot*, *Ketubot* 11a, to the effect that the fetus of a pregnant women who undergoes conversion is itself a convert but nevertheless inherits its mother's estate. Quite obviously the child can be an heir only if a maternal-filial relationship has been established and in the case of a pregnant proselyte that relationship can come into being only by virtue of parturition.

It might, however, be argued that although this source amply demonstrates that generation of the ovum is not the definitive criterion of the existence of a maternal relationship, nevertheless, it may be gestation rather than parturition that constitutes the factor serving to establish such a relationship. The convert would then be considered to be the mother of the child on the basis of having nurtured the fetus in her womb during the post-conversion period of gestation. This would lead to the conclusion that a naturally conceived fetus that is subsequently transferred from the womb of one woman to that of another would have two mothers for purposes of Halakhah. There are, however, aggadic sources that speak of the intrauterine transfer of Dinah from the womb of Rachel to Leah and of Joseph from Leah to Rachel.[15] Subsequent scriptural references to Dinah as the daughter of Leah and of Joseph as the son of Rachel ostensibly indicate that each child had but a single mother. If so, it must be parturition, rather than gestation, that establishes the maternal relationship.[16] Of course, aggadic sources are not dispositive with regard to matters of Halakhah and, accordingly, the matter cannot be regarded as entirely resolved.

## III.  GESTATION AS A DETERMINANT

In an article published in *Tehumin*, vol. V (5744), R. Zalman Nechemiah Goldberg cites one significant source in support of the position that gestation establishes a maternal relationship even prior to parturition and, accordingly, that source would support the conclusion that a woman who carries a fetus in her womb for any portion of the gestational period—at least during the last two trimesters of pregnancy—is regarded as the baby's mother for purposes of Halakhah.[17]

The Gemara, *Hullin* 113b, declares that the biblical prohibition against cooking and eating commingled milk and meat is not attendant upon meat cooked with the milk removed from an animal that has been slaughtered. Milk derived from a slaughtered animal is excluded from the prohibition because, according to talmudic exegesis of the verse "you shall not cook a kid in the milk of its mother" (Exodus 23:19; Exodus 34:26; Deuteronomy 14:21), the biblical prohibition applies only to the milk of an animal "that has the capacity to become a mother" (*re'uyah lehiyot em*). Obviously, a dead animal can no longer bear a child and hence lacks the capacity to become a mother.

In his notes on *Shulhan Arukh, Yoreh De'ah* 87:6, R. Akiva Eger queries whether the milk of a live animal that is a *treifah* is similarly excluded from the prohibition. The talmudic principle is that a *treifah*, (i.e., an animal that suffers from one of a number of specified anatomical defects either congenitally or as the result of trauma causing loss or perforation of the organ) cannot conceive and carry a fetus to term. Hence, comments R. Akiva Eger, since a *treifah* cannot become a mother, it might be assumed that the milk of a *treifah* is excluded from the prohibition against cooking or consuming commingled milk and meat. Nevertheless, R. Akiva Eger cites a statement of the Gemara, *Sanhedrin* 69a, to the effect that a male who has sired a fetus is to be termed a "father" immediately upon expiration of the first trimester of pregnancy. If the male parent of a fetus is a "father" it would stand to reason that the female parent is similarly to be regarded as a "mother." As applied to the question before him, R. Akiva Eger remarks that the talmudic reference to a parental relationship vis-à-vis a fetus may be limited to a relationship with a viable fetus and hence, since the fetus of a *treifah* is not viable, there may well be no halakhic relationship between the fetus of a *treifah* and its gestational mother. Nevertheless, it would appear that, in the case of a viable fetus, such a relationship does indeed exist. Thus R. Akiva Eger's comment serves to establish that the gestational mother is a mother in the eyes of Jewish law. However, insofar as a child born of in vitro fertilization is concerned, since the Gemara recognizes a paternal relationship only subsequent to the expiration of the first trimester and R. Akiva Eger equates inception of the maternal relationship with that of the paternal relationship, R. Akiva Eger's comments do not serve to establish the existence of a halakhically recognized relationship with the genetic mother. By virtue of the nature of in vitro fertilization, the physiological relationship between the donor of the unfertilized ovum and the fetus is severed long before the end of the first trimester of pregnancy.

Rabbi Goldberg points out that R. Akiva Eger's position is contradicted by at least one authority. R. Joseph Engel, *Bet ha-Otzar, erekh av,* argues that, although the sire of a fetus is a "father," nevertheless the female carrying the fetus in her womb is not recognized as a "mother" in the eyes of Jewish law until the moment of parturition. The Gemara, *Megillah* 13a, notes the redundancy inherent in the phrases "for she did not have a father or a mother" and "upon the death of her father and her mother"

(Esther 2:7) and indicates that the second phrase is designed to convey additional information to the effect that Esther did not have a father or mother for even a single day. The Gemara comments that Esther's father died as soon as her mother conceived and that her mother perished upon her birth. The Gemara carefully spells out that Esther is described as never having had a father because her father died following conception before he could properly be termed a "father," i.e., before the end of the first trimester of pregnancy, and that she is described as never having had a mother despite the fact that her mother survived until the end of the gestational period. Esther is described as not having a mother because her mother died in childbirth. Hence this talmudic passage clearly indicates that a woman may properly be termed a "mother" only upon parturition. Presumably, the distinction between the male and female parent is based upon the fact that the male's role in reproduction ceases upon fertilization of the ovum and, accordingly, he is termed a "father" as soon as the fetus has reached a significant stage of development, whereas the female's role remains incomplete until the moment of birth.[18] Why R. Akiva Eger ignored the discussion in *Megillah* is unclear.[19] He may have regarded that discussion as aggadic in nature and hence as not being a proper source for derivation of a halakhic principle.

It should also be noted that the comments of Maharal of Prague in his explication of this verse in his commentary on the Book of Esther[20] suggest that he understood the Gemara's statement as being predicated upon the position that a fetus is an integral part of the mother (*ubar yerekh imo*). It then follows that during gestation mother and fetus constitute an undivided entity; accordingly, the maternal progenitor cannot become a "mother" until a physiological separation occurs, i.e., parturition. If, however, the opposing view is adopted and the fetus is not regarded as an integral part of the mother (*ubar lav yerekh imo*) there is no reason to assume, according to Maharal, that the maternal relationship is established any differently from the paternal relationship with the result that according to that view the maternal-filial relationship is established at a much earlier stage of gestation.

## IV. DUAL MATERNAL RELATIONSHIPS

Although, as discussed earlier, there is strong evidence supporting the position that parturition serves to determine maternal relationship, those sources serve only to establish that parturition establishes a maternal-child relationship but do not preclude the possibility that Halakhah may recognize two or more maternal relationships, i.e., a relationship arising from parturition and an additional relationship or relationships arising from gestation or provision of a gamete.[21]

The possibility of "doubtful" dual maternal relationships is raised in one recent discussion of this issue, albeit on the basis of entirely different considerations. A talmudic discussion regarding a similar quandary in the area of agricultural law is cited by Professor Ze'ev Low, *Emek Halakhah*, II (Jerusalem, 5749), 165–169, as reflecting the principle to be employed in resolving the issue of maternal identity. It is forbidden to consume newly harvested grain crops until the *omer* has been offered in the Temple on the second day of Passover. That offering renders permissible not only already harvested grain but also grain in the field that has taken root but which has, as yet, not fully matured. Any crop planted subsequent to the offering of the *omer* does not become permissible for use as food until the following Passover. The Gemara, *Menahot* 69b, posits a situation in which a stalk of grain is planted and has reached a stage of development equal to a third of its ultimate growth (i.e., the stage at which the produce has reached a state of maturity at which it is recognized, for halakhic purposes, as a grain product); having reached this stage of development, the stalk is removed from the ground before the *omer* is offered and replanted after the offering of the *omer* whereupon it continues to mature and ultimately reaches its normal state of growth. The question posed by the Gemara is whether the *omer* renders the entire plant permissible since the primary growth of the stalk occurred before the time of offering of the *omer* or whether, because of its enhanced growth subsequent to the offering of the *omer*, the produce may not be eaten. The Gemara identifies a similar problem with regard to *orlah*, the fruit of a tree that is forbidden during the first three-year period after planting. The problem involves a situation in which a young sapling already bearing fruit is grafted onto a mature tree and that fruit subsequently greatly increases in size. The question is whether the newly grown portion of the fruit produced by the grafted sapling is to be regarded as the product of the mature tree and hence permissible or whether, since the identity of the fruit has been established as *orlah* prior to grafting, the newly grown portion of the fruit is also infused with that identity. A third problem occurs with regard to *kilayim,* produce that is forbidden because of mingling in the planting of diverse species. The situation discussed by the Gemara involves a vegetable that has been planted in a vineyard; the vines are then uprooted and the vegetable continues to grow after the vine has been removed. Both the vegetable and the grapes become forbidden upon mingling of the species in planting. The question is whether the additional growth of the vegetable subsequent to removal of the grape vine is permissible since that portion of the vegetable was never commingled with grapes or whether the identity of the vegetable was established as forbidden produce upon its planting in the vineyard and hence all subsequent growth acquires the same identity.

A number of talmudic commentators make it clear that they regard the issue in each of these related cases, not as involving a question concerning the admixture of a small quantity of a forbidden foodstuff with a much larger quantity of a permitted foodstuff, as might perhaps be presumed, but as a question of determination of identity in cases in which there is continued growth and development. Is the identity of a stalk of grain determined with finality as soon as it is halakhically recognized as grain? If so, then, having acquired identity and status as grain before the offering of the *omer,* it retains the identity of "pre-omeric" (and hence presently permissible) grain even if a significant portion of its growth occurs after the offering of the *omer,* much in the same manner that we regard a person who gains a considerable amount of weight to be the same person after the weight-gain as before or in the manner that we regard an infant who grows to adulthood as retaining the same identity he possessed as a child. Or do we regard the portion of the grain added as a result of accretion or incremental growth of the grain as having an independent identity since that growth occurs subsequently to a second "post-omeric" (and hence as yet forbidden) planting? Has the identity of the fruit of the sapling been irreversibly determined upon its first appearance so that it predetermines the identity of the even much greater portion of the fruit that develops after grafting with the result that the entire fruit is forbidden *orlah* or does the added portion of the fruit that grows after grafting have its own identity as a permitted fruit? A vegetable planted in a vineyard acquires identity as a forbidden planting of diverse species. But does that identity infuse even the portion of the vegetable that comes into being after the grapevine is removed or docs the newly developing portion of the vegetable acquire an identity of its own, *viz.*, an identity as a vegetable that has not been compromised by diverse planting in a vineyard? These questions are left unresolved by the Gemara with the result that, in any given case, the stringencies of both possible resolutions of the issue must be applied, i.e., the grain is forbidden because of the possibility that the previously-acquired status does not control the enhanced growth of the grain, but the fruit of the grafted sapling and the increased growth of the vegetable are forbidden because the earlier acquired identity may indeed control the identity of that which is a natural outgrowth of the old.

If this analysis of these talmudic questions is accepted as correct, the question of maternal identity of progeny born as the result of in vitro fertilization of a donated ovum may be regarded as analogous. Maternal identity is established in the first instance by production of the gamete. The question is whether that determination is also dispositive with regard to the identity of the fetus whose later physical development is attributable to the gestational host or whether the identity of the developing fetus is derived from its nurturer, *viz.*, the host mother, in which case the child could be regarded as having two mothers just as, for example, a single grain of wheat may be, in part, "pre-omeric" and, in part, "post-omeric." Since the Gemara leaves the basic issue unresolved and, accordingly, rules that the stringencies of both possible identities must be applied, a child born of in vitro fertilization, on the basis of this analogy, would to all intents and purposes be regarded as having two mothers.

However, the analogy does not resolve the issue of its entirety. Presented in this manner it assumes as axiomatic that, in the first instance, motherhood is genetically determined but that the original relationship can perhaps be nullified by establishment of a subsequent maternal relationship. The thrust of the analogy is to establish that the earlier relationship is not extinguished. The crux of the question, however, is whether Halakhah at all recognizes a maternal relationship based upon donation of an ovum, i.e., a relationship based solely upon genetic considerations. That is an issue with regard to which there may well be no evidence in rabbinic sources.[22] Only after it is established that there exists halakhic cognizance of a maternal relationship based upon donation of an ovum can the question of possible subsequent nullification or supersedure be addressed. Nevertheless, the analogy does serve a valuable purpose. The thrust of this analogy, if it is properly understood, is to demonstrate that Halakhah may recognize two maternal relationships with the effect that the possibility of a maternal relationship based upon a genetic relationship cannot be regarded as excluded simply because there is evidence that Halakhah recognizes a different maternal relationship based upon parturition or gestation. The analogy to agricultural laws does not, however, serve to provide affirmative evidence demonstrating that Halakhah recognizes a maternal relationship based upon genetic considerations.[23]

Although some scholars are reported as questioning the aptness of any analogy based upon determination of species or status with regard to agricultural law, Prof. Low concludes that the analogy cannot be dismissed out of hand and that, accordingly, at least for purposes of halakhic stringency, the child must be regarded as having two mothers. This writer would concur in that conclusion even in the absence of any analogy to agricultural law.[24] The halakhic (as distinct from aggadic)[25] evidence supporting parturition as determining motherhood does not serve to preclude the possibility of a dual maternal relationship. Hence the possibility of such a relationship cannot be ignored unless evidence of its non-existence is adduced.

This point notwithstanding, it seems to this writer that the analogy to the provisions of agricultural law fails entirely with regard to in vitro fertilization if the statment of the Gemara, *Yevamot* 69b, categorizing an embryo within the first forty days of gestation as "mere water" is to be understood literally. If the fetus is entirely lacking in status and identity during this period it would stand to reason that no maternal relationship can be established during that period. It is only logical that an entity that has no identity cannot be the subject of a relationship, or better, it stands to reason that that which is "mere water" knows no mother. On the other hand, if, as many authorities maintain, categorization of an embryo in the early stages of development as "mere water" is limited in application and, for example, does not serve to prohibit destruction during that period,[26] the analogy is quite apt.

Moreover, an entirely different analogy may be offered in demonstrating that, at least for some authorities, the child born of in vitro fertilization should be regarded as having two mothers. The Gemara, *Hullin* 79a, in discussing the classification of the offspring born as a result of the interbreeding of different species, records one opinion which maintains that the identity of the male partner is to be completely disregarded in determining the species of the offspring. According to this view, since it is the mother who nurtures and sustains the embryo, it is the female parent alone who determines the species of the offspring. It is thus the identity of the mother which is transferred to members of an inter-species.

There is, however, a conflicting opinion which asserts that "the father's seed is to be considered" (*hosheshin le-zera he'av*). Presumably, according to this view, "the father's seed is to be considered" because the father plays a dynamic role in the birth of the offspring. In an analogous manner, a similar line of reasoning may be applied in determining the maternity of a child born of a fertilized ovum implanted in the womb of a host mother. It is the host mother who nurtures the embryo and sustains gestation. However, the role of the genetic mother in the determination of identity is a dynamic one and analogous to that of "the seed of the father." It may therefore be argued according to those who assert with reference to the classification of hybrids that "the seed of the father is to be considered" that, in the case of a donated ovum, the maternal relationship between the child and the donor mother is to be "considered" no less than "the seed of the father." Of course, the result of consideration of that principle in situations involving implantation of an already fertilized ovum would be to establish, not a paternal relationship, but rather a second maternal relationship between the child and the donor of the ovum.

## V.  A NON-JEWISH OVUM DONOR

Yet another complication arises in cases of in vitro fertilization in which the donor of the ovum is a gentile. Ova produced by another woman and donated to the childless couple are utilized in situations in which the infertile woman does not ovulate, or does not produce viable ova, but her uterus is capable of receiving a fertilized ovum and carrying it to term. In such situations the couple may seek a gentile donor, fertilize her ovum with the sperm of the infertile woman's husband by means of an in vitro procedure and implant the zygote in the wife's uterus. If parturition is accepted as the sole criterion to be employed in determining maternal identity it might be assumed that, since the child has a Jewish mother, the child is also Jewish. However, if the donor mother also enjoys a maternal relationship with the child and the child, in effect, has two mothers, the resulting status of the child of two mothers, one a Jewess and the other a non-Jewess, is far from clear. Moreover, there is reason to conclude that some early authorities would maintain that a child whose genetic mother is non-Jewish requires conversion even if the child is regarded by Halakhah as the child of a Jewish mother. There may even be reason to infer that this conclusion is compelled by statements of the Gemara itself.

This rather anomalous conclusion is based upon the position formulated by Ramban in his commentary on *Yevamot* 47b. Ramban maintains that a male child born to a woman who has converted to Judaism during pregnancy requires circumcision for purposes of conversion. Ramban acknowledges that immersion of the mother in a *mikveh* for the purpose of conversion constitutes immersion of the fetus as well but that, in the case of a male, circumcision is required in order to complete the conversion process. However, as noted earlier, the Gemara, *Yevamot* 97b, declares that, should the same woman give birth to twins, a fraternal relationship exists between the children. If so, Ramban's position is problematic. If, as he maintains, the conversion is as yet incomplete, how can a fraternal relationship arise? Upon completion of the conversion process, each of the children is deemed to be "a newly born child" and, in the eyes of Jewish law, lacks any familial relationship with previously born relatives even if they, too, become converts to Judaism.[27]

Addressing himself to the problem presented by Ramban's position, Rabbi Moshe Sternbuch, *Be-Shevilei ha-Refu'ah*, no. 8 (Kislev 5747), resolves the difficulty by suggesting that the maternal relationship—and consequently any other maternal blood relationship—is indeed established at the time of parturition and therefore the baby is not "a newly born child" bereft of blood relatives. Nevertheless, since the child's genotype is non-Jewish, the child requires conversion in order to eliminate "impurity" associated with the gentile state. Similarly, a child born of in vitro fertilization would be deemed the child of the Jewish birth mother but would yet require conversion because of its non-Jewish genetic origin.[28]

Rabbi Sternbuch's discussion is unclear with regard to one point, i.e., the problem that he addresses exists even if Ramban's position with regard to circumcision is not accepted.[29] The Gemara, *Yevamot* 78a, clearly states that immersion of the mother for purposes of conversion constitutes immersion of the fetus. Implicit in that statement is the proposition that the fetus requires conversion. Yet, as noted earlier, the Gemara, *Yevamot* 97b, declares that if the pregnant proselyte gives birth to twins they are regarded as maternal siblings. If the fetus is a proselyte lacking blood relatives, including a mother, how can it later acquire a brother at the time of parturition? To be sure, absent Ramban's position maintaining that conversion is not complete until circumcision is performed, the problem might be resolved by postulating that, since parturition gives rise to a maternal-filial relationship, parturition subsequent to conversion also serves to generate a maternal relationship even though the fetus is a proselyte. However, that solution gives rise to a further problem: If parturition generates a maternal relationship, why does it not also serve to establish the status of the neonate as a Jew? If so, antecedent conversion of the fetus in utero, as posited by the Gemara, *Yevamot* 78a, would be superfluous. This problem is resolved if it is understood that conversion is required in all instances in which the maternal genetic origin of the child is non-Jewish in nature. If so, that conclusion follows directly from the discussion of the Gemara itself rather than from Ramban's analysis thereof.

Rabbi Sternbuch points to an interesting historical parallel in illustrating his thesis. Our ancestors became "converts" to Judaism at the time of revelation on Mount Sinai and, indeed, many of the principles concerning conversion are derived from biblical passages concerning that event. Nevertheless, asserts Rabbi Sternbuch, prohibitions concerning incest were fully binding upon our ancestors at that time and encompassed blood relatives who themselves became "converts" contemporaneously. In accordance with the talmudic dictum "A proselyte who converts is comparable to a newly born child" (*Yevamot* 22a and *Bekhorot* 47a) the recipients of the Torah at Mount Sinai should, ostensibly, have been regarded as "newly born children" lacking blood relatives. Rabbi Sternbuch suggests that the status as Jews enjoyed by our ancestors at Mount Sinai was assured by virtue of the fact that they were the progeny of Abraham the Patriarch and that "conversion" at Sinai was necessary only in order to remove the "impurity" associated with the gentile state and concludes that conversion required solely for the purpose of eliminating such impurity does not give rise to status as "newly born children" that would, in turn, serve to render consanguineous relationships permissible.

In point of fact, Rabbi Sternbuch's assertion that our ancestors did not have the status of "newly born children" at Mount Sinai is a matter of some dispute. Rabbi Sternbuch's position echoes that of Maharal of Prague, *Gur Aryeh, Parashat Va-Yigash* (Genesis 46:8), cited by the author of *Shev Shematata* in section 9 of his introduction to that work. Maharal of Prague is of the opinion that, unlike subsequent proselytes, the recipients of the Torah at Mount Sinai did not acquire status as "newly born children" and, accordingly, they were forbidden to marry close relatives. However, Maharal offers a rationale entirely different from that advanced by Rabbi Sternbuch in explaining why those who became Jews at Mount Sinai were not deemed to be "newly born children." Acceptance of the commandments at Sinai is described by the Gemara, *Shabbat* 88a, as having been coerced. Status as "newly born children," asserts Maharal, is acquired only when acceptance of commandments is voluntary. Nevertheless, R. Meir Simchah of Dvinsk, *Meshekh Hokhmah, Parashat Va-Et'hanan* (Deuteronomy 5:27), espouses an opposing view in declaring that previously existing consanguineous relationships were not terminated at Sinai as evidenced by the fact that all participants were directed "Return to your tents" (Deuteronomy 5:27), i.e., they were granted permission to resume conjugal relations prohibited in the preparatory period before receiving the Torah at Mount Sinai. Indeed, *Meshekh Hokhmah* points to that directive as the biblical source of the talmudic dictum "A proselyte who converts is comparable to a newly born child."[30]

The thesis advanced by Rabbi Sternbuch in postulating two types of conversion is remarkably similar to that expounded by R. Naphtali Trop in his *Shi'urei ha-Granat, Ketubot* 11a,[31] save that Reb Naphtali's comments are expressed in the positive rather than in the negative.[32] Rabbi Sternbuch's analysis of the principle "A proselyte who converts is comparable to a newly born child" and his conclusion that it is inapplicable to the recipients of the Torah at Mount Sinai are also identical to those of Reb Naphtali. In resolving a number of problems involving the difficulty associated with Ramban's position, Reb Naphtali explains that there are two forms of conversion: 1) conversion for the purpose of becoming a Jew, i.e., a member of the community of Israel; and 2) conversion for the purpose of acquiring sanctification as an Israelite (*kedushat Yisra'el*). Reb Naphtali suggests that one who enjoys the status of a member of the Jewish community is under obligation to undergo conversion in order to acquire the "sanctity of an Israelite." Presumably, the implication of that position is that obligations pertaining to fulfillment of commandments are contingent upon acquiring the "sanctity of an Israelite." Thus he asserts that even those authorities who maintain that the child of a Jewess whose father is a non-Jew requires conversion agree that conversion of such a child for purposes of membership in the Jewish community is unnecessary since membership in the Jewish community is transmitted by virtue of matrilineal succession. According to those authorities, Reb Naphtali asserts, conversion is necessary solely for the purpose of acquiring "sanctity of an Israelite" which is acquired automatically upon birth only if both parents are Jews. Similarly, maintains Reb Naphtali, even according to Ramban, a child born to a proselyte who was pregnant at the time of her conversion acquires status as a member of the community of Israel by virtue of having been born to a Jewish mother and, accordingly, a maternal-filial relationship is also established by virtue of parturition for all genealogical purposes. Conversion, according to Ramban, asserts Reb Naphtali, is necessary only for the purpose of acquiring the "sanctity of an Israelite."[33] Reb Naphtali similarly asserts that conversion at the time of revelation at Mount Sinai was solely for the purpose of acquiring the "sanctity of an Israelite" and, accordingly, prohibitions with regard to sexual relations with blood relatives remained in effect.

On the basis of the thesis developed by R. Naphtali Trop it would follow that a fetus transplanted from a gentile woman to a Jewess would require conversion for purposes of *kedushat Yisra'el*. It would appear to be the case that such conversion might be performed even during pregnancy by means of immersion of the pregnant mother in a *mikveh* as is the case with regard to the fetus of a pregnant non-Jewess who converts to Judaism.[34] According to this thesis, the same would be true of a fetus conceived from an ovum donated by a gentile donor.[35]

In a contribution to *Tehumin,* vol. V, devoted to a discussion of the status of a child born as the result of in vitro procedures, Rabbi Abraham Kilav accepts the basic principle that a maternal relationship is established by virtue of parturition. Nevertheless, Rabbi Kilav denies that parturition serves to establish such a relationship in situations in which the ovum was donated by a non-Jewish woman.[36] The fact that a fetus carried by a proselyte at the time of her conversion itself requires conversion leads to the conclusion that a fetus born of in vitro fertilization of an ovum donated by a gentile also requires conversion. Yet, maintains Rabbi Kilav, a maternal relationship exists in the case of the pregnant proselyte but not in the case of an implanted ovum of gentile origin. In the former case, conversion takes place during pregnancy and at the time of birth the child is already Jewish. In the case of in vitro fertilization, the gestational mother is Jewish and no conversion of the fetus takes place during pregnancy. Since conversion of the fetus does not occur prior to parturition, argues Rabbi Kilav, no relationship to the mother is established by parturition. Rabbi Goldberg, on the other hand, maintains that, although the child requires conversion, parturition nevertheless serves to establish a maternal relationship even in such circumstances.

The conclusion reached by Rabbi Goldberg seems to be compelled according to the position of Ramban. Ramban maintains that conversion of a male fetus is not complete until circumcision is performed after birth. Nevertheless, as has been noted earlier, the existence of a maternal relationship between a proselyte and the children converted with her as fetuses during pregnancy is clear. According to Ramban, that relationship exists despite the fact that circumcision for the purpose of conversion did not occur.[37] Hence, the same relationship should exist even if the conversion process has not commenced, e.g., a non-Jewish fetus is implanted in the womb of a Jewish mother, or, according to *Dagul me-Revavah, Yoreh De'ah* 268:6, if the *Bet Din* was unaware of the pregnancy at the time of the mother's conversion. Similarly, if R. Naphtali Trop's thesis is accepted, the identical conclusion may be reached even without reliance upon Ramban's position. According to that thesis, membership in the community of Israel is established on the basis of parturition while conversion is necessary for purposes of *kedushat Yisra'el*. Hence, in the case of the implantation of an ovum donated by a non-Jewish woman, parturition would serve to establish membership in the community of Israel and would simultaneously serve to establish a maternal relationship with the birth mother while conversion would be required for purposes of *kedushat Yisra'el*.[38]

Rabbi Goldberg adds one caveat that is apparently not accepted by either Rabbi Sternbuch or Rabbi Kilav. Rabbi Goldberg asserts that according to those who maintain that the fetus is an integral part of the mother's body (*ubar yerekh imo*) a fetus implanted in the womb of a Jewess does not require conversion in situations in which the donor of the ovum is a non-Jewess. Rabbi Goldberg argues that, upon implantation, the fetus becomes part of the mother and, hence, part of a Jewish body with the result that conversion of the fetus becomes unnecessary. In making this point without further discussion, Rabbi Goldberg seems to ignore the possibility that, if non-Jewish identity is established prior to implantation in the uterus of a Jewish woman, transformation into a limb of the gestational mother may not *ipso facto* result in negation of previously acquired identity as a gentile.

Prof. Low reports an intriguing opinion with regard to a hypothetical question involving a Jewish woman who becomes pregnant as the result of in vitro fertilization utilizing an ovum donated by a non-Jewish woman and who wishes to accomplish conversion of the fetus prior to its birth by undergoing immersion in a *mikveh* during the course of her pregnancy. Prof. Low cites an oral opinion expressed by R. Shlomo Zalman Auerbuch to the effect that "for [the purpose of conversion] the immersion of the host mother is of no effect" insofar as the fetus is concerned but fails to report the grounds supporting the conclusion. A communication from Rabbi Avigdor Nebenzal is also cited by Prof. Low in which Rabbi Nebenzal expresses a similar view even with regard to a situation in which an already fertilized ovum is removed from the non-Jewish natural mother and subsequently reinserted into her own uterus. Rabbi Nebenzal apparently maintains that, in such circumstances, immersion of the mother is not efficacious on behalf of the fetus. The more usual case, of course, is a situation in which the donor of the ovum is a gentile woman and the Jewish gestational mother would prefer to immerse the child in utero rather than delay the immersion of the neonate until medically advisable.

In each of these cases it is difficult to comprehend why the mother's immersion should not *ipso facto* be deemed immersion of the fetus. The Gemara, *Yevamot* 78a, certainly recognized the efficacy of fetal conversion in the case of natural pregnancy. In the course of that discussion the Gemara questions why the mother's body shall not be deemed a barrier between the fetus and the water of the *mikveh* since, because of the interposition of the mother, the fetus does not at all come into contact with the water. The response of the Gemara is, "A fetus is different. That is the way it grows (*hainu reviteih*)." The import of that response is that, whether or not the fetus is regarded as an "organ of the mother," i.e., as an integral part of her body, the mother's body is not a foreign entity separating the fetus from the water. Since attachment to the uterine wall is normal, natural and essential to the fetus, the mother's body does not constitute an interposition (*hatzitzah*) for purposes of immmersion.

As a ramification of the laws of interposition, the talmudic ruling permitting conversion of the fetus in utero would appear to be entirely unrelated to the principles that serve to determine maternal identity. It is certainly arguable that immersion of the pregnant woman may serve to effect a valid conversion even if she is not the genetic mother and even if the fetus is subsequently transferrerd to the uterus of another woman prior to term. Although there is no report to that effect, one may speculate that those who are quoted as adopting an opposing view regard the Gemara's statement regarding interposition as limited to natural pregnancy.[39] That, too, is difficult to comprehend since, assuredly a skin graft, or hypothetically, a graft of an entire limb, that has become a functioning part of the recipient's body does not constitute an interposition invalidating immersion in a *mikveh.* This would be true even if the skin graft covered the entire surface of the body. The fact that the mother's body will ultimately become separated from the fetus at birth while the graft is destined to remain in place throughout the recipient's life should not serve to negate the underlying rationale expressed in the dictum "That is the way it grows," i.e., since pregnancy by its nature is transitory the ultimate separation of the fetus from its mother should not interfere with the noninterposing status of the mother's body.

## VI. IMPLANTATION WITHIN THE FIRST FORTY DAYS

R. Aaron Soloveichik is quoted by his son, R. Moshe Soloveichik, *Or ha-Mizrah,* Tishri-Tevet 5741, p. 127, as being of the opinion that, although the status of the fetus of a pregnant woman who converts to Judaism is that of a convert, nevertheless, the status of a fetus of the proselyte who converts within the first forty days of pregnancy is not that of a convert but is that of a child born to a Jewish mother. That position is based upon the statement of the Gemara, *Yevamot* 69b, categorizing a fetus during the first forty days following conception as "mere water." Hence, it is argued, at the time that it acquires the status of a fetus, i.e., following the expiration of the first forty days of gestation, it is the fetus of a Jewish mother.[40] If so, it would logically follow that, *mutatis mutandis,* a host mother in whom the developing zygote has been implanted immediately after fertilization should be regarded as the halakhic mother of the child, not necessarily because the host mother is the birth mother, but because at the time of implantation the fetus has as yet not acquired identity with the result that at the stage of development that it can acquire identity it acquires identity in relationship to the gestational mother. Since, at least at present, implementation of the fertilized ovum in the uterus of the gestational mother takes place in the very early stages of cell division, the effect of this position is to eliminate the need for conversion in all cases involving non-Jewish donors.

This line of reasoning is best understood if it is assumed that the prohibition against feticide does not apply during this early period of gestation because the fetus is "mere water." However, if, as is the opinion of many authorities, the prohibition against feticide applies even during this early stage of pregnancy[41] because, although the fetus may be "mere water" with regard to other matters of Halakhah, it is nevertheless regarded as a nascent life from the moment of conception, that conclusion may serve to establish the principle that the developing fetus is a "person" in its own right and hence may, even at that early stage of development, enjoy a status independent of that of its gestational mother.

Moreover, if, as is the position of many authorities, including Rabad, *Hilkhot Avadim* 7:5, Rabbenu Nisim, *Hullin* 8a, R. Akiva Eger, *Ketubot* 11a, and others, a fetus is not an integral part of the mother's body (*ubar lav yerekh imo*)[42] it is not clear that the child becomes a Jew other than through conversion, (i.e., the conversion of the mother which serves concomitantly as conversion of the child as well) even though the mother's conversion occurs within the first forty days of gestation. To be sure, even according to the authorities who maintain that a fetus is not regarded as an integral part of the mother's body, a child conceived by a Jewish mother is Jewish by virtue of the fact that it springs from the ovum of a Jewess. Even though the ovum itself is "mere water," the developed fetus is nevertheless the product of a Jewish maternal forebear. However, halakhically speaking, the embryo within the uterus of a woman who converts to Judaism is regarded as *sui generis*. Accordingly, if the fetus is not regarded as an integral part of the mother there is no apparent reason why the embryo should automatically acquire her status.[43]

In his article published in *Tehumin*, Rabbi Kilav explicitly rejects any distinction between situations involving implantation of a developing embryo during the first forty days following conception and implantation during later periods of gestation.[44] The Gemara, *Kiddushin* 69a, posits a situation in which a Jewess may give birth to a child whose status is that of a slave. The Sages, whose opinion in this regard is accepted as normative, declare that a master may emancipate a female slave who is pregnant without simultaneously emancipating the fetus. The master thereby reserves the fetus to himself as a slave subsequent to birth. There is no hint in the Gemara or in the subsequent codifications of this halakhic provision that such a reservation is ineffective if the female slave is less than forty days pregnant. Hence it cannot be assumed that because the nascent embryo is described as "mere water" it lacks independent status and identity. Similarly, R. Ezekiel Landau, *Dagul me-Revavah, Yoreh De'ah* 268:6, in discussing a related situation, fails to distinguish between the various states of pregnancy. *Dagul me-Revavah* expresses doubt with regard to the efficacy of the mother's conversion vis-à-vis her child in situations in which the pregnancy was not made known to the members of the *Bet Din* at the time of her immersion in a *mikveh,* but does not indicate that failure to disclose this information is immaterial if conversion takes place within the first forty days of pregnancy. In his contribution to *Be-Shevilei ha-Refu'ah,* no. 8, Rabbi Sternbuch similarly maintains that conversion of the fetus is required even if the mother becomes a convert within the first forty days of gestation.

## VII. A JEWISH DONOR AND A NON-JEWISH GESTATIONAL MOTHER

As yet, there has not appeared a detailed discussion of the status of a child born to a non-Jewish gestational mother by means of in vitro fertilization of an ovum donated by a Jewish woman. On the basis of the foregoing discussion it may be assumed that the child would require conversion in order to be recognized as a Jew. That conclusion would be the necessary result of acceptance of parturition as the determining factor with regard to a maternal-child relationship. Even if the possibility of a dual maternal relationship is recognized, conversion would appear to be required at the very minimum for the purpose of acquiring *kedushat Yisra'el* because of the existence of a non-Jewish genealogical relationship. That conclusion would follow *a fortiori* from the requirement for conversion of the fetus of a proselyte who converts while pregnant and for the conversion of a non-Jewish fetus implanted in a Jewish gestational mother. It is also entirely conceivable that a dual maternal relationship would result in a status of "half-Jew, half-gentile" analogous to the status of "half-slave, half-freeman," posited by the Gemara in other contexts. If so, the "half-gentile" would require the usual form of conversion. However, Rabbi Kilav, in a cryptic statement, expresses the opinion that in such circumstances the child is a Jew.[45] That view is consistent with his position that in the converse situation of a non-Jewish ovum donor the child is a gentile and that parturition determines only maternal identity but not religious status.

At issue is not simply the status of such a child. Determination of that question has obvious and serious implications with regard to the issue of ovum donations by Jewish women on behalf of non-Jewish infertile couples. Obviously, such donations cannot be sanctioned if they result in situations in which a Jewish child, or a child who is "half-Jew, half-gentile," is reared as a gentile and allowed to become "assimilated among the nations." On the other hand, if the child's status is that of a non-Jew, the permissibility of such a donation is far from clear and, at the very minimum, the procedure is contrary to ideological norms of Judaism. In the case of idol-worshippers, the Gemara, *Avodah Zarah* 26a, censures various forms of assistance in the propagation of pagan children because the mother "gives birth to a child for idolatry." Permission for such assistance is granted only when withholding of necessary services would result in enmity toward Jews.

Indeed, even donation of an ovum to a Jewish infertile couple in situations in which the child will not be provided with a Jewish education and reared in an observant home is fraught with both halakhic and ideological difficulties that are beyond the scope of this discussion. Moreover, if a maternal-filial relationship between the donor and the child is recognized by Halakhah, suppression of the identity of the genetic mother would be forbidden because of the potential for an incestuous marriage at some future time,[46] not to speak of the general odium associated in Jewish teaching with interference with, and distortion of, normal familial relationships.

## VIII.   ANIMAL GESTATION OF A HUMAN EMBRYO

The possibility of dual maternal relationships may acquire particular significance when, and if, implantation of a human fetus in a member of an animal species becomes an empirical possibility. Gestational development would then occur in the uterus of the animal which would serve as a sort of living incubator. Although, at present, the possibility seems extremely remote, recent developments in science and technology amply demonstrate that the science fiction of today may become the reality of tomorrow. Development of immuno-suppressive drugs has made zenografts a distinct possibility and, although some may find such a procedure repugnant, those developments may conceivably lead to use of animals for gestational purposes. In such an eventuality the crucial question will be whether the product of such gestation is to be accorded status as a human being.

It is evident from the discussion of the Gemara, *Niddah* 23b, that identity as the member of a particular species is determined, not by distinguishing physical characteristics, but by birth. Thus, an animal-like creature born to a human is regarded as a human being. The Gemara clearly recognized the theoretical possibility of a converse situation, *viz.*, of a human-like creature being born to an animal. If born to a member of a kosher species the Gemara questions whether or not the offspring may be slaughtered for food since, although it possesses a "hoof," it does not have the characteristic split hoof of a kosher species. From the very formulation of the question it is manifestly evident that the Gemara did not regard a creature of this nature as enjoying the status of a human being.

Thus, if parturition is regarded as the sole determining criterion in all matters of personal status to the exclusion of genetic considerations, the Gemara's discussion may one day become entirely germane to the determination of the status of a human zygote implanted in an animal uterus. If, on the other hand, the possibility of dual maternal relationships is accepted, such offspring may acquire the identity of the genetic mother as well as that of the gestational mother.

## IX. CONCLUSIONS

In the opinion of this writer, the preponderance of evidence adduced from rabbinic sources demonstrates that parturition, in and of itself, serves to establish a maternal relationship. Nevertheless, the possibility that Jewish law may recognize a second maternal relationship based upon donation of an ovum cannot be excluded and indeed there is some evidence indicating that such an additional relationship is recognized. It is also possible that an additional non-genetic and non-parturitional relationship, or even multiple relationships of that nature, may be established on the basis of gestation. Thus, for purposes of Jewish law, the relationship arising from parturition must be regarded as firmly established whereas genetic and gestational relationships must be regarded as doubtful (*safek*). The primary effect, but by no means the sole implication, of recognition of this "doubtful" relationship is to prohibit marriage between genetic siblings and other genetic relatives.

A child born of an in vitro procedure in which the ovum was donated by a non-Jewish woman requires conversion. Although the grounds are not entirely clear, such authorities maintain that, in such cases, immersion for purposes of conversion must be performed after birth but not by the mother during pregnancy. Whether or not there exists a maternal relationship with the Jewish birth mother in such cases is a matter of dispute.

This endeavor addresses only issues of maternal identity and conversion in situations in which a child has been born as the result of in vitro fertilization. A comprehensive analysis of the various issues that must be addressed in discussing the permissibility of utilization of in vitro procedures or ovum donations in order to overcome problems associated with infertility is beyond the scope of this undertaking. Those issues represent matters of grave halakhic and moral significance requiring informed halakhic guidance.

## NOTES

1. *Tradition*, vol. 13, no. 2 (Fall, 1972) and vol. 19, no. 4 (Winter, 1981), reprinted respectively in this writer's *Contemporary Halakhic Problems*, I (New York, 1977), 106–109 and *Contemporary Halakhic Problems*, II (New York, 1983), 91–93.

2. See R. Shlomo Goren, *Ha-Tzofeh*, 7 Adar I 5744. See also R. Joshua Feigenbaum, *Sha'arei Torah*, vol. IV, no. 4; Prof. Ze'ev Low, *Emek Halakhah*, II (Jerusalem, 5749), 163–172; Dr. Itamar Warhaftig, *Tehumin*, V (5744), 268–269; and R. Ezra Bick, *Tehumin*, VII (5746), 266–270.

3. In addition to the sources cited herein, see R. Moshe Hershler, *Halakhah u-Refu'ah*, I, (Jerusalem, 5740), 316–320; R. Menasheh Grossbart, *Sha'arei Torah, Sha'ar Menasheh*, XV (5684), no. 3; R. Zevi Hirsch Friedling, *Ha-Be'er*, VI (5691), no. 3; and R. Batzalel Ze'ev Safran, *Ha-*

*Be'er*, VII (5692), no. 2, reprinted in *Teshuvot ha-Rabaz* (Jerusalem, 5722), *Teshuvot mi-Ben ha-Mehaber*, no. 5.

4. See, for example, R. Moshe Sternbuch, *Be-Shevilei ha-Refu'ah*, no. 8 (Kislev 5747), p. 33 and *Tradition*, vol. 13, no. 2, pp. 128–129, reprinted in *Contemporary Halakhic Problems*, I, 108. This possibility will be discussed in a later section of this article.

5. This responsum originally appeared in *Assia*, vol. 9, no. 1 (Tammuz 5742) and is reprinted in *Sefer Assia* (Jerusalem, 5746) V, 84–93. Cf. the comments of R. Avigdor, Nebenzal, *Assia*, vol. 9, no. 2 (Tishri 5743), reprinted in *Assia*, V, 92–93.

6. It is indeed true that culture media are required in order to enable cell division to occur. The specific components of the medium used for this purpose vary widely from one in vitro center to another but usually include human blood serum or, in some places, fetal calf serum to which antibiotics and other chemical products are added. Frequently, but not always, the serum is derived from the patient's own blood. Nevertheless, there is no reason to assume that nutrients utilized to support metabolism constitute a "third power" effecting parental relationships. It is not inconceivable that medicine may find a way to introduce artificial nutrition intravenously into the fetus in utero in order to compensate for certain natural deficiencies. Indeed, in utero blood transfer is already employed as a means of overcoming certain incompatibilities between fetal and maternal blood. No rabbinic decisor has suggested that introduction of blood or nutrients from a source other than the bloodstream of the mother casts doubt upon the maternal-filial relationship.

7. This article is reprinted in Rabbi Gershuni's *Kol Tzofayikh* (Jerusalem, 5740), pp. 361–367.

8. The primary source affirming a paternal relation is *Hagahot Semak*, cited by *Mishneh le-Melekh*, *Hilkot Ishut* 15:4, *Bah*, *Yoreh De'ah* 195, and *Bet Shmu'el*, *Even ha-Ezer* 1:10. A similar view is expressed by *Helkat Mehokek*, *Even ha-Ezer* 1:8; *Teshuvot Tashbaz*, III, no. 263; *Turei Even*, *Haggigah* 15a; *Bnei Ahuvah*, *Hilkhot Ishut* 15; *Arukh la-Ner*, *Yevamot* 10a; *Mishneh le-Melekh*, *Hilkhot Issurei Bi'ah* 17:13; *She'ilat Ya'avez*, II, no. 97; *Maharam Shik al Taryag Mitzvot*, no. 1, *Teshuvot Divrei Malki'el*, II, no. 107; R. Shlomo Zalman Auerbach, *No'am*, I (5717), 155; R. Israel Zev Mintzberg, *No'am*, I, 129; R. Joshua Baumol, *Teshuvot Emek Halakhah*, I, no. 68; R. Avigdor Nebenzal, *Assia*, V (5746), 92–93; and R. Ovadiah Yosef, quoted by Moshe Drori, *Tehumin*, I (5740), 287, and Abraham S. Abraham, *Nishmat Avraham*, *Even ha-Ezer* 1:5, sec. 3. An opposing view is expressed by *Taz*, *Even ha-Ezer* 1:8; *Birkei Yosef*, *Even ha-Ezer* 1:14; R. Ovadiah Hedeya, *No'am*, I, 130–137; R. Moshe Aryeh Leib Shapiro, *No'am*, I, 138–142; and R. Ben Zion Uziel, *Mishpetei Uzi'el*, *Even ha-Ezer*, no. 19, reprinted in *Piskei*

*Uzi'el* (Jerusalem, 5737), pp. 282–283. *Teshuvot Helkat Ya'akov,* I, no. 24, regards the issue as a matter of doubt.

9. In his previously cited article in *Be-Shevilei ha-Refu'ah,* p. 30, R. Moshe Sternbuch presents an argument quite similar to that advanced by *Divrei Malki'el* in rejecting a paternal relationship between the donor of the semen and the child born of subsequent in vitro fertilization even when the zygote is implanted in the donor's wife. Rabbi Sternbuch argues that "the act of conception takes place in the sterile petri dish which acts to commence conception, to unite both of them (i.e., the ovum and the sperm) as in the womb. This is not in the manner of conception since another power is combined therein, that is the petri dish."

The effect of denying paternal identity, asserts Rabbi Sternbuch, is to prohibit in vitro fertilization entirely. Rabbinic authorities who permit ejaculation of semen by the husband for purposes of artificial insemination sanction that procedure only because it leads to procreation. However, if in vitro fertilization does not result in a father-child relationship it does not serve to fulfill the commandment to "be fruitful and multiply" and hence ejaculation of semen for purposes of in vitro procedures is not permissible. See sources cited above, note 8. With regard to artificial insemination, some authorities, including *Arukh la-Ner, Yevamot* 10a, and *Maharam Shik al Taryag Mitzvot,* no. 1, maintain that although the child is considered the son of the donor, the donor does not fulfill the precept of procreation because no sexual act is involved. Rabbi Gershuni, although he too denies that artificial insemination results in a paternal-filial relationship, nevertheless regards the procedure as permissible for a married couple. Rabbi Gershuni argues that although artificial insemination does not serve to fulfill the commandment to "be fruitful and multiply," nevertheless, since the procedure results in procreation of the human species, it serves to fulfill the prophetic mandate "He created [the universe] not to be a waste, He formed it to be populated" (Isaiah 45:18) and hence ejaculation of semen for that purpose is not for naught.

For a vaguely similar reason Rabbi Sternbuch, p. 29, opines that destruction of an embryo fertilized outside of a woman's body is not prohibited. He states that ". . . the prohibition against abortion is in the woman's uterus, for the [embryo] has the potential to develop and become complete in her womb and it is destroyed. But here, outside the womb, an additional operation is required to implant [the embryo] in the woman's uterus and without this it will . . . of its own not reach completion. . . ." Rabbi Sternbuch cites no sources in support of that distinction. A similar view is advanced, without elaboration or citation of sources, by R. Chaim David Halevy, *Assia,* vol. 12, no. 3–4. One source that might be cited in support of such a conclusion is *Teshuvot Hakham Tzevi*, no. 93. Citing *Sanhedrin* 57b, *Hakham Tzevi* rules that destruction of a *golem* does not constitute an act of homicide and is not prohibited because its gestation is not in the form of "a man within a man," as evidenced by the fact that the Gemara, *Sanhedrin* 65b, reports that Rabbi Zeira commanded a person created by utilization of *Sefer Yetzirah* to return to dust. That statement, however, cannot be taken as definitive since *Hakham Tzevi* concludes that a *golem* lacks status as a Jew or as a human being for other purposes as well. See also R. Joseph Rosen, *Teshuvot Tzofnat Pa'aneah* (Jerusalem, 5728), II, no. 7. Genesis 9:6 is cited by the Gemara and rendered "Whosoever sheds the blood of a man within a man his blood shall be shed" in establishing feticide as a capital transgression in the Noahide Code. Accordingly, there would be strong grounds to assume that a Noahide does not incur capital punishment for destruction of an embryo fertilized in vitro, but not for support of the position that a person born of in vitro fertilization may be destroyed with impunity or even for the position that there is no halakhic consideration forbidding a Jew to destroyed a developing embryo outside the human body. Moreover, Ramban, cited by Ran, *Yoma* 82a, and Rosh, *Yoma* 8:13, maintains that Sabbath restrictions and the like are suspended for the purpose of preserving the life of a fetus. Those comments clearly reflect the view that there is an obligation to preserve fetal life. Thus, there are no obvious grounds for assuming that nascent human life may be destroyed with impunity simply because it is not sheltered in its natural habitat, i.e., its development takes place ouside the mother's womb. R. Samuel ha-Levi Wosner, *Teshuvot Shevet ha-Levi*, V, no. 47, expresses the opinion that Sabbath restrictions are not suspended for the preservation of a zygote that has as yet not been implanted in the gestational mother on the grounds that the vast majority of such zygotes are not viable but adds the cautionary note that the empirical situation, and hence the halakhic ruling, may change with advances in the development of reproductive knowledge and techniques. The clear implication of his position is that destruction of such nascent life cannot be countenanced. For a further discussion of the propriety of destroying fertilized ova see this writer's article, "Ethical Concerns in Artificial Procreation: A Jewish Perspective," *Publications de l'Academie du Royaume du Maroc*, Vol. X: *Problèmes d'Éthiques Engendrés par les Nouvelles Maîtrises de la Procreation Humaine* (Agadir, 1986), pp. 143–145.

There are, however, strong reasons to assume that there is no prohibition against the destruction of a nonviable fetus, as is stated by Rabbi Sternbuch, *loc. cit.* See Abraham S. Abraham, *Nishmat Avraham, Hoshen Mishpat* 425:1, sec. 19, and R. Zalman Nechemiah Goldberg, *Tehumin*, V,

p. 250. Nevertheless, such a conclusion is contrary to the view expressed by R. Eleazer Fleckles, *Teshuvah me-Ahavah*, no. 53 with regard to a nonviable neonate. See also *Teshuvot Radbaz*, II, no. 695.

10. R. Chaim Soloveitchik is reported to have resolved an entirely different issue by declaring that this statement is limited to the case of a woman who converts to Judaism within the first forty days of gestation. See R. Elchanan Wasserman, *Kovez He'arot*, no. 73, sec. 12, and below, note 27. According to Reb Chaim's interpretation of this source, no further conclusion can be drawn with regard to determination of maternal identity. However, Reb Chaim's understanding of the limited application of the Gemara's statement is not reflected in the compilations of any of the codifiers of Jewish law, in the responsa literature or in the talmudic commentaries.

11. In a note appented to the articles published in *Tehumin*, the editor, Dr. Itamar Warhaftig, expresses the opinion that, logically, the biological mother, i.e., the donor of the ovum, should be considered to be the mother of a child born of in vitro fertilization. Without offering demonstrative proof, he assumes that any sources indicating that parturition establishes a maternal relationship serve to establish only that parturition gives rise to a maternal relationship vis-à-vis a biological child or vis-à-vis a child with regard to whom Halakhah abrogates the biological relationship, *viz.*, a convert. He entirely fails to consider the possibility of dual maternal relationships. See also R. Ezra Bick, *Tehumin*, VII, 267–268.

Dr. Warhaftig does however point to what he considers to be a halakhic anomaly. Biblical law provides financial compensation to be paid to the father in cases of fetal death resulting from battery of the mother. Rambam, *Hilkhot Hovel u-Mazik* 4:2, rules that, in the event that the father has died before the miscarriage occurs, compensation is to be paid to the mother. Although all authorities agree that compensation is to be paid to the mother in the case of the miscarriage of a pregnant convert or in the case of the wife of a convert who is deceased, Rambam's position is novel in a situation in which the Jewish husband has died leaving heirs. *Kesef Mishneh, ad locum*, explains that in describing this untoward event Scripture employs the phrase "and her children emerge" thereby indicating a possessive relationship vested in the mother. That source, however, does not at all serve to establish a halakhic relationship for other areas of Jewish law. Compensation for loss of fetal life is rooted in a property interest established by Scripture solely for that purpose. Establishment of that property interest is not necessarily predicated upon a familial relationship recognized for other purposes of law. Moreover, as Rabbi Goldberg points out, miscarriage of the fetus is tantamount to parturition and hence miscarriage itself serves to establish a maternal relationship. Cf. also, below, note 12.

12. It would be reasonable to assume that delivery of a viable fetus by means of a cesarean section similarly serves to establish a maternal relationship since such delivery is equated with normal birth for other purposes of Jewish law. See R. Abraham Kilav's response to Prof. Ze'ev Low, *Emek Halakhah*, II, 173. Indeed, *Tosafot, Niddah* 44a, declare that, if a pregnant woman predeceases her fully-developed fetus, the fetus inherits its mother's estate and causes it to pass to the fetus' maternal relatives. The fetus inherits, according to *Tosafot*, because upon the mother's death its vitality is no longer derived from the mother. Clearly, there could be no inheritance in the absence of a filial relationship. That relationship, then, is established, not by parturition *per se*, but upon termination of gestation regardless of how that event occurs. Cf., R. Zalman Nechemiah Goldberg, *Tehumin*, V, 252, note 4. However, contrary to the presumption of R. Ezra Bick, *Tehumin* VII, 269, there is no basis upon which to assume that termination of gestation at a stage at which the fetus is as yet not viable is tantamount to parturition; assuredly, this could not be the case when the embryo is as yet "mere water." Accordingly, removal of an as yet non-viable embryo and subsequent artificial gestation in an incubator or the like in a manner similar to that portrayed by Aldous Huxley in his *Brave New World* might well result in a situation in which the child has no mother for purposes of halakhic provisions predicated upon the existence of a maternal relationship. Cf., however, Prof. Ze'ev Low, *Emek Halakhah*, II, 164–165 and R. Abraham Kilav, *Emek Halakhah*, II, 173. Rabbi Kilav asserts that, under such conditions, a halakhically recognized maternal relationship exists between the child and its genetic mother but offers no evidence in support of that view. Rabbi Kilav rejects the existence of a maternal relationship with the donor of the ovum in usual circumstances because the birth mother or the gestational mother is regarded as the mother for halakhic purposes and, he asserts, a child cannot have two mothers. He, however, offers no concrete support for those views. As will be shown in a later section, the possibility that a child may well have two mothers for purposes of Halakhah cannot be summarily dismissed. By the same token, if Halakhah does not recognize a maternal relationship based solely upon contribution of the ovum, a fetus nurtured in an incubator may well have no mother in the eyes of Halakhah. Cf., R. Ezra Bick, *Tehumin* VII, 270.

13. Cf., however, R. Zalman Nechemiah Goldberg, *Tehumin*, V, 253–255, who tentatively suggests that the Gemara, in postulating such a fraternal relationship, may be doing so only according to the view that maintains that the fetus is an integral part of the mother's body (*ubar yerekh imo*). See, for example, *Avnei Milu'im, Even ha-Ezer* 4:3 and 13:4; and *Beit Ya'akov, Ketubot* 11a, who maintain that although the Gemara

*Yevamot* 78a speaks of the fetus as itself a convert, that description is accurate only according to the talmudic position that maintains that the fetus is not an integral part of the mother's body. If so, he argues, parturition may establish a maternal relationship only if the fetus is in reality an integral part of her body, i.e., if the fetus is biologically her own, but not in situations in which the fetus is conceived outside of her body and subsequently implanted in her uterus. Nevertheless, there is considerable discussion with regard to whether Rambam maintains *ubar yerekh imo* or *ubar lav yerekh imo* (see *Lehem Mishneh, Hilkhot Avadim* 7:5 and later sources cited below, note 42) despite the fact that in *Hilkhot Issurei Bi'ah* 14:14 Rambam clearly rules that a fraternal relationship does indeed exist. Hence it may be assumed that the principle that parturition establishes a maternal relationship is not a product of that dispute. Cf., R. Joshua Ben-Meir, *Assia*, Nisan 5746, pp. 28–29 and p. 39.

14. R. Zalman Nechemiah Goldberg, *Tehumin*, V, pp. 255–256, endeavors to show that the statement of the Gemara, *Yevamot* 97b, regarding the fraternal relationship between fetal converts is not dispositive according to the novel position of one latter-day authority regarding another matter of personal status. R. Jacob of Lissa, in a responsum published in *Teshuvot Hemdat Shlomoh, Even ha-Ezer,* no. 2, opines that a child born to a Jewish mother but fathered by a gentile requires conversion despite the fact that the Gemara, *Bekhorot* 47a, declares that if such a child is the first-born child of its Jewish mother it requires redemption of the first-born. Since converts do not require redemption, postulation of a requirement for redemption would seem to contradict the thesis advanced by R. Jacob of Lissa. R. Jacob of Lissa responds by stating that, prior to conversion, the child of a Jewish mother and a non-Jewish father is a gentile by virtue of his status as the son of a non-Jewish father and, as a gentile, the child does not require redemption. R. Jacob of Lissa further states that, as a non-Jewish issue of a gentile father, the child can have no Jewish relatives. However, asserts R. Jacob of Lissa, conversion has the effect of severing all prior relationships, including the paternal one. At that point, a maternal relationship is automatically and retroactively established. As the firstborn of a Jewish mother the child requires redemption. If so, argues Rabbi Goldberg, it is conceivable that, according to R. Jacob of Lissa, parturition establishes a maternal relationship only in situations in which the fetus undergoes conversion during the course of pregnancy and hence has no already existing filial relationship, but that under different circumstances a preexisting maternal relationship established genetically or on the basis of gestation precludes any other maternal relationship, just as a non-Jewish paternal relationship precludes the genesis of a Jewish maternal relationship. However, Rabbi Goldberg's argument is not compelling. Even according to R.

Jacob of Lissa, it is only the child's status as a gentile that precludes the genesis of a parental Jewish relationship; there is no evidence whatsoever that an already existing paternal or maternal relationship prevents the existence of a second relationship of a like nature. Cf., R. Ezra Bick, *Tehumin*, VII, 268.

15. For a discussion of those sources see *Contemporary Halakhic Problems*, II, 92–93, and R. Sholomo Goren, *Ha-Tzofeh*, 7 *Adar* I (5744).

16. Cf., R. Moshe Soloveichik, *Or ha-Mizrah*, Tishri-Tevet 5741, p. 125 and R. Abraham Kilav, *Tehumin*, V, 267.

Cf. also the comments of R. Isaac Berger, *Seridim*, no. 4 (5743), who assumes that either parturition or "pregnancy" may serve to establish a maternal relationship. Accordingly, he concludes that the donor of the ovum has no maternal relationship to the child. However, neither his sources nor his analysis serve to demonstrate that it is "pregnancy," i.e., gestation, rather than contribution of the ovum that serves to establish the relationship.

17. *Tehumin*, V, 249.

18. See R. Yitzchak Ya'akov Rabinowitz, *Zekher Yitzhak*, I, no. 4.

19. See Maharal of Prague, *Or Hadash*, s.v. *va-yehi omen*. Indeed, even if no compelling evidence can be adduced demonstrating recognition of dual maternal relationships, the possibility of dual relationships cannot be excluded unless there is evidence to that effect.

20. *Loc. cit.;* see also R. Mier Dan Plocki, *Klei Hemdah, Parashat Toldot*, sec. 1.

21. Even the statement recorded in *Megillah* 13a serves to establish only that the maternal relationship comes into being at the *time* of parturition but not that such a relationship is limited to the birth mother. It should be remembered that the paternal relationship arises upon termination of the first trimester of pregnancy. No "paternal" act is performed at that time; it is simply the moment at which the relationship is halakhically recognized. Similarly, parturition may be the moment at which all maternal relationships are recognized, including a maternal-filial relationship based upon contribution of the ovum from which the fetus developed.

22. R. Joshua Ben-Meir, in a critical review of earlier published material concerning this issue that appears in *Assia*, Nisan 5746, cites a comment of Rashi, *Yevamot* 98a, in support of the view that maternal identity is determined at conception. Rashi comments simply that recognition of consanguineous maternal relationships in the case of a pregnant proselyte and her fetus is evidence that the fetus does not enjoy the status of a "newly born child" bereft of any halakhically recognized blood relatives, as is the case with other converts. Although Rabbi Ben-Meir expresses astonishment that other discussants have not cited Ra-

shi's comment in their discussion of this issue, this writer finds Rashi's comment to be entirely irrelevant to the matter under discussion. Rashi states only that the fetus of a proselyte is not a "newly born child." He does not declare or imply that the relationship is established at conception—much less so at the time of the sexual act—rather than at parturition. See *Assia,* pp. 36–37 and p. 40.

23. Cf., R. Abraham Kilav, *Emek Halakhah,* II, 174, who fails to distinguish these points as separate issues, possibly because he declines to recognize the possibility of dual maternal relationships.

24. In point of fact, there may be evidence pointing to similar principles specifically with regard to determination of identity and status of animal species as well. It is clear that identity in terms of classification as a members of a particular species is determined at the beginning of life. Thus, a mature non-kosher animal is intrinsically non-kosher rather than merely the *yotzeh,* or derivative, of the infant from which it developed. Accordingly, if the animal is eaten as food, the culpability incurred is that associated with partaking of food that is intrinsically non-kosher rather than for violation of the less stringent prohibition associated with derivatives of non-kosher species, e.g., the milk of a non-kosher animal.

Moreover, there is evidence that identification in terms of a particular forbidden status is determined at the earliest stage of existence to the exclusion of other prohibitions that might be generated by other causative factors. It is a general principle that, in ordinary circumstances, a prohibition cannot be superimposed upon an already existing prohibition (*ein issur hal al issur*) of equal severity. One example discussed by the Gemara, *Hullin* 90a, is the nature of the prohibition against partaking of the sciatic nerve of the progeny of a sacrificial animal. If not for a specific exception to the general principle, the prohibition regarding eating the sciatic nerve would not apply to the offspring of sacrificial animals. Rashi, *ad locum,* explains: "For from the moment that it comes into being it is sanctified, but the nerve is, as yet, not generated for one observes that the creation of the embryo precedes the generation of the nerve." The embryo undergoes repeated cell divisions and at some point in the early stages of gestation there is a differentiation with regard to the characteristics of cells destined to become diverse organs and tissues. The nerve cells, and indeed the matter of which they are composed, do not exist at conception or in the earliest stages of gestation. The cells of the nascent sciatic nerve are new, not only to the nerve in the sense that cells possessing such characteristics do not exist at a previous stage, but to the embryo itself in the sense that they are newly generated from nutrients derived from the mother's blood stream. Thus, when those cells come into being, they are generated as being simultaneously both cells of a sanctified animal and cells of a sciatic nerve. Yet, for purposes of Halakhah, their identity as an integral part of a sacrificial animal is regarded as prior to their identity as a sciatic nerve. It follows, then, that the earlier identity and status of the animal determines the identity and status of newly formed cells despite the interposition of a new casual factor that would otherwise govern status and identity, i.e., appearance of the distinctive characteristics of the sciatic nerve.

Here, then, according to Rashi's analysis, is an example of an instance in which the identity of an organisim is determined with finality by the earliest casual factor and in which that organism's identity serves to control the organism throughout its life despite the fact that, absent the earlier acquisition of identity and status, the identity of later growths or developing appendages would be determined by other factors. Indeed, while with regard to plant identification and agricultural law the issue is regarded by the Gemara as unresolved and hence, in practice, this principle is applied only as a matter of "doubt" and stringency, with regard to animal species it appears to be the normative rule. This in no way contradicts the earlier conclusion that parturition serves to establish maternal identity. It means only that Halakhah may recognize two mothers, viz., a birth mother and a "generative" mother.

However *Tosafot*, as well as several other early commentaries on that talmudic discussion, speak of the sciatic nerve and other fetal tissues as coming into existence simultaneously and explain the priority of other prohibitions over that pertaining to the sciatic nerve on the basis of the fact that in early stages of development the sciatic nerve lacks the distinctive features associated with that structure. Since none of those authorities offers an explicit reason for diverging from Rashi's analysis, it is not possible to ascertain the precise nature of their disagreement with Rashi. It is, however, entirely possible that the controversy is precisely with regard this point, i.e., that they reject the notion that identity and status of animal structures are determined from the earliest moment of existence in a manner that unalterably determines the identity of later accretions as well.

25. See above, note 15.

26. For a discussion of the status of the fetus during this period see *Contemporary Halakhic Problems*, I, 339–347.

27. R. Chaim's thesis that a fraternal relationship exists only if the mother converted during the first forty days of pregnancy was advanced as a resolution of this difficulty inherent in Ramban's position; see above, note 10.

28. An identical thesis is advanced by Rabbi Kilav, *Tehumin*, V, p. 263, in resolution of a different problem.

29. The same point may be made with regard to Reb Chaim's assertion cited above, note 10. Reb Chaim is quoted as having raised the problem only in conjunction with Ramban's position.

30. See R. Zalman Nehemiah Goldberg, *Tehumin* p. 255, note 5.

31. Three versions of Reb Naphtali's *shi'urim* as recorded and transcribed by his students have been published: 1) *Shi'urei ha-Granat* (Jerusalem, 5715); 2) *Sefer Duda'ei Mosheh: Shi'urei ha-Granat he-Hadashim,* 2nd edition (Bnei Brak, 5745); 3) *Hiddushei ha-Granat ha-Shalem* (Jerusalem, 5749), edited by R. Moshe David Dryan.

32. Cf., *Zekher Yitzhak,* I, no. 4, who expresses a similar concept in speaking of conversion, not for purposes of becoming a Jew, but in order to remove "disqualification as a gentile" (*pul akum*).

33. This material first appeared in *Ha-Metivta,* Heshvan 5703.

34. The sole question is whether such conversion is biblically valid or whether the status is that of a "rabbinic" conversion. R. Akiva Eger, *Ketubot* 11a, maintains that biblical conversion of a fetus is possible only when the conversion is simultaneously performed on behalf of the mother. Cf. however, below, note 38.

35. Acceptance of this thesis in explanation of the requirement for conversion of the fetus of a pregnant proselyte may have a significant practical halakhic ramification with regard to in vitro fertilization. The authorities who permit ejaculation of semen by the husband for purposes of artificial insemination do so only because, in their opinion, the procedure serves to fulfill the commandment to be fruitful and multiply." Cf. above, notes 8 and 9. Hence emission of semen for the insemination of a gentile woman could not be sanctioned for the simple reason that, since Jewish law does not recognize a paternal relationship between a Jewish father and his non-Jewish progeny, ejaculation does not lead to fulfillment of the obligation to "be fruitful and multiply." If a fetus that develops from an ovum donated by a non-Jewish woman requires conversion despite the fact that the gestational mother is Jewish, the ostensive halakhic implication is that there is no paternal relationship between the child and its biological father and hence ejaculation of semen by the husband for utilization for the purpose of in vitro fertilization could not be sanctioned in such situations. If, however, identity as a member of the community of Israel as well as a maternal-filial relationship is established on the basis of the gestational mother's identity as a Jewess, the birth of such a child may serve to fulfill the commandment to "be fruitful and multiply" as well. Accordingly, if a paternal relationship is recognized in usual cases of artificial insemination, Jewish law would recognize a paternal-filial relationship between the Jewish donor of the semen and the child of a Jewish gestational mother for all other aspects of Jewish law even though the ovum was donated by a non-Jewess.

On the other hand, if there is no maternal relationship between the Jewish gestational and birth mother and the child born of an ovum donated by a non-Jewish woman, ejaculation for purposes of fertilizing such an ovum cannot be sanctioned.

36. *Tehumin,* V, 263–264.

37. Rabbi Kilav apparently maintains that in the case of a pregnant proselyte conversion of the fetus is accomplished, according to Ramban, by immersion of the mother and Ramban intends only to indicate that failure to perform circumcision prior to immersion does not serve as a barrier to conversion. See *Tehumin,* V, 264.

38. R. Akiva Eger maintains that conversion of the fetus is valid in biblical law only if conversion is simultaneously performed on behalf of the mother and, accordingly, only under such circumstances can there be a maternal-filial relationship. See above, note 34. If R. Akiva Eger does not accept Reb Naphtali's thesis, conversion of the fetus or neonate conceived from a gentile ovum would not result in a maternal-filial relationship with the gestational mother. Insofar as biblical law is concerned, the child remains a non-Jew even if conversion takes place during pregnancy. Were a biblically valid conversion to occur subsequent to parturition it would clearly result in status as a "newly born child" and serve to sever any possible maternal relationship. Nor is there evidence that rabbinic law established a maternal-filial relationship in cases of in vitro fertilization or embryo transplants. See R. Joshua Ben-Meir, *Assia,* pp. 30–33 and p. 40.

39. Rabbi Kilav, *Emek Halakhah,* II, 174, suggests that, to be valid for the fetus, the immersion must be efficacious for some other purpose, e.g., conversion of the mother. It is however, difficult to comprehend the reason for such a requirement since, if the mother's body is not an interposition, the fetus should be regarded as if it has come into direct contact with the water of the *mikveh.*

40. R. Aaron Soloveichik's view seems to reflect that of his grandfather, R. Chaim Soloveitchik, as reported by R. Elchanan Wasserman, *Kovetz He'arot,* no. 73, sec. 12; see above, note 10.

41. For a discussion of this issue see *Contemporary Halakhic Problems,* I, 339–347.

42. Cf., however, *Tosofot, Baba Kamma* 47a, *Hullin* 58a and *Sanhedrin* 60b; *Taz, Yoreh De'ah* 89:5; *Shakh, Yoreh De'ah* 89:8; and *Lehem Mishneh, Hilkhot Avadim* 7:5. See also *Sedei Hemed, Kuntres ha-Kellalim, ma'arekhet ha-ayin,* no. 62; *Melo ha-Ro'im,* "Ubar Yerekh Imo," secs. 6–8; and *Kesef Nivhar, kellal* 132, sec. 9.

43. Dr. Abraham S. Abraham, author of *Nishmat Avraham,* graciously acceded to my request to contact Rabbi Auerbach for clarification of his position. In a communication dated 22 Shevat 5751, Dr. Abraham writes

that Rabbi Auerbach expressed doubt with regard to the efficacy of conversion of the fetus during pregnancy "because perhaps she is not its mother and she has no jurisdiction over it" (my translation). Rabbi Auerbach's hesitation is apparently born of reservations with regard to the conditions necessary for the conversion of gentiles during their minority. It may be inferred from the comments of Rashi, *Ketubot* 11a, that the application of the child's father or, in his absence, of the mother is necessary in order to effect a valid conversion of a minor. Some authorities maintain that a minor may present himself for conversion while other authorities maintain that the *Bet Din* may act on its own initiative. See sources cited in *Encyclopedia Talmudit*, VI, 445. An obvious problem arises in situations in which a child is surrendered for adoption but the natural parents do not know that the child is to be adopted by a Jewish couple and certainly do not formally consent to conversion. A number of contemporary decisors have expressed the view that all authorities agree that when the gentile parents have abandoned their interest in the child, parental application or permission is not required. See, for example, R. Meir ha-Levi Steinberg, *Likkutei Me'ir* (London, 5730), pp. 68–69. If this concern is the sole impediment to conversion during pregnancy it would appear that it may be obviated by obtaining permission from the donor mother for conversion.

Parenthetically, Rabbi Auerbach seems to have no question with regard to the efficacy of conversion if performed after birth, presumably because parturition establishes a maternal relationship between the child and the birth mother. If, however, the child has two mothers it is not clear that the rights and prerogatives of the donor mother become extinguished (unless, of course, Reb Naphtali's thesis to the effect that conversion is required only for purposes of *kedushat Yisra'el* is accepted). If, on the other hand, parturition and only parturition establishes a maternal-filial relationship, the fetus has no mother before parturition and there is scant reason to assume that a minor "orphan" cannot be converted. Moreover, according to R. Akiva Eger, the selfsame problem may remain after birth as well since, according to R. Akiva Eger, parturition may not establish a maternal-filial relationship in such cases; see above, note 38.

44. *Tehumin*, V, 262.

45. *Tehumin*, V, 267.

46. The statement of the Gemara, *Yevamot* 37b, forbidding a man from establishing multiple families whose identities are not known to one another serves as the basis for a ban upon any suppression of information that might prevent an incestuous relationship. See, for example, R. Moshe Feinstein, *Iggerot Mosheh, Yoreh De'ah*, I, no. 162, regarding a similar application of that principle in cases of adoption. See also, R. Shlomo Goren, *Ha-Tzofeh*, 7 Adar I (5744).

# 4

# *Ovum Donations: A Rabbinic Conceptual Model of Maternity*

Ezra Bick

A

The new reproductive technologies introduced by modern medicine offer bold new approaches to medical problems associated with infertility. Rather than treating the couple to cure infertility, they circumvent the problem by utilizing other people—other ovaries, wombs, or testes—to replace the malfunction of the couple. These techniques bring with them a host of moral and halakhic problems. For example, in the procedure known as IVF, a donated ovum can be fertilized in vitro and implanted in a woman who did not contribute the egg. In such a case, who is the mother, the genetic donor or the woman who carried the fetus and gave birth to it?

In a recent review[1] of the halakhic literature on this subject,* Rabbi J. David Bleich comes to the conclusion that "the preponderance of evidence adduced from rabbinic sources demonstrates that parturition, in and of itself, serves to establish a maternal relationship." He concedes that there are other opinions, and suggests that indeed there might be room to rule that the genetic mother is *also* the halakhic mother. He basically dismisses the po-

---

Rabbi Bick, a member of the editorial board of *Crossroads*, gives a *shiur* at Yeshivat Har Etzion in Alon Shevut, Israel.

*Chapter 3 in this volume.

sition that it is the donor alone who is the halakhic mother (or that there is no halakhic mother at all).

While I do not necessarily take issue with all of his specific conclusions, I believe that the whole issue demands a different conceptual approach. Essentially, this question is not susceptible to the classical halakhic approach of analogy with an existent halakhic ruling. Not only does a "preponderance" of halakhic sources not exist in favor of parturition as the maternal determinant, practically speaking, no halakhic sources exist for this or any competing candidate for the determinant. A different approach must therefore be attempted. Before showing how that might be done, I must, however, first explain why the methodology exhibited by R. Bleich fails to adequately solve the problem.

The major proof cited by R. Bleich that birth is the determinant of maternity is from the Gemara in *Yevamot* (97b), which states that twins born to a woman who converted during pregnancy are considered brothers. Since the twins are considered to have converted in the womb (see *Yevamot* 78a), and conversion annuls all preexisting familial relationships (*"ger she-nitgayer ki-tinok she-nolad dami"* [a convert has the status of a newborn baby"]), their relationship to each other and to their mother must have been created subsequent to conception and the conversion in utero. The proof assumes that halakhically this case is analogous to the implantation of a fetus in a woman.

Were this proof to be valid, it would represent a legitimate use of conventional halakhic methodology and I would have nothing to add. However, the conclusion is not supported by this source. This can be shown in several ways. Firstly, the analogy of a convert mother to a transplant mother is flawed. Perusal of the footnotes to R. Bleich's article shows that he agrees that the source is compatible with the possibility that both parturition and conception are independent determinants of maternity. In fact, he appears to favor this conclusion. He further mentions an opinion that takes for granted that dual motherhood of one child is an impossibility, an assumption that appears to me to be eminently logical. The conjunction of these two opinions gives rise to the conclusion that although in the case of the pregnant convert (where the determinant of conception has been annulled by conversion) maternity is determined by birth, in our case, maternity will be determined immediately at conception in favor of the genetic mother, and any subsequent determination by birth is therefore precluded.

Secondly, the principle that a convert has the status of a new-born only serves to eliminate previous familial relations, but not to erase historical facts. That the children born to a pregnant proselyte are brothers only indicates that the relationship between them and their mother is established at the *time* of birth, but not that birth is the cause of the determination. It is possible that ovum donation determines maternity, but the relationship is established only when the child is born. If that is true, conversion during pregnancy would not prevent the establishment of maternity at the time of birth based on the pre-conversion ovum donation.

Indeed, the cogency of this proof begs the solution to the question. If ovum donation determines maternity, that would suggest that the meaning of motherhood depends on the genetic origin. Therefore, one might argue that although conversion erases the relationship established by ovum donation, the relationship that is ultimately established at birth must be based on the reality of genetic motherhood and can be effected only if in fact the child and the mother are genetically related. This would be true in the case of the pregnant convert, but not in the case of ovum donation. Even if birth alone determines maternity, it might be argued that genetic continuity is a necessary condition for such determination. Bleich rejects this possibility as unsupported. However, the same consideration that underlies the argument that ovum donation is an independent determinant of motherhood—that to the modern scientific mind genetic continuity seems to be a basic component of the concept "parenthood"—raises the possibility that any other determinant (such as birth) should include genetic continuity as a necessary condition. According to this possibility, a child born to a woman who had received a donor ovum would either have the donor as a mother, or have no mother at all.

Bleich himself (footnote 13), in a different context, allows that birth could be merely the time of maternity determination. He points out that sperm donation is undoubtedly the determinant of paternity, yet the time of the actual determination is only at the end of the first trimester.[2] A similar deferral could be true of the mother, with the time of determination postponed to the birth. This extended deferral could be due to a number of reasons. Rav Yosef Engel, cited by Bleich in support of his position, explicitly states that maternity is determined at birth because "*ubar yerakh immo* (the embryo is a limb of its mother)"; in other words, the determination must be delayed as a woman cannot be the mother of a part of herself. Birth, then, is not the determinant of maternity, but merely the removal of the impediment to its establishment by some previous factor, presumably the woman's role in conception, parallel to that of the male. Another reason could be that the entire pregnancy is the parallel to the male's role; that is, conception (rather than ovum donation) is the determinant. Birth would then be not an event which determines maternity; it would be simply the conclusion of the extended determinant. Accordingly, a woman who did not conceive could not be a mother, even if she did "give birth."

Thirdly, the proof is based on two assumed premises not explicitly stated in the source: first, that the embryos are considered to have converted; second, that hence all pre-conversion relationships are annulled. Rashi (Yevamot 97b), however, studiously refuses to apply the principle that a convert is like a new-born to a conversion in utero. He uses this principle (in order to annual relationship with the mother) only where the conversion was after birth. In the case of the twins whose mother converts, Rashi states that they are not related to the father because of a different principle, one which applies only to paternity. Accordingly, this source is completely compatible with the assumption that maternity is established by, and even at the time of, conception. The *Zera Yitzhak* (4) denies the first assumption, stating that there is no such thing as conversion in utero. A child born to a woman who converted during pregnancy is Jewish by virtue of the birth. This does not imply that the child is *her* child by virtue of the birth, and in the absence of a conversion of the child, the proof, based on the principle that a convert is like a new-born, evaporates.

There exist two sources which explicitly deny that birth alone is the determinant of maternity, although without conclusively demonstrating what the determinant is. The Talmud (*Hullin* 70a) asks: "What is the law [regarding the sanctity of a first-born animal] if two wombs were affixed and [the fetus] went out of one and entered the other? *Its own womb* is exempted [from future status of a first-born, as this was its first-born], the one not its own is not exempted, or perhaps the one not its own is also exempted." The very term "its own womb" indicates that conception creates a relationship between the mother and the embryo; the question of the Talmud is whether the laws of the first-born, which are dependent on "that which opens the womb (*peter rehem*), could apply to a womb of an animal that was not the mother ("not its own"). The Rambam is even more explicit—"If two wombs were affixed . . . or is (the second) not exempted as its womb was not opened *by its child*" (*Hil. Bekhorot* 4:18).[3]

At the very least, this source demonstrates that in a case of embryo transfer, where an embryo is removed from a woman who conceived it, she is considered the mother. This could, however, be due to the fact that the removal from the first woman is in fact a birth, although the term, "its own womb" does not support this interpretation.[4]

Bleich quotes the aggada that Dina was originally conceived by Rachel and subsequently transferred to the womb of Leah. Since the Torah refers to Dina as the daughter of Leah, it could be argued that this proves that birth, and birth alone, determines maternity. Bleich correctly points out that an aggada cannot serve as a source of a halakhic ruling, but there is a further difficulty in relying on this source.

The aggada does not state that Dina is the legal daughter of Leah. The proof rests on the assumption that the narrative discription of Dina as the daughter of Leah should be understood halakhically. Yet it is possible that the verse refers to Dina as Leah's daughter only because she was generally considered so, especially sinced no one knew about the switch. In fact, one medieval commentator, referring to this aggada, discloses his *halakhic* assumption that birth is not a determinant of maternity. The Tur, in his commentary to the Torah (Gen. 46:10), asks how Shimon was permitted to marry Dina, since even non-Jews are forbidden to marry a sister of the same mother. He answers that since Dina was conceived in Rachel's womb, she was in actuality Rachel's daughter; hence, Shimon and Dina did not have a common mother.

This source was introduced into the literature concerning parenthood over thirty years ago by Rav Yisrael Zev Minzberg[5] and subsequently ignored. Rav Minzberg assumes that the aggada states that Rachel's ovum was transferred to Leah prior to fertilization. Since the Tur states that the ovum-donor is the legal mother, he inferred analogously that the sperm-donor in artificial insemination is the legal father. If this were correct, it would also be an explicit source that ovum-donation determines maternity in in vitro fertilization.

However, the aggada actually states that the embryo which was Dina was transferred from Rachel to Leah. Hence, it is possible that the assumption of Rachel's motherhood is based on her having conceived the child and not merely donated the ovum. This same aggada is used to explain why Dina's birth is described without the customary introduction "and Leah conceived . . ." (Gen. 30,21); that is, according to the aggada, Leah had not conceived Dina, although she did give birth to her. We may therefore conclude that according to the Tur, birth is not the determinant of maternity. Some earlier connection, as exemplified by the relationship of Rachel to Dina, is the maternal determinant. This is, to the best of my knowledge, the only classical halakhic source relevant to the question.[6]

The other proofs offered by Bleich are striking by reason of their *a priori* inappropriateness. In the absence of a persuasive analogy from a case of maternity, various authors attempt to produce a proof by analogy—the conventional method of halakhic reasoning—with vegetative relationships. This seems to be a desperate attempt to maintain conventional halakhic reasoning procedures. It is however, totally invalid. There is no reason that the halakhic age of a grafted branch, for example, should bear any relationship with the concept of maternity. Aside from the obvious difference between plants and animals, our topic is identity—who you are—and not age. The fact that in our case there is also a father (i.e., a child is the result of sexual reproduction) is a further difference. In fact, I think it is pointless to list differences. The question is why should there be even a prima facie basis for imagining that the two concepts are analogous.

If conventional halakhic method fails, the result should not be desperate attempts to preserve a semblance of halakhic reasoning. There may be questions to which conventional halakhic methodology provides no sources, no solutions. The question is whether there is an alternative halakhic methodology available. The rest of this article will be devoted to that question.

B

If we come to the conclusion that there exists no clear indisputable halakhic source for our question of motherhood, how do we go about analyzing the problem? The first step is to formulate the conceptual question involved. I would like to suggest the following approach.

At first glance, it seems axiomatic that the concept of parenthood is basically the same for mothers and fathers. Under normal circumstances, we know that the parents are the people who conceived the baby. The question then is, how does the Halakha understand the act of conception? Only by answering that can we determine what is the role of each parent.

I believe that there are two possibilities. The first is parallel to the biological explanation of sexual reproduction. A new human being is conceived when genetic material from two donors is combined. Accordingly, the father and the mother are the two donors of the genetic material. In artificial insemination, the sperm donor is the father, and in in vitro fertilization (IVF), the ovum donor would be the mother.[7] This, in light of modern medical knowledge, is the simplest solution to our problem.

There is, however, no clear source in rabbinic literature which suggests that a woman has ova. Inasmuch as the rabbis certainly had a concept of motherhood, such a concept must be definable without reference to the ovum. This in and of itself might argue for birth as the sole determining factor for motherhood.

However, there is another conceptual model of parenthood, one based on the model of fertilization rather than donation and combination. This model perceives the role of father and mother as essentially parallel to what takes place in agriculture, where a seed is placed in a fertile environment. A man fertilizes a woman by placing his seed in her. The man is the donor of the seed, the woman the recipient. Accordingly, paternity may be determined by sperm donation, but maternity is determined by becoming pregnant, by producing life through the act of receiving the male seed. The roles of the mother and the father are complementary rather than identical. The analogy is to planting a seed in the ground rather than to mixing ingredients in a laboratory.

Of course, this "agricultural" model is not based on the accepted modern scientific understanding of what takes place in fertilization. It is therefore important to point out that this should not be a factor in rejecting it as a halakhic model. This is not a case of basing a halakhic conclusion on incorrect information. If halakhic maternity were based on the transfer of genetic material and the Sages believed that this transfer took place in a manner inconsistent with scientific belief and consequently determined maternity in accordance with that manner, there would be a problem of whether to revise the halakhic conclusion to agree with our new knowledge. But here the question is what is the *principle* for determining maternity, not which facts fulfill that principle. There is no dispute as to the facts, but only as to which facts are relevant.

I mentioned before that the Sages were apparently unaware of the existence of human ova. Therefore, in determining maternity they did not have a model which was an exact parallel to the male role. It is quite possible that they saw the female role as complement (rather than the parallel) of the male role, as receiving what the male donates and converting or being affected by it. In that case, even if we could construct a new model based on our different scientific knowledge, there would be no reason to do so, as there exists a valid halakhic model that historically was accepted and developed without in any way having been rendered obsolete.

In both the biological and agricultural models, the basic assumption is that parenthood is determined by fulfilling the male and female roles in conception. The question is how we are to view those two parallel roles; as two donors combining their respective contributions, or as a male donation to a female receptor, who in turn produces life.

It would not necessarily follow from acceptance of the agricultural model that only the moment of fertilization is relevant for maternity. It is not the physical reception of the seed that constitutes the woman's role but rather the production of life as a result. Hence it is possible that the entire period of gestation is the determinant of maternity, as that is the process whereby the woman turns the seed into life. Accordingly, the actual moment of determination may be birth, when the seed bursts out of the "ground."

The "biological" model would seemingly imply that the sperm donor is the father in artificial insemination. In fact, many of the arguments advanced to deny paternity in cases of artificial insemination assume that sperm donation should in principle determine paternity, but claim that some further reason abrogates the natural connection between the donor and the child.

The "agricultural" model permits the argument that paternity is dependent on an act of impregnating a woman, and in artificial insemination, the male has not done this even though his sperm was used. On the other hand, it is fully consistent with this model to claim that donation of the sperm is the determinant of paternity, as it is the sperm that constitutes the seed which gives rise to life in the woman. In effect, by donating sperm, the male is the (material) cause of the woman's impregnation.

In a case of in vitro fertilization, the "biological" model would presumably recognize the two donors as the respective parents of the child. Under the "agricultural" model, at the time of fertilization, there is no determinant of either paternity or maternity, as the woman (as opposed to the ovum) has not been inseminated ("planted"). However, it might be argued that implanting the fertilized zygote in the woman's uterus constitutes her insemination. She receives a seed and turns it into life. Since this model does not recognize the existence of the donor's ovum, and in any event does not consider it to be a determinant of maternity, it would not matter that the "seed" that is planted in the recipient has an ovum constituent as well as a sperm constituent. Hence, the recipient could be the mother—not because she gives birth to the child, but because she is considered to have conceived it. Before returning to the first question, let me briefly address this latter point.

For implantation to be considered insemination, I think we must agree that the zygote not be considered a live human being. The determinant of maternity is being the source of life, the ground from which it springs. If a fertilized ovum is a live human being, the woman has not received a seed as the ground does, but has only been the home for a developing human being. Our model defines the woman's role not as nurturing a baby, not gestation per se, which is not parallel to the role of the father, but as producing a human being through the act of reception of something that does not have that status. Hence, if the zygote is already a baby, no subsequent action can establish a ground for the production of life.

One way to guarantee this conclusion would be to accept the

forty day limit as a halakhic definition of human life. Those who permit abortion before this point, at least in relation to the prohibition of murder, would surely agree. However, even if the forty day limit is not used in questions of abortion, and the phrase "mere water" is not taken literally, it may be possible to rely on the halakhic requirement of forty days which appears in the laws relating to birth-*tum'a* (ritual defilement). If a woman who aborts spontaneously before forty days is not *tamei* and her subsequent child is considered a first-born, it is reasonable to conclude that she has not given birth. One might reason that this is because, lacking "the form of a human," the embryo is not considered a human being. Alternatively, one might conclude that prior to forty days, a woman is not pregnant, and, according to this model, that is because human life has not flowered within her. There may indeed be a prohibition in abortion before forty days, even if the embryo is considered no more than potential life. However, for our purposes, an implanted embryo may be considered to be generated in the womb where it grows from the fortieth day on. Before that date, there was no baby.

Implantation in in vitro fertilization is performed far earlier. The zygote is microscopic at that point,[8] and, as Rabbi Bleich has pointed out elsewhere, "an organism that can be seen only by means of a magnifying glass or under a microscope is an organism of which Jewish law takes no notice. . . . [Hence] when the developing [human] organism is still sub-visual, the law takes no cognizance of its existence."[9] Essentially, a fluid without any particular components is being injected into the woman. (This would not necessarily imply that abortion could be performed in the first few days of pregnancy, as the prevention of the development of life may also be prohibited under the rubric of destroying seed.)

Furthermore, the fact that the zygote has no mother while in vitro would itself be a reason to deny it personal identity. This, in turn, might allow us to view the implantation into a human womb as the equivalent of organ transplant, where the transplanted material loses its original identity and becomes part of the host. If this takes place in the recipient womb, the subsequent development of the embryo is the equivalent of giving forth life from the ground of the recipient mother.

The implication of being without a mother in the stage before implantation may be quite radical. If a fertilized egg were incubated artificially and consequently had no mother, it is not clear that the resulting child would be halakhically human. In animals, species is determined solely by descent—the offspring of a cow is a cow (Hullin 79a). The fact that an animal looks like a pig in no way determines that it is one. If it were born by a cow, it is a cow, though somewhat deformed. If we applied the same conclusion to in vitro fertilization and incubation, such a baby, though produced from human cells, might be the halakhic equivalent of a *golem.* The question is whether birth determines species identity, or origin—for our purposes, genetic origin. It could be claimed that if cell donation is not considered descent, then this baby has been manufactured, rather than conceived.

Of course, the implications of not being human are extreme. The Talmud (*Yevamot.* 65b) states that Rav Zeira killed a *golem* sent to him by Rava. Hakham Tzvi (no. 93) concluded from this that the life of the *golem* was of no significance. He also claims that even if the *golem* is human, the prohibition of murder extends only to humans who were born in pregnancy, based on the verse, "He who sheds the blood of a man, by a man shall his blood be shed (Gen. 9:6)," reading "He who sheds the blood of a *man in a man,* his blood shall be shed" (cf. Sanhedrin 57b). This leads to the conclusion that fertilized eggs not needed could be discarded prior to implantation in the mother.[10] For our purposes, this would be another reason to conclude that implantation of the fertilized ovum in a woman would therefore be its conception, as it had not previously achieved the status of a human being.

Hence, it seems to me logical to conclude that according to the "agricultural" model, where the fertilization was in vitro, no one other than the recipient woman could be considered the mother. This would not necessarily be true if a fertilized embryo was transferred from one womb to another. Here, the previous determination of maternity in favor of the donor would prevent subsequent determination. Transfer following uterine lavage might occur early enough to deny the conceiving women maternal status. Determining the exact cut-off time is beyond our consideration here.

(The equivalent conclusion for paternity is not as clear. Even assuming that in artificial insemination the sperm donor is the father, that is because he was the sole source of the "seed" which impregnated the woman. In our case, the woman is inseminated by a fertilized zygote, for which the father is not the sole source. It might be claimed that if the ovum does not exist halakhically, then the only material being injected in to the woman derives from the male. However, the sperm has been changed from its original state and hence the father is not the sole cause of the woman's impregnation. Of course, if the sperm donor is not the father in artificial insemination, he is surely not the father in in vitro fertilization. Hence, it is possible that the host woman is the mother, but there is no father at all.)

There is however one possible objection to this argument. This model ignores the scientific understanding of the role of the ovum. This, as I stated above, is acceptable when constructing the model. However, it is not as clear that we can ignore the difference between insemination and zygote implantation when deciding whether the model is appropriate for the latter. Our knowledge today indicates that there is a radical difference between them, relative to the agricultural model. In the case of insemination, life is being produced within the host woman. With zygote implantation, life *appears* to develop in utero, but we know that in fact a major step—fertilization—has taken place elsewhere, without the woman's participation. The argument that halakhically the ovum does not exist carries less weight here. The process of implantation is still significantly different from that of insemination precisely in that area relevant to the model. The existence of the ovum will not entail a revision in the halakhic model, but it well may be relevant to deciding whether a particular case meets the model.

In other words, one can have a valid concept of motherhood without specific knowledge of the existence of ovum; however, it is not clear that one can apply that concept to a case where knowledge of the role of the ovum would contradict the model. Since ova are invisible, it may make sense, for that reason or others, to define a process on the basis of the visible phenomena. The definition of maternity then is the production of life, rather than the donation of ova. However, this is not the same as saying that invisible objects do not exist, are never taken into account, and hence we are interested only in outward appearances. It might be argued that in zygote transplantation, life is not in fact produced by the host woman at all, whether that is apparent to an outward observer or not; in other words, the model constructed without reference to ova is not being fulfilled. I am not sure that modern scientific knowledge should not prevent us from blithely ignoring the difference between insemination and implantation. Accepting this distinction will lead to the conclusion that since only the production of life determines maternity, neither the ovum-donor nor the host is halakhically the mother. The child would have no mother at all.

This objection is potentially valid only against the line of reasoning which viewed implantation as equivalent to insemination, but not against the argument which viewed it as equivalent to organ transplantation.

A finer distinction may be required here. Is the definition of motherhood in the agricultural model the ground from which life springs, or the source of that life? In other words, is it sufficient that a live human being appear out of a ground where none existed before, or is it necessary that the woman be considered to have produced, created the child, from within herself, If the first, I believe the arguments presented will be sufficient to demonstrate that the zygote was not a live human being before implantation, and hence, the host mother was the ground from which the human being emerged. According to the latter definition, I am doubtful if the condition of maternity is met in a case where the essential ingredient, the ovum, is donated by another woman. Although the analogy with the earth in agriculture would suggest the former definition, it is far from clear that the latter definition is not closer to the truth. Of course, if we seriously suggest that invisible objects have no halakhic existence at all, there will be no problem. I am not sure what would be the basis for such an assertion.

The preceding discussion referred to the original method of IVF, where a fertilized zygote was implanted into the host mother. An increasingly popular alternate method is called GIFT, gamete intra-fallopian transfer, where the ovum and sperm are injected as a mixture into the fallopian tube of the host-mother before the ovum has been fertilized. In this case, it is clear that there is no human being before the transfer, as fertilization takes place in the body of the host mother. Furthermore, the last objection is significantly deflected as well, as it is far easier to utilize the argument of organ transplant in relation to an unfertilized ovum than for a fertilized zygote; and as we have seen, this objection is not

valid against the argument from organ transplant. Even without
the analogy to organ transplant, the fact that fertilization takes
place in the host mother makes it easier to see her as not merely
the ground from which the child emerges, but as the cause of the
emergence of life. It would appear that, given the agricultural
model, one would be justified in concluding that in cases of GIFT,
the host mother is the halakhic mother.


# C


Returning to the major question of the halakhic model of conception, is there any halakhic source sufficient to resolve it? The answer is no. I propose instead to attempt to discover the general
conceptual framework of the Sages concerning conception, on
the assumption that, in the absence of negative evidence, the
proper legal definition of conception in regard to the determination of parenthood will be congruent with that general framework.

In support of the "agricultural" model, I claimed that the
Sages were not aware of the existence of the human ovum. The
Talmud (*Nidda* 31a) states: "If the woman is *mazria* first, she will
bear a male child; if the man is *mazria* first, she will bear a female
child." The phrase "*mazria*," applied to the male, clearly means
ejaculating, i.e., producing sperm. Applied to the female, the
term would seem to mean ovulation, i.e., producing her seed, an
ovum. The statement of the Talmud would accordingly mean that
if ovulation precedes intercourse, a male child will be born. This,
however, is not a generally accepted explanation. The Talmud
continues (op.cit.): "Is it in a man's power to increase his sons
and grandsons? Rather [the verse refers] to their custom of hold-
ing back [from ejaculating (Rashi)] so that their wives should be
*mazria* first and their children would be male. . . ." It is apparent
that *mazria* is something that takes place during intercourse. The
Talmud continues: "Rava said: One who wishes to ensure that all
his children be male should have intercourse twice. (Rashi: As a
result of sexual passion, she will be *mazria*, and . . . her *hazra'a* will
precede the second intercourse)."[11] *Mazria* is therefore associated
with the heightening of passion during intercourse. Clearly, the
*biblical* term *mazria* does not refer to ovulation, as the verse (Lev.

12:12) states: "If a woman is *mazria* and bears a male child," without mentioning explicitly the need for male impregnation. The reference here is to receiving (fruitfully) the seed of the man.

Ramban (Lev. 12:12) comments on this verse:

> It is not the Sages' intention to imply that a child develops from the seed of a woman, for even though a woman has "eggs" similar to those of a male (i.e., testicles), either they do not produce any seed or the seed is inert and has no affect on the embryo. The term *mazria* refers to the blood of the womb, which is gathered at the conclusion of intercourse and is conjoined with the seed of the male, for the Sages believe that the baby is formed from the blood of the female and the white of the male and both are called "seed."

Ramban here states his own belief that no female ovum is involved in conception, and explains the term in the Talmudic statement as referring to the development of the lining of the uterus prior to conception. This could be translated into modern terms in one of two ways. One might claim that the Sages agree that the mother donates a substance which combines with a male donation to form a child. Based on scientific discovery, we have substituted ova for blood. Substituting ova for blood, however, does not permit translation of the statement of the Gemara in *Nidda*. A translation that does not involve loss of meaning would suggest that the term *mazri'a* means producing the necessary environment for the reception of the seed. This implies that the female role in determining the sex of the offspring is associated with her being the receptor of the male seed. This would parallel the claim that her role as a receptor is the determinant of maternity. This statement of the Sages is not only not a refutation of the "agricultural" model, it lends a certain measure of support to it.

Ramban continues:

> In the opinion of the Greek philosophers, the body of the embryo is totally derived from the blood of the woman, and the man only provides the power called in their language *hyle,* which gives form to the matter, as there is no difference between a fertilized chicken egg and an unfertilized one; yet one produces a chick and the other does not, as it lacks the essential heat which is its *hyle.* Accordingly, the word *tazria* (in the biblical verse) means "growing its

(received) seed." This is how Onkelos translated it: 'A woman who becomes pregnant. . . .'

This alternate understanding of the process of conception, which Ramban ascribes to the Greek philosophers and to the Targum, provides a model exactly equivalent to the "agricultural" model. A mother is she who physically provides the substance of the child's body out of herself, having been fertilized by the seed of a male.[12]

The first opinion of the Ramban, in terms of the agricultural model, perceives the woman as receiving and nurturing the seed of a man; the second opinion sees her as being transformed, fertilized, by it.

It is worth noting that the Hebrew word for parent is *hore*, which is derived from the verb meaning to be pregnant.[13] The female parent is one who is pregnant with child, and the male parent is the one who fulfills the male role in that state. *Moshe Rabbenu* exclaims, "Have I *horiti* (conceived) all this people (Num. 11:12)," which Onkelos translates as, "Am I the father of all this people." To be a father and to impregnate are here seen as synonyms.[14]

It may appear strange to utilize an analogy to agriculture to illustrate the model described above, when it is clear to us that in fact the earth is merely the environment for the development of the seed, which is exactly the opposite of the relationship of the seed and the mother described by Ramban as the opinion of the Greeks. However, this in fact illustrates the difference between a halakhic model and a scientific one. Clearly, the Sages were aware that seeds develop into plants; after all, seeds develop roots and shoots without being planted at all, in water or even in the air. Nevertheless, the Sages consistently speak of the earth as bringing forth plants. An agricultural curse is addressed to the fruitfulness of the earth.[15] This derives, of course, from the language of the Torah itself, both in creation (Gen. 1:11–12; "Let the earth bring forth grass . . .") and in destruction (Gen. 3:17–18; "cursed is the ground for your sake. . . . Thorns and thistles it shall bring forth to you. . . .").

Moreover, this conception of the plant being a product of the earth is apparently reflected halakhically as well, as the status of a plant or a fruit is dependent on the earth in which it is planted.

If a plant grows not in earth but in water or in a closed pot, it is not considered a normal plant in many respects. The scientific picture of the earth as merely a conduit for water and nutrients fails to justify the important role the earth has in determining the "identity" of a plant or fruit. Clearly, the Halakha views a plant as being the "fruit of the earth," of the particular earth in which it is grown. In an analogous manner, we can claim that the identity of a baby is dependent on the ground out of which it grows.

There are numerous references in rabbinic literature to the principle of the female as being identified with receptivity, as well as the relationship of the earth to the heaven (or to the rain) as being equivalent to that of a female being vitalized by a male activating principle. A striking example is the following:

> R. Levi said: the upper waters are male and the lower female. The one says to the other, "Receive us; you are God's creatures and we are His messengers." Immediately, they receive them, as is written (Isa. 45:8), "[Drop down, heavens, from above, and let the skies pour down righteousness,] let the earth open"—as a female opening herself to a male—"and be fruitful with salvation"—they procreate.[16]

We find here a clear aggadic picture of a woman receiving from a man and in that way becoming "fruitful." I am suggesting, in order to reach a halakhic conclusion, two additional steps. First, we accept this picture as defining halakhically the sexual roles in conception. Second, the sexual roles in conception define parental identity.

I think it important to note that what I have attempted to do in the previous section is totally different to the comparison offered in R. Bleich's article between maternity and plant identification in cases of grafting. As a normal halakhic proof, the analogy to vegetative reproduction is simply too loose to be convincing. For one thing, grafting is not reproduction at all. Secondly, we are investigating sexual reproduction, which is not necessarily the case in plants. The concept of parenthood, as understood in the animal world, has no exact halakhic parallel in the vegetative world. Specifically, we wish to determine if there is a difference between paternity and maternity, which is meaningless in plants. The end result is not the same either. The question in plants was the age of the branch grafted unto an older tree; the question for us is familial identity. Who you are and how old you are are not equivalent questions. No one doubts that animal age is measured from birth—even though paternity is determined by the donation of sperm. Finally, as pointed out in the first section, even if maternity is determined at birth, that does not conclusively imply that the mother is she who gives birth.

My comparison to vegetation, the "agricultural" model, would be even weaker were it offered as a proof by analogy; however, I had no intention of doing so. I merely offered it as a model, as a way of perceiving how the Sages may have viewed a similar process. The launching point for what I have done is the conclusion that no normal halakhic proof exists for deciding the question of maternity. Having accepted that as a starting point, I posited that it would be valid to use an entirely different method in order to reach a conclusion.

What does one do when there are no sources for a halakhic answer to a pressing question? Our usual answer is "*hafokh ba, hafokh ba*"—keep looking! There is always a source. But are there not dozens of halakhot and legal principles in the Talmud which have no apparent scriptural source? Are we to assume that there must have been a source, or that the Sages of the Talmud were granted a unique (prophetic?) ability to originate Halakha? One would be hard-pressed to find a source for such a position. There are a limited number of specific instances where the Tosafot, for example, state that a particular talmudic Halakha is based presumably on some scriptural text, although unknown.[17] That is because the Halakha in question strikes Tosafot as not being particularly self-evident, or even logical. In numberous other cases, however, the only source of a Halakha is Reason, although it does not represent, strictly speaking, the only logical possibility. The Sages have certain conceptions of law and understanding of various concepts which underlay halakhic conclusions. Our topic is in fact a perfect example. If it is true, as R. Bleich claims, that the Sages consider birth to be the determinant of motherhood, what is their source? If sperm donation determines paternity without intercourse, or vice-versa (the question of paternity in artificial insemination), what are the (pre-Talmudic) sources?

Halakha is riddled with concepts that reflect the assumed conception of the Talmudic Sages on a particular topic. In our halakhic investigations, we attempt to base all our conclusions on the determination of the Talmudic concepts, because we accept implicitly the legal formulations of the Sages. Rarely does a contemporary halakhic discussion investigate the sources of Talmudic concepts.[18] It is simply accepted that certain basic assumptions underlie many halakhic formulations, and we accept those assumptions if they are evinced in Talmudic Halakha.

What then do we do if there is no Talmudic Halakha relevant to the assumptions needed for a decision in our question? It appears to me that we are justified in trying to determine the Talmudic assumptions, the base conceptions of the Talmudic worldview, from other sources. This is not the same as the oft-rejected aggadic source for halakhic conclusions. To derive a Halakha from a single aggadic source is misleading, as we cannot be sure what the intent or precise factual meaning of the aggada is. To use the aggada to determine a general approach of the Sages to a question, in order to determine what Halakha must necessarily arise from that approach, is, although risky and lacking the certitude we are accustomed to expect in halakhic discourse, in principle as valid as what the Sages would have done in the first place had they faced the question we are facing today. Were there to exist absolutely no Talmudic guidance for our question, neither in halakhic or aggadic sources, in principle we would have to formulate for ourselves the proper way to understand the necessary concepts, in the same way that the Talmudic scholars did. I cannot imagine any serious Torah scholar being happy with such a situation; we depend upon direct Talmudic sources as a fish depends on water. Nonetheless, I believe it is a valid way to derive Halakha; indeed, it is one of the bases for Talmudic Halakha itself.[19]

What is the difference between an "agricultural" model and a "biological" model? The latter either denies or at least attaches no importance to the differences between male and female. They both donate genetic material and together constitute the embryo. Maternity and paternity are identical; simply the different names we give to the same position when filled by members of the two sexes, like shepherd and shepherdess. A mother is a female father, at least at the level of the determining factors.

The former model, while positing parallel roles, so that it is only through the joint participation of the two that an embryo can be formed, nonetheless defines the roles in a radically different, almost opposite way. It seems to me that this dual model, an impregnator and the impregnated, the spark of life and the ground of life, form and matter, most closely corresponds with the metaphors the Sages associate with female and male. Although these metaphors have no halakhic validity, it is logical to conclude that they could underlie halakhic concepts based on male and female as well. We surely have the right to expect conceptual uniformity over the aggadic-halakhic divide.

If it is fair to derive philosophical concepts from the Halakha, it must be because these underlying concepts are basic to the world-view of Torah and not only Halakha in the strictly legal sense. There is a stricter level of logical rigor required in halakhic definition than in aggadic definition; hence it is risky going from less-well defined aggada to the strict domain of Halakha, but it is not excluded in principle. If the Halakha has a world-view and a conceptual basis, which is the conceptual framework of the Sages, there may be cases where there is no other way to determine that conceptual basis other than to examine the wider framework as expressed in aggada.

This is completely different from trying to derive the Halakha directly from an aggadic comment or story. Since the purpose of the aggada is not to decide Halakha, the halakhic conclusion may be totally irrelevant and not necessarily accurate. However, the conceptual conclusion is not incidental to the aggada but directly implied by it, and if the same conceptual conclusion has halakhic ramifications, they are in principle valid. There are two problems here, first in determining the conceptual conclusion with the desired degree of precision, and then determining the halakhic ramification, which necessitates a further degree of specificity not always possible for philosophic concepts. The conclusion will be almost unavoidably tentative. In cases where direct legal analogy or derivation is non-existent, there may be no choice.

One of the basic endeavors of contemporary talmudic research is the attempt to uncover the conceptual models of halakhic conclusions. This consists not only in proposing a *svara* for a given Halakha, but in formulating the second-layer conceptual assumption of the first-level *svara*. Unless this is a merely intellectual exercise, it implies that the underlying conceptual model has halakhic validity; i.e., that further halakhic conclusions may be derived from it. Students of modern talmudists—especially those of the Rav, Rabbi Joseph B. Soloveitchik,—are familiar with this process; it is a daily exercise in advanced talmudic reasoning.

This then is our first assumption, that the Halakha is based on conceptual models. Our second assumption is that the conceptual model is not in itself a halakhic statement. Hence, it is in principle not limited in operation only to the realm of Halakha. One consequence of this assumption is that we could, on the basis of conceptions derived from the Halakha, formulate a proper Jewish philosophy; i.e., derive aggada from the Halakha. This, of course, was the basis for most of the Rav's philosophic endeavors, and in fact is, in his opinion, the most, perhaps only, valid way to discover the philosophy of Judaism. A second consequence is that in principle it would be possible to derive the conceptual model from the aggada. If the conceptual framework has applications in the Halakha and the aggada, it may be derived, at least in principle, from either. Hence, eventually, in this way, we will reach halakhic conclusions based ultimately on aggadic source material.

## NOTES

1. J. David Bleich, "In Vitro Fertilization: Questions of Maternal Identity and Conversion," *Tradition*, 25:4, Summer 1991, pp. 82–102.

2. Rav Bleich seems to imply that the Gemara in *Megilla* 13a states explicitly that paternity is established only at the end of the third trimester. Actually, this is not the case. On the contrary, Rav Yosef Engel (*Bet Otzar*, 4) considers the Gemara in *Megilla* to be a proof that paternity is established immediately. The assumption that paternity is established only at the end of the first trimester is based on Rashi (*Sanhedrin* 69a); cf. R. Yosef Engel, ad. loc.

3. Cf. Rav Zalman N. Goldberg, *Tehumin* 5:253 (in English, *Crossroads* 1:74), who arbitrarily limits this case to a full term embryo; cf. Bick, *Tehumin* 6:268 (*Crossroads* 1:82).

4. Bleich argues that surgical removal of the fetus is considered birth only if it is viable when removed from the first woman. Accordingly, he concludes that if a non-viable fetus were to be removed from a woman and placed in an artificial incubator "similar to that portrayed by Aldous Huxley in his *Brave New World*," it might have no mother at all in the halakhic sense.

But, of couse, in every major hospital, non-viable babies in the fifth and six months of pregnancy are placed in incubators. There must be thousands of these "motherless" babies alive today, in our brave old world. There should be no reason to distinguish between natural delivery at any stage of development and surgical removal of the fetus. If caesarean section is considered birth for viable babies, and natural delivery is birth for non-viable babies, caesarean section or ovarian lavage should be considered birth for non-viable babies. A more logical division point might be removal before forty days. However, the halakhic significance of the forty day boundary is not clear, as Bleich himself points out. In any event, this source is not relevant to in vitro fertilization, where an unfertilized ovum is removed from the woman, so that if birth is indeed the determinant of maternity, the fertilized ovum in vitro will be without a mother.

5. Rav Yisrael Zev Mintzberg, "Artificial Insemination," *Noam,* vol. 1, 5718 (1958), p. 159.

6. The *Targum Yonatan* actually states that Dina, conceived by Rachel, and Yosef, conceived by Leah, were transposed. For non-halakhic reasons, it is very difficult to claim that Yosef is not the legal son of Rachel. It should be noted however that the textual support for the aggada—the absence of the phrase, "she conceived" in reference to the birth of Dina to Leah, is absent in the case of Yosef. The *Meshekh Hokhma* (Gen. 46:22), however, discovered a textual reference to the conception of Yosef by Leah.

7. This approach could be alternatively defined not in terms of sperm and ova, but by the sex of the parents. Sexual reproduction is a process of combination of the genetic material from two donors; they are the parents. The male donor is the father, the female donor the mother, i.e., mother is merely the feminine form of the word father (like *hore* and *hora*—parent). The *Minhat Hinukh* (168) appears to maintain a variant of this position when he states that were a man to give birth, he would consequently be a father.

8. The human ovum is in fact barely visible to the unaided eye. Nonetheless, practically I do not believe that a dot without visible shape can be the object of a halakhic determination, and surely is not a human being.

9. J. David Bleich, "Ethical Concerns in Artificial Procreation: A Jewish Perspective," *Publications de l'Academie du Royaume du Maroc, vol. X: Problemes d'ethiques Engendres par les Nouvelles Maitrises de la Procreation Humaine* (Agadir, 1986), pp. 144f.

10. Reduction after implantation of multiple embryos would not be included in this conclusion. Cf. Richard V. Grazi and Joel B. Wolowelsky, "Multifetal Pregnancy Reduction and Disposal of Untransplanted Embryos in Contemporary Jewish Law and Ethic," *American Journal of Obstetrics and Gynecology,* Nov. 1991, v. 165, pp. 1268–71, where several halakhic

authorities are quoted (without their arguments) as permitting both procedures.

11. There is some evidence that during the course of intercourse the vaginal passage becomes increasingly alkaline, which seems to favor the Y-sperm.

12. Cf. *Tosafot, Nidda* 13a, s. v. "VeNashim" and other commentators ad. loc., where the issue is whether a woman is liable for "destruction of seed." Some of the commentators are referring explicitly to the destruction of the man's seed. From Rabeinu Hananel, it would appear that the discussion refers to the possibility of induced menstruation, which would not necessarily imply knowledge of the existence of the ovum. As we have seen, the Sages understood that the blood, i.e., the menstrual lining, is necessary for conception. Even those commentators, like the Rosh, who refer to the destruction of the woman's seed, are not necessarily referring to the ovum, but merely to the possibility that through some action of hers she will interfere with the possibility of her immediate fertilization; i.e., she will bring on her menses.

13. Most commentators derive the verb from *har*, meaning mountain describing the shape of the pregnant woman.

14. The possibility exists, of course, that Onkelos deliberately changed the metaphoric use of conception and pregnancy because he thought it inappropriate to use a distinctly female verb in relation to Moshe.

15. Cf. *Bereshit Rabba* 5:9, "Why was the earth cursed? Because it transgressed the command. God said to it: 'Let the earth bring forth grass . . . and fruit trees bearing fruit'—the tree was to be as edible as the fruit—but it did not do so; rather: 'the earth brought forth grass . . . and trees bearing fruit'—the fruit was edible but not the tree." Because the earth was not fruitful enough, it was cursed that it would produce "thorns and thistles." The implication of both the Midrash and the verse is that the production of plants is inherent in the earth.

16. *Bereshit Rabba* 13:13.

17. Cf. Bava Kamma 22a, s.v. "*lav.*"

18. The *Meshekh Hokhma* is a distinguished exception.

19. The different opinions concerning the use of electricity on Shabbat reflect such as process. Although the definition of *boneh* (building) may be derived from the Talmud, the Hazon Ish's extension of it to electricity is based on a completely new conceptualization of the nature of an electric current, which obviously has no basis in the Talmud itself. The Hazon Ish has a model for electricity and tries to decide what the Talmud Sages would have said about it.

# 5

# *Maternal Identity Revisited*

## J. David Bleich

The ongoing discussion of halakhic determination of maternal identity and its application in situations involving host mothers and donated ova has been broadened by Rabbi Ezra Bick's article titled "Ovum Donations: A Rabbinic Conceptual Model of Maternity" published in the preceding issue of *Tradition*, vol. 28, no. 1 (Fall, 1993).* In the course of that discussion Rabbi Bick takes issue with a number of points made in my earlier article "In Vitro Fertilization: Questions of Maternal Identity and Conversion" that appeared in *Tradition*, vol. 25, no. 4 (Summer, 1991) as well as in my "Survey of Recent Halakhic Periodical Literature" published in *Tradition*, vol. 19, no. 4 (Winter, 1981). I use the passive voice advisedly since, despite the impression made by Rabbi Bick's comments, the points that he questions have all been made by earlier writers and have been attributed to them.

Although it was candidly stated that certain statements to the contrary do exist, it is indeed my conclusion that "the preponderance of evidence adduced from rabbinic sources demonstrates that parturition, in and of itself, serves to establish a maternal relationship." That is the conclusion of a long list of contemporary rabbinic scholars cited in my article. Whether or not the donor of the ovum (a term that I regard as, halakhically speaking, more precise than "genetic mother") is also a mother is, as I have shown, an issue that is open to discussion.

1. The major source serving to establish parturition as a deter-

---

*Chapter 4 in this volume.

minant of motherhood is the statement of the Gemara, *Yevamot* 97b, establishing that twins born to a woman who becomes a convert to Judaism during pregnancy are regarded for halakhic purposes as maternal siblings. Since familial relationships are nullified upon conversion, and since a fraternal relationship cannot exist without a concomitant filial relationship, it follows that the maternal relationship must have come into being subsequent to conversion.

Rabbi Bick raises a number of objections to this argument. Assuming for the purpose of his argument that a child can have but one mother, he contends that when motherhood is established at conception (or, it may be added, at an early stage of gestation), the existence of such a relationship serves to bar any second maternal relationship. Only in the case of a pregnant convert does parturition establish a maternal relationship since it has not been preempted by a previously existing relationship.

The response to that argument is quite simple. Having conceded that birth is, at least in some circumstances, a determinant of motherhood, it becomes necessary to prove: a) that a child cannot have two halakhic mothers; and b) that conception (or gestation) is indeed itself a determinant of maternity; and c) that it preempts any subsequent maternal relationship. *Yevamot* 97b establishes parturition as a determinant of maternal relationship. The contention that this relationship is established with the birth mother only if it is not preempted by a biological mother is an additional proposition. Methodologically, that proposition cannot be entertained unless supported by proof. Such proof is not adduced.

Rabbi Bick further argues that the maternal relationship may well be established at the *time* of birth, but only between the child and the woman who is the source of the ovum from which the child develops. I would rephrase that position in somewhat different terms and express it in the proposition that birth is the cause (*sibah*) of the maternal relationship but that the biological relationship is a condition precedent (*tenai*). The response to that argument is: 1) The burden of demonstrating the existence of such a condition has not been fulfilled, particularly if a baby may have two (or more) halakhic mothers. 2) Were it indeed the case that generation of the ovum is a condition of maternal identity, I fail to understand how birth can establish a maternal relationship between a mother and her proselyte child. It must be clearly recognized that Halakhah takes no direct cognizance of genetics as a significant factor in and of itself. There is no evidence that what Rabbi Bick calls "historical facts" are at all of halakhic relevance. There is no support of which I am aware for the notion that "genetic continuity" is, halakhically speaking, a *sina qua non* of parenthood. Consequently, since conversion nullifies any preexistent relationship, if it be insisted that continuity of identity between the donor (or gestational mother) and the birth mother is a necessary condition of halakhic motherhood, the inescapable conclusion would be that the child born to a pregnant convert has no (halakhic) mother.

The contention that the fetus of a pregnant proselyte undergoes conversion simultaneously with the mother is substantiated by the statement of the Gemara, *Yevamot* 78a, questioning the absence of a requirement for separate immersion of the child. The Gemara establishes that the mother's body does not constitute an interposition or barrier (*hazizah*) between the waters of the *mikveh* and the child because "that is its natural growth." This is the normative halakhic position as reflected in the comments of *Dagul me-Revavah, Yorah De'ah* 268:6, and is in no way contradicted by Rashi, *Yevamot* 97b. However, assuming, as cited in the name of *Zera Yitzhak,* that "there is no such thing as conversion *in utero*" it then certainly follows that "A child born to a woman who converted during pregnancy is Jewish by virtue of birth." That position also yields the conclusion that parturition is a determinant of motherhood. Indeed, such an interpretation of *Yevamot* 97b understands birth as establishing a maternal relationship and *ipso facto* Jewish identity. The linchpin is parturition as the determinant of maternal identity.

[Despite the diligent efforts of the Gottesman Library's prodigious Rabbi Bernard Mandelbaum, the statement cited in the name of *Zera Yitzhak* (4) (sic) eludes me. I suspect this is a typographical error and should read *Zekher Yitzhak,* I, no. 4. However, *Zekher Yitzhak* does not deny that a fetus undergoes conversion in utero. His statement reads, ". . . for whoever was a fetus in the innards of a proselyte who converted became sanctified with the sanctity of Israel." The sanctification to which reference is made is the sanctification of conversion undergone simultaneously with the fetus' mother. Moreover, *Zekher Yitzhak* declares explicitly:

"But that the child is a relative of the mother, this is not by virtue of [its] origin in intercourse, but rather by virtue of the fact that it was born from her." Thus, as accurately indicated in footnote 18 of my earlier article and explained in the accompanying text, *Zekher Yitzhak* represents another prominent authority who unequivocally supports the thesis that the maternal relationship is established at the time of parturition.]

2. Both R. Joseph Engel and Maharal state that a pregnant woman cannot be termed a "mother" because the fetus is yet an integral part of the mother. Maharal explicitly states "and at the time that she became [Esther's] mother, *at the time she was born* (emphasis added), for at the time of conception she could not yet be termed a mother since the fetus did not separate [itself] from her." Those words are cited by R. Joseph Engel in declaring that his view is identical with that of Maharal. Contrary to Rabbi Bick's assertion, not only do these authorities declare that parturition is a determinant of motherhood, they also declare that any earlier maternal relationship is an impossibility. That declaration effectively precludes the possibility of a child having two halakhic mothers. Rabbi Bick seems to be saying that, according to R. Joseph Engel, motherhood is established by donation of genoplasm in the ovum, then nullified by the fetus' integration in the body of the mother, only to be reestablished upon separation from the mother at birth. That takes us back to square one, i.e., the absence of any proof for a genetic theory of halakhic motherhood. Moreover, even if such support were available, any attempt to read that theory into the words of Maharal would be a bit strained, to say the least.

3. Rabbi Bick argues that the Gemara, *Hullin* 70a, explicitly denies that birth alone is the determinant of maternity. The Gemara queries:

> What is the law [regarding the sanctity of a first-born animal] if the two wombs were affixed and [the fetus] went out of one and entered the other? Its own womb is exempted [from future status of a first-born, as this was its first-born], the one not its own is not exempted, or perhaps the one not its own is also exempted."

If any proof is to be brought from this text it must be in support of the proposition that maternal identity is established by birth.

The issue left unresolved by the Gemara is then whether a fetus can be "born" twice by emerging from two different uteruses and thereby precluding any future first-born to the second mother as well. The phrase "its own womb," upon which Rabbi Bick dwells, connotes nothing more than the notion that parturition is a phenomenon of halakhic significance only as the culmination of gestation in utero.

This source is discussed in a somewhat peripheral vein by R. Zalman Nechemiah Goldberg in his contribution to *Tehumin*, vol. V. Rabbi Goldberg certainly does not find that it contradicts the thesis that motherhood is determined at parturition. In point of fact, no halakhic writer has cited this text as a source for the definition of maternal identity. They have not done so for the good and sufficient reason that status as a *"peter rehem"*, i.e., a fetus that "opens a womb" has no bearing on maternal identity. No one has suggested that a neonate—even one which has no mother, if such is halakhically possible—subsequently inserted into the uterus of a woman acquires a mother simply by emerging from the birth canal of its host. One must assume that it is birth in the mode of disengagement from the physiological systems of the host, or at least as the result of labor, that is a determinant of a maternal identity. The question posed by the discussion in *Hullin* is whether *"peter rehem"* is to be defined in the same manner or whether mere opening of the womb by a fetus suffices to exempt future fruit of that womb from the status of a *"peter rehem."* The term "its own womb" employed by the Gemara and the transmuted term "its own child" found in Rambam connote nothing more than a gestational fact and have no import whatsoever for the determination of halakhic motherhood.

4. The conflicting halakhic inferences drawn by various writers from the aggadic statement to the effect that Dina was originally conceived by Rachel and subsequently transferred to the womb of Leah, including the comments of *Tur*, were cited and discussed in detail in this column in the Winter, 1981 issue of *Tradition*.

The statement that the aggadic source "was introduced into the literature concerning parenthood over thirty years ago by Rav Yisrael Zev Mintzberg and subsequently ignored" is factually incorrect. In actuality it was first cited by R. Menasheh Grossberg some seventy years ago in a contribution to *Sha'arei Torah, Sha'ar Menasheh*, XV (5684), no. 3, and subsequently discussed by R.

Joshua Feigenbaum, *Sha'arei Torah,* XV, no. 4; R. Zevi Hirsch Friedling, *Ha-Be'er,* VI (5691), no. 3; and R. Betzalel Ze'ev Safran, as reported by his son in *Ha-Be'er,* VII (5692), no. 2. Nor has it been ignored in more recent times. This source is cited and discussed by R. Moshe Hershler, *Halakhah u-Refu'ah,* I (Jerusalem, 5740), 319-320, by R. Abraham Isaac ha-Levi Kilav, *Tehumin,* V (5744), 267 and others.

I do not place any great weight upon this aggadic source because of the general inappropriateness of aggadic statements as a basis for halakhic inferences and also, as I have carefully shown in my earlier contribution to *Tradition,* because of the conflicting conclusions drawn from this source by earlier scholars. My own inclination lies with those who cite it coupled with the phrase "Dinah the daughter of Leah" in Genesis 34:1 as indicative of the fact that motherhood is governed by parturition because the Pentateuch is first and foremost a legal document and not given to surplusage. However, at best, the evidence is merely confirmatory.

5. Rabbi Bick dismisses proofs by analogy to vegetative relationships out of hand because of their "*a priori* inappropriateness" and describes such arguments as "desperate attempts" to "present a semblance of halakhic reasoning." In point of fact, those arguments were made by, and cited in the name of Professor Ze'ev Low, not by myself. Rabbi Bick seems to be concerned that, rather than consign that approach to the theater of the absurd, I dignify it by presenting an analysis and reasoned critique of those arguments.

Rules pertaining to plants and animals are not automatically analogous. But no serious and knowledgeable student of Halakhah should question "why there should be even a prima facie basis for imagining that the two concepts are analogous." Laws of *orlah* are predicated upon the identity of one living, growing organism, or of a part thereof, becoming submerged in an identity of another living, growing, organism. The primary question with regard to these problematic cases of *orlah* is not age, as Rabbi Bick seems to think; it is first and foremost identity. With regard to these problematic cases of *orlah,* age is directly contingent upon identity. Absent reasons to the contrary or overreaching in the construction of inappropriate analogies, such principles apply with regard to matters pertaining to animals and humans as well.

The methodology is not really reasoning by analogy at all, but rather the identification of an operative principle equally applicable in non-agricultural situations. It is for that reason that as early as 1928, Rabbi Yekutiel Aryeh Kamelhar, *Ha-Talmud u-Mada'ei ha-Tevel*, pp. 44–45, cited regulations pertaining to *orlah* in writing that the recipient of a successful ovarian transplant must be regarded as the halakhic mother of any subsequent issue. Rabbi Bick himself enthusiastically embraces this principle with regard to organ transplants in which "the transplanted material loses its original identity and becomes part of the host." That principle is formulated and expressed with regard to agricultural laws.

6. Rabbi Bick asserts that the impossibility of dual motherhood is "eminently logical." Whether or not Halakhah recognizes dual motherhood is certainly a matter for detailed discussion as I have shown. There is, however, nothing "eminently logical" about either position. The discussion, it must be remembered, is not with regard to the empirical possibility of two biological or genetic mothers. Even with regard to that (at present) entirely theoretical question, *Tosafot, Sotah,* 42b, maintains that it is physically possible for two sperm to penetrate a single ovum. It would undoubtedly be technically much more difficult—but hardly logically or biologically impossible—for genetic material in the form of different chromosomes to be drawn from the ova of two different women. The result will be a child who draws maternal genes from two different women.

Our discussion, however, concerns halakhic rather than biological motherhood. There are indeed legal systems that find nothing illogical about dual legal motherhood. Unlike Roman law that recognized adoption as extinguishing all legal consequences of the natural relationship and consequently permitted consanguineous marriages between adopted children and their natural parents or siblings, Western society does not regard the natural relationship as having been completely destroyed in the legal sense. Nevertheless, many American jurisdictions prohibit marriages between individuals whose sole relationship with one another is the product of adoption. Such marital relationships are regarded as legally incestuous for sound psychological and social reasons. In effect, the law recognizes the existence of two sets of parents for at least some legal purposes. Were it to be established that Halakhah regards both the biological mother and the birth mother to be "legal" mothers, both the geneticist and the psychologist would find such a halakhic determination to be eminently logical.

7. The balance of Rabbi Bick's comments require no detailed response. Despite his valorous attempt to distinguish between an "analogy" and a "model" he offers us, at best, an analogy and as an analogy even he concedes his "model" to be weak. In reality, he offers us a metaphor.

One may indeed formulate philosophical conceptions on the basis of Halakhah. We cannot, however, derive Halakhah from the conceptual model of the *aggadah* for reasons that should be obvious and are, in any event, beyond the scope of these comments. Rabbi Bick's example of the *Hazon Ish*'s position with regard to electricity is entirely inapt. *Hazon Ish*'s position is not at all based upon "a completely new conceptualization of the nature of an electric current." It is based upon the notion of the pragmatic and utilitarian effect of completing a circuit. It does involve a teleological concept of *boneh* (building). At the risk of oversimplifying his position, *Hazon Ish* argues that, once the teleological concept is accepted, creation of an entity capable of performing virtually any new function is a form of *boneh*. *Hazon Ish*'s position has indeed been severely criticized by many, but not because he attempts to construct a "model" in order "to decide what the Talmudic sages would have said about it." The debate is about what they *did* say, not what they would have said. The question of the permissibility of opening a refrigerator door on *Shabbat* requires no knowledge of, or model for, the nature of an electric current. Neither does determination of the status of completion of an electric circuit. In both cases, resolution of the question requires elucidation of already known and accepted principles, not construction of models based upon philosophical concepts.

Rabbi Bick has verbalized the problem, but has presented the wrong solution. There may be—and there probably are—questions to which conventional halakhic methodology provides no solutions. When that occurs there is only one solution: confession of ignorance. That, too, is a halakhic answer. The matter is then to be treated by application of the halakhic canons governing situations of doubt. The one thing that we must not do is engage in "desperate attempts to preserve a semblance of halakhic reasoning"—including the drawing of inappropriate analogies, construction of conceptual models and derivation of halakhic norms from philosophical or aggadic notions.

## NOTES

1. Two volumes devoted to the particular and unique problems encountered by *ba'alei teshuvah* (or better, returnees to Jewish observance) and their mentors are to be highly recommended: R. Moshe Newman and R. Mordecai Becher, *Avotot Ahavah* (Jerusalem, 5752); and R. Moshe Weinberger, *Jewish Outreach: Halakhic Perspectives* (Hoboken, 5750).

2. For additional sources see R. Isaac Elijah ha-Kohen Adler, *Lifnei Iver* (Ofakim, 5749), chap. 3, sec. 5.

3. See, however, *Sedei Hemed, Ma'arekhet ha-Vav, klal* 26, sec. 7, and cf., *Lifnei Iver,* chap. 4, sec. 4.

4. See also the discussion presented in *Lifnei Iver,* chap. 20.

5. Cf., *Lifnei Iver,* chap. 7, sec. 1.

6. Cf. *Teshuvot Imrei Yosher,* II, no. 115, and *Hazon Ish, Shevi'it* 12:9.

7. Cf. also, R. Abraham I. Kook, *Shabbat ha-Aretz* 7:5 as well as sources cited in *Lifnei Iver,* no. 13, sec. 3 and *ibid., Birurim ve-Hakirot,* no. 1, sec. 8.

8. See *Lifnei Iver,* no. 13, sec. 3, p. 75.

9. Cf., *Lifnei Iver, Birurim ve-Hakirot,* no. 1, sec. 8.

10. A less literal translation of this letter is published in *Jewish Outreach,* p. 80.

11. For an examination of sources discussing the *mitzvah of tokhahah* see *Lifnei Iver,* Part 4 and *Jewish Outreach,* pp. 1–30.

# 6

# Male Infertility: Halakhic Issues in Investigation and Management

YOEL JAKOBOVITS

## INTRODUCTION

Difficulties in the male partner are recognized as contributing to infertility in over forty percent of barren couples,[1] and hence the husband is frequently the focus of consideration in the evaluation of the couple. Notwithstanding the plethora of tests currently available to analyze these problems, successful treatment of male infertility remains restricted to only a few correctable conditions. Some of these diagnostic and therapeutic interventions prompt significant halakhic concerns. As in other areas of medical ethics, Judaism's attitudes are often distinctly inconsonant with prevailing secular ethico-legal systems. However, some principles are shared with other religious groups.[2]

For the practitioner used to managing the "average" member of contemporary society, the unusually intense longing for children exhibited by their observant Jewish patients—even quite early in their marriage—requires clarification. The approach to this group of patients demands a sensitive understanding of their particular concerns and aspirations.

Dr. Jakobovits, an internist and gastroenterologist, holds academic appointments at Sinai Hospital of Baltimore and the Johns Hopkins University School of Medicine, and is physician-in-residence on the campus of Ner Israel Rabbinical College.

## 1. THE LONGING FOR OFFSPRING

Judaism regards the gift of children as one of life's preeminent endowments—and challenges. Fecundity is among the most cherished of blessings, an attitude graphically amplified in Psalm 128 which speaks of "a wife as fruitful as a vine," whose "children are as olive plants around the table" leading to the ultimate joy of seeing "children to thy children." This is vividly emphasized by the belief[3] that there is a predestined number of people who must be born before the Messiah can come. Therefore, having more children hastens his arrival.

It has been postulated that the Jewish approach to procreation is, in addition, partially shaped by a legacy of lamentable historical conditions.[4] Frequent physical assault by massacres and pogroms coupled with equally devastating forced conversions and not-so-forced assimilation constitute an enormous—and alas, persistent—depletion of Jewish demographics. A collective, subconscious instinct may exist to replenish these losses by achieving birth rates far in excess of the growth of the ambient society. Interesting and attractive as this theory is, its validity as an historically valid social force remains conjectural: the thesis has not yet been tested by comparing different Jewish communities in separate periods.

The most distinctive defining characteristic of the observant Jew is, of course, loyalty to the dictates of Jewish law. Though not the only reason for marriage,[5] bearing children fulfills three specific religious imperatives—and sets the stage for many others—and is therefore the quintessential ambition of a religious couple. Indeed, the primacy of the mitzva of procreation is reflected in its being the first mitzva in the Torah.[6] Actually, the Mishna[7] regards the biblical references in Bereshit as merely exhorting, as a minimum, the reproduction of the couple by having at least two children. However, the Talmud explicates two supplementary ordinances. One, of biblical origin, known as *lashevet*, is based on the verse in Isaiah 45:18: "Not for void did He create the world, but for habitation *(lashevet)* did He form it." The second, of rabbinic derivation, is known as *la'erev* and is based on the verse: "In the morning, sow thy seed, and in the evening *(la'erev)* do not withhold your hand" (Eccl. 11:6). Subsequently these precepts were codified by Maimonides: "Although a man has fulfilled the mitzva of *pru urvu*—be fruitful and multiply—he is commanded by the Rabbis not to desist from procreation while he yet has strength, for whoever adds even one Jewish soul is considered as having created an entire world."[8]

The pressure, therefore, on Jewish devout infertile couples is often more intense than that which is found among the population at large. Indeed, the opposite calculations may pertain. Whereas a modern, secular couple might choose to "protect" against pregnancy during their first few years of marriage, the Jewish allegiant couple yearns for early parenthood. Actually, both prototypes are motivated to solidify their as yet tenuous relationships. The secular couple maintains that the premature arrival of children would likely undermine their vulnerable ties. By contrast, the religiously inclined pair believe that early parenthood is more apt to cement their marital bonds through the commonality of offspring. These divergent positions can be traced to the fundamentally differing views of the marital covenant itself. On the one hand, the secular couple thinks of the *privileges* of marriage as paramount—if indeed the privileges of conjugal sharing are delayed until the formality of matrimony altogether. On the other hand, a religiously sensitive couple regards marriage's *responsibilities* as preeminent. Consequently, the secular view emphasizes the couple's fulfillment in one another; the religious view stresses their fulfillment in their offspring.

These sociologic features are ubiquitous in the religious Jewish community, fostering an unusual urgency to the resolution of infertility difficulties. It is common for childless couples to seek early counsel, perhaps even within the first few months of marriage. The urge to ignore such entreaties as premature must be tempered by the recognition that these cultural phenomena are deeply rooted in religious law and custom.

Mindful of these fundamental influences we proceed to consider the halakhic intricacies which can develop when evaluating an apparently infertile male.

## 2. GENERAL OVERVIEW OF MALE INFERTILITY

The perception of the degree of male involvement in infertility has undergone a number of revisions in the past 50 years. Initially, and still in the minds of many, infertility was considered primarily a female problem. As we shall see, however, the halakhic aspects are much more serious in the male than in the female.

The extent of male "liability" is hard to quantify with precision. For example, it is estimated that 40% of infertility is wholly or partly due to male factors.[9] On the other hand, there have been attempts to redefine, in a downward direction, the lower limit of "normal" sperm counts. Thus, many men who previously would have been considered as sub-fertile are now considered normal, and the focus has turned back again to the females.[10] Some conditions adversely affecting seminal function include changes in hormonal levels, genetic or congenital anatomic abnormalities, including retrograde ejaculation, and drug use, toxins, infections, and surgical sequalae; some are discussed below in more detail.

## 3. BLOOD TESTS

Subsumed under male infertility is a diagnostically heterogeneous group of disorders. One key basis of discrimination within this group rests upon widely available blood tests. Chief among these are assays of gonadotrophins.[11] A defect in the production of gonadotrophins can be measured in the blood by finding low levels of these hormones. Approximately 9% of infertile males belong to this category. Causes include brain tumors and several rare congenital syndromes. Treatment by injections of gonadotrophin may be effective in selected cases.

On the other hand, patients with testicular failure will have high levels of circulating gonadotrophin hormones.[12] Such patients comprise about 14% of the total number of infertile males. Causes include, in particular, radiotherapy, chemotherapy, and post-infection such as after mumps orchitis. Treatment is currently not possible.

By far the largest group of infertile males—77%—have normal gonadotrophin levels. These patients are said to have "post-testicular dysfunction," that is, impairment of the outflow or production of sperm, in spite of normal pituitary and testicular structures. This category encompasses men with mechanically obstructed ejaculatory ducts (6%), infections such as prostatitis and epididymitis, which are often transient, varicoceles (37%), and idiopathic (25%).

## 4. VARICOCELE

Celsus, in the first century, described superficial and deep varicoceles and noted the presence of testicular atrophy on the affected side. A varicocele is an abnormal dilation of veins within the spermatic cord. This cord consists of nerves, blood vessels, and spermatic ducts through which the testes are attached to and communicate with the body. These deformities, which probably exert their deleterious effects on sperm production by raising the temperature around the testes,[13] occur on the left side in 90% of cases because of the direct insertion of the spermatic vein into the renal vein on that side. By contrast, the right testicular drainage is through the right iliac veins, a venous system with lower resistance pressure. This asymmetric vascular arrangement may also be the basis of the halakhic ruling that injuries to the left testicle (the "weaker one") are less problematic than injuries to the right one which can bar conjugal union within the genetically Jewish community.[14]

The exact significance of a varicocele—and hence of the indications for surgical obliteration—in the management of infertility is controversial. Approximately 10-15% of males in the general population have a varicocele. There is no evidence that males with normal semen characteristics need corrective treatment even if a varicocele is present.

In men with varicoceles and documented impairment of fertility, surgical correction results in a 30–50% pregnancy rate, although this response rate is very controversial.[15] In spite of lingering questions,[16] current practice is to offer correction of varicocele in such men. Surgical interruption of the internal spermatic vein is the usual treatment for clinically apparent varicoceles; there is also a nonsurgical approach that utilizes embolization to occlude the vein.

Halakhically speaking, varicocele repair presents little difficulty. Provided that the medical risks are low and the possibility of fertility improvement is real, one would give every encouragement to correction of this potentially significant impairment.

## 5. SPERM EVALUATION

Most infertility problems, however, are multifactorial in orgin—a virtual axiom in all of medicine. Thus varicocele patients often demonstrate specific sperm abnormalities as well, the recognition of which can help in selecting patients for varicocele treatment.[17] The evaluation of sperm characteristics lies at the center of male infertility testing—and at the crux of the halakhic concerns.

Van Leeuwenhoek, the inventor of the microscope, first observed sperm with his new instrument in 1677. However, it was not until 1929 that the modern era of sperm analysis really began.[18] In addition to the initial exclusive emphasis on the sperm itself, attention is now paid to the noncellular biochemical components of the seminal fluid as well.

## 6. SEMEN PROCUREMENT

The proper collection of sperm is described in detail in many texts. The following extract from a book[19] on infertility testing is instructive in that it directs us immediately to some of the special problems with which Jewish law is concerned.

> The specimen may be obtained at home or in the physician's office, but it should be kept warm during transit. It is very unusual for a patient to object to masturbation as a form of inducing ejaculation. When there is an objection, coitus interruptus is an alternative method of obtaining the specimen. If the patient has religious objections to both masturbation and withdrawal, he can use a perforated plastic condom manufactured by the Milex Corporation of Chicago, and if he is of the Catholic faith, he may have the condom perforated by a priest. In the rare situation in which none of these methods is satisfactory to the patient, the physician will have to rely on post-coital examination of the ejaculate in the vagina. The patient should understand that an incomplete collection is not only worthless but also misleading.

Although there is no parallel to clerical boring (this type of boring, at any rate!) in Jewish sources,[20] halakhic misgivings are prompted by every option summarized in this excerpt. The collection of sperm, masturbation, coitus interruptus, and the use of condoms are all of concern to the Halakha. Notwithstanding the strongly pro-procreative attitudes outlined earlier, there are several halakhic principles which pull in the antithetical direction, curtailing any routine or automatic authorization to investigate male infertility.

By omitting explicit condemnation of masturbation, the Torah[21] has promoted much discussion as to the precise categorization of this prohibition. The "improper emission of genital seed"[22] is regarded as fitting within the general heading of prohibited sexual relations by some,[23] as a "freestanding" prohibition by others,[24] or as merely of rabbinic origin by yet others.[25] In addition to these negative aspects, improper emission of seed may be forbidden as a breach of the obligation to have children.[26] However, another authority[27] holds that the ban on conscious wastage of seed is entirely unrelated to the mitzva of procreation. Other candidates for the classification into which masturbation properly fits are the interdictions forbidding wastage in general,"[28] and censuring eroticism even when only by contemplation,[29] let alone by performance.

The tradition records its condemnation of the wasting of seed in two historical settings. This was the sin which is thought by many commentaries to have been a principal reason for the Flood in Noah's days.[30] Secondly, it was the transgression of both Er and Onan[31] which gave rise to the term "onanism." Chief among the several sinful ingredients in Onan's act is its association with coitus interruptus, a topic which prompts apparently contradictory views in the Talmudic literature.

Despite the Onan story, with its unequivocal censuring tones, there is a Talmudic[32] record of R. Eliezer's opinion which actually recommended the practice of coitus interruptus! He taught so in order to protect a lactating mother from a second pregnancy which could endanger the existing infant by diminishing the mother's milk supply. Rabbi Moshe Feinstein, the recently-deceased, universally acknowledged premier halakhic adjudicator comments: "Since this is the same R. Eliezer in whose name the Talmud quotes a dictum warning against even unintentional improper emission of seed, his endorsement of coitus interruptus for reasons of the health of the child is all the more instructive. It means that, to him at least, seed is not said to be "uselessly" destroyed if a proper purpose is served thereby, and if this is the only manner in which that purpose can now be served. Marital relations is that purpose; since normal intercourse would cause a hazard to health, the emission of seed for such relations, where there is no alternative, is not wasteful; where there is an alternative, it is wasteful, even according to him."[33]

The normative ruling, however, is in accordance with the Sages' dissenting opinion. Ergo Maimonides prohibits the practice without equivocation: "It is forbidden to destroy seed. Therefore, a man may not practice coitus interruptus, etc."[34]

The strict attitudes regarding coitus interruptus[35] should be considered alongside, and in contrast with, the somewhat more lenient attitudes towards "unnatural intercourse" *(bi'a shelo kedarka)*. The prevailing Talmudic view is that "a man may do with his wife as he wishes."[36] Tosafot[37] records two notable formulae proposed by R. Yitzhak to resolve the law's permissiveness in *Nedarim* as compared with the restrictive attitude held in *Yevamot*. Firstly, the tolerant view sanctioning unnatural intercourse may have assumed that no semination occurs. Alternatively, semination is in fact tolerated provided unnatural intercourse is resorted to only on occasion and that the contraceptive intention of the husband is not constant.

This second answer of R. Yitzhak—highlighting both 'intent' and 'irregularity'—may constitute broad foundation for authorization to practice unnatural intercourse within marriage when it fulfills a "purpose." Even the assuagement of the husband's sexual desire may be included within the parameters of acceptable standards of sexual relations, this being reaffirmed by many authorities.[38] All authorities emphasize, however, that this general license is controversial and certainly applies only to occasional sexual expression.[39]

There are several instances where prominent early sources sanctioned masturbation—and the inevitable spillage of seed to which it leads—to achieve an overriding "purpose." A man may resort to masturbation in order to relieve an otherwise uncontrollable sexual desire, thereby avoiding an even graver transgression of a prohibited sexual relationship.[40] The Talmud[41] itself recommended masturbation for the investigation of sexual impotence (erectile dysfunction), a disability which can preclude marriage within the genetically Jewish community. Some authorities[42] also sanctioned masturbation in order to ascertain whether post-coital vaginal bleeding derives from the male or from the female. Post-coital bleeding in the female may pose restrictions on the resumption of sexual relations.

Other specific "purposes" may also be acceptable reasons to sanction a lenient attitude. Medical[43] considerations—though not specified—would be generally pardoned and can provide halakhic grounds for sanctioning this method for temporary birth control. This is clearly articulated by Rabbi Isaiah da Trani[44] who writes:

> How [in the light of the sin of Er and Onan] did the Sages permit unnatural intercourse [as when using a diaphragm] when it involves [wasteful] emission of seed? The answer is: Wherever the husband's intent is to avoid pregnancy so as not to mar his wife's beauty and he does not want to fulfill the mitzvah of procreation, it is forbidden. But if his intent is to spare her physical hazard, then it is permitted. So also if he does so for his own pleasure [unnatural intercourse is permitted] . . . for 'a man may do with his wife what he wishes.'

Strikingly, as Feldman[45] points out, though this passage was written in the thirteenth century but remained unpublished until 1931, it nevertheless reflects an off-repeated mainstream opinion. It has been used to provide significant support for lenient rulings by several twentieth century halakhic masters such as Rabbi Isaac Herzog,[46] the late Chief Rabbi of Israel, and Rabbi Moshe Feinstein.[47]

It should be noted, however, that there is a notable body of extra-halakhic Kabbalistic literature[48] which inveighs heavily against any spillage of seed under any circumstance. Reflecting this view is the comment[49] of R. Yosef Karo: "Had R. Yitzhak seen what the Zohar says about the gravity of *hash-hatat zera*, namely that it is the most severe of sins, he never would have written what he did." Both the permissive and restrictive opinions are recorded by Rabbi Moshe Isserles.[50]

These considerations form the foundation upon which the halakhic position regarding masturbation is based. Of paramount importance is purpose. When the intention is procreation, either directly through artificial insemination and in vitro fertilization or indirectly when evaluating male infertility, there is significant room for leniency within the halakhic guidelines. A large body of rabbinic literature exists delineating the Jewish attitude to artificial insemination.[51] Briefly: most authorities[52] would sanction this technique, provided there are rigid safeguards insuring that only the husband's sperm is introduced into his wife. Conversely, artificial insemination using the sperm of a donor from outside the marriage (AID) is strongly condemned.[53] However, note the remarkable, and at first glance paradoxical, leniency of one leading halakhist[54] permitting—nay, recommending—using the sperm of a non-Jewish donor. The prohibition of using "outside" Jewish sperm arises from concerns regarding adultery and/or incest. In addition the identifiable lineage of the offspring would be severely compromised, leading to potentially dreadful situations of personal status and marriageability.[55]

It is important to recognize that no *carte blanch* regarding the method of semen procurement, even under conditions of need and sanction, is granted. Justification for a tolerant approach exists only in special circumstances, as in the investigation of male infertility. For example, by recommending either warm perianal applications (Rava) or visually evocative stimuli (Abaye) to arouse ejaculation, the Talmud[56] itself appears to be deliberately avoiding any suggestion of direct penile stimulation to avoid conflict with the Talmud's (*Niddah* 13a) express admonition against such contact. A similar reluctance may have prompted the "teach us our Rabbi" phrase used to establish an acceptable method of penile evaluation. The expression assumes that there is difficulty with the seemingly obvious technique, masturbation.[57]

Specifically germane to our discussion here are the expressed rabbinic positions regarding procurement of sperm by masturbation in the medical investigation of male infertility.[58] Mindful of the pro-procreative intent of the procedure, where no other technique is appropriate, many[59] authorities sanction such artificial collection of sperm. Others,[60] however, disagree, arguing that because of the many technical uncertainties[61] coupled with the strongly condemnatory Talmudic and, in particular, Kabbalistic pronouncements, masturbation can never be sanctioned—even in the interest of siring offspring. Similarly, some[62] even have argued that because of the severity of the sin of masturbation, one would rather recommend that a childless couple divorce and remarry someone else! Mindful of the limited likelihood of helpful medical intervention, several authorities[63] are similarly disinclined to sanction masturbation even with the intention of aiding procreation.

On the other hand, contrary, more lenient views exist as well. Chief among these opinions are the previously quoted views of Rabbi Yaakov Emden and Rabbi Chaim O. Grodzinski. The latter suggests that, if possible, it is better to collect seminal fluid from a condom[64] worn during intercourse, thereby avoiding masturbation. More contemporaneous decisors[65] have also suggested this method as most acceptable. In addition, Bet Shmuel,[66] citing the same Talmudic passages, also deduces a liberal attitude with respect to semen procurement in pressing circumstances. Accordingly, where post-coital bleeding is detected, he permits the noncoital ejaculation of sperm to establish whether hematospermia is responsible. This license may only be appropriate when the evaluation of the female companion is not conclusive.[67]

A leading contemporary halakhist, Rabbi S. Z. Auerbach,[68] has ruled "that even when he has a male and a female child [the halakhic minimum], a man is permitted to obtain sperm [notwithstanding the severe restrictions which normally apply] in order to fulfill the imperative of *lashevet* (see earlier discussion) or where his wife is in significant [psychological] distress from not having more children." However, the precise method of procuring sperm is not indicated.

Yet another approach might be applied in situations of infertile couples where investigations already undertaken fail to identify any female disorder. Here it may be fair to assume, that the male either has no viable sperm or has defective sperm. In either case, wastage of his seed would not constitute *zera l'vatalah,* there likely being no viable seed to speak of. This line of reasoning is developed by Rabbi S.B. Sofer[69] who concludes by advising that "where it is possible, a postcoital diaphragm may be used; even during coitus one may be lenient for this purpose. . . . But if it is impossible [to use the semen collected] by a diaphragm—then my opinion is to be lenient [about manual masturbation]. . . . However, since I failed to find absolute proof, and due to the gravity of the issue I would solicit additional [concurring] opinions. . . ."

## 7. SUMMARY OF SEMEN COLLECTION METHODS

The reader may be excused if he is left quite bewildered by the foregoing account of widely differing views. A workable algorithm of graduated choices along the lines of Rabbi E. Waldenberg's[70] is suggested:

> The preferred method of semen collection is from the vagina following normal coitus.[71]
>
> Where that is not possible because of technical or emotional reasons, sperm may be procured after coitus interruptus.[72]
>
> Where that is unsuitable, the collection should be made using a condom—preferably one with a perforation—worn during intercourse.[73]
>
> If that is impossible a collecting receptacle should be placed intra-vaginal.
>
> Finally, if that too is impractical, sperm may be obtained by masturbation. Penile stimulation should preferably be achieved by a mechanical stimulator, though self-stimulation is also permitted.[74]

## 8. TESTICULAR BIOPSY

Occasionally, biopsy of the testicle is indispensable to accurate diagnosis. It is usually recommended in azoospermic men with normal-sized testes to discriminate between ductal obstruction and spermatogenic failure. In men with poor quality sperm or very low counts, results of histological evaluation will rarely, if ever, alter therapy. The biopsy will assist, however, in making a definitive diagnosis which can aid the physician in providing the patient with a reliable prognosis, thereby avoiding needless treatment in unsalvageable circumstances.

Evidently, the futility of testicular biopsy was assumed by one early halakhic writer[75] who reports that "none of the physicians of my town are familiar with such a test." Nevertheless, he proceeds to discuss the halakhic concerns in some detail. The obstacles relate in particular to the biblical injunction proscribing marital bonds with a genetically Jewish woman by any man who has "wounded testes or severed membrum."[76] The Talmud[77] elaborates this injunction to include any wounding or crushing injury to the penis, testes or cords of the testes. The author concludes that testicular biopsy would be permitted from a "wounded or crushed" point of view in that the perforation in the testes heals completely. However, he regards this method of semen procurement as "unnatural" emission of seed and therefore rules against it. He does not speak of actual biopsy of the testicle.

Arguments allowing the procedure because testicular sperm are immature prior to their maturation in the collecting ducts, and therefore would not be subject to any restrictions on sperm emission, have been advanced.[78] Furthermore, the prohibition on surgical damage to the genitalia might be applicable only where the patient has reproductive capacity, a precondition clearly not extant in the investigation of an infertile male.[79] Similarly, Rabbi Feinstein[80] also sanctions testicular biopsy, arguing that the Talmudic constraints are applicable only when the perforation of the testis results in infertility; nowadays the procedure has the reverse likelihood, being designed to help alleviate infertility.


## 9. METAPHYSICAL AND PSYCHOLOGICAL CONSIDERATIONS

The mysterious nature of the miracle of procreation instinctively prompts many infertile couples to first seek guidance and blessing from spiritual rather than medical sources. An ancient axiom states that "a blessing is only effective on that which is concealed from the eye."[82] The psychological sensitivity of intimate human relationships cannot be over-emphasized. Great care must be exercised in advising a couple to embark on the trail of infertility investigation. A precise recommendation as to how much time should elapse before infertility investigations are begun cannot be made. Though, by convention,[83] couples who remain childless after one year of a regular, sexually active married life are called infertile, the point at which the diagnosis of infertility is earned is quite variable.

Regarding the "right time" at which to initiate the various stages of infertility testing, the rabbinic opinions are quite variable. For example, while some[84] allow semen analysis only after ten years, others urge only a five[85] or even a two[86] year period. Rabbi Waldenberg[87] underscores the need to tailor one's approach to the individual cases at hand.

Even though the Halakha may have no technical opposition to some investigations, there are some important psychological aspects to consider. The confirmation, particularly during the early months of marriage, by objective scientific testing of aspermia or azoospermia can have a devastating impact on the male and hence on the marriage itself. Consequently, great deliberation must be exercised when agreeing with—or advising—a couple asking for fertility testing.

We have already emphasized the degree to which a religious Jewish infertile couple may feel compelled to seek medical help. The couple will often first seek the counsel of their rabbi. Indeed, infertility difficulties, in particular, are associated with prayer and spiritual exertions. The very concept of supplication in prayer to the Creator finds roots in our principal matriarchs, Sarah, Rebecca, and Rachel, all of whom were infertile through many years of marriage. The Bible chronicles their yearning for the blessing of children through anguished prayer, prompting the Rabbis to declare that "God is desirous of the prayer of the righteous."[88] These moving passages were eventually regarded as the paradigm of prayer and were therefore incorporated into the High Holiday services.[89] All who are involved in advising such people must be sensitive to these metaphysical aspects of their petitioner's needs and aspirations.

## NOTES

1. G. S. Berkowitz, "Epidemiology of Infertility and Early Pregnancy Wastage," in *Reproductive Failure*, A. H. DeCherney, ed. London, Churchill Livingstone, 1986, pp. 17–40. In the U.S., today, approximately 10%–20% of couples are infertile. Infertility is defined as the inability to conceive after one year of regular coitus without contraception. This definition is based on an expected monthly pregnancy rate of 20%–25% in normal couples attempting pregnancy. (See: S. B. Jaffe and R. Jewelewicz, "The basic infertility investigation," *Fertility and Sterility* 56:599, 1991.)

2. The Roman Catholic Church's generally restrictive attitudes in

matters of procreation are well known. Less widely appreciated are the fairly detailed Church proscriptions bearing upon infertility testing. These are often remarkably similar to Judaism's teachings. A brief review by G. Kelly, *Medico-Moral Problems* (St. Louis, 1966), pp. 218–228, reflects the view of the Catholic Hospital Association.

3. *Yevamot* 62a, 63b; *Avoda Zara* 5b; *Nidda* 13b.

4. See David M. Feldman, *Marital Relations, Birth Control and Abortion in Jewish Law.* (NY: Schocken Books, 1974), p. 51.

5. See, for example, the series of expositions on the inherent value of marriage for the male partner in Yevamot 62b where one who is unmarried is regarded as being without joy, blessing, good, Torah protection, and peace. Likewise, the Talmud (e.g., *Yevamot* 118b; *Kiddushin* 7a, 41a) often assumes that marriage is beneficial for the female partner: *"tav l'metav tan du mil'metav armelu"*—It is always to her advantage to be part of a tandem, married, rather than alone. Both references focus on companionship, a non-procreative aspect of marriage.

6. Rashi and Tosafot (*Yevamot* 65b) and Ramban (*Bereshit* 9:7) hold that the verses addressed to the Noachidic survivors of the Flood (*Bereshit* 9:1 and 7) and to Jacob (*ibid.*, 35:11) are the source of this injunction. Contrary to the common assumption, the charge to Adam and Eve (*ibid.*, 1:28) is actually a blessing, not a commandment.

7. *Yevamot* VI, 6 (61b).

8. *Yad HaHazaka, Hil. Ishut,* 15:16.

9. R. F. Blackwell and M. P. Steinkampf, "Infertility: Diagnosis and Therapy," in *Controversies in Reproductive Endocrinology and Infertility,* M. R. Soules, ed. (NY: Elsevier, 1989), p. 15.

10. C. M. K. Nelson and R. G. Bunge, Semen Analysis: Evidence for Changing Parameters of Male Fertility Potential," *Fertility and Sterility,* 25:503, 1974.

11. Gonadotrophins are a set of hormones secreted by the pituitary gland in the base of the brain which stimulate ( = trophic) the testicular apparatus ( =gonads) to produce seminal fluid ( =sperm and the fluids in which it is suspended).

12. Because the pituitary gland tries to drive the unresponsive testes, unrestricted by the negative biofeedback which successful spermatogenesis would provide.

13. Alternative suggestions—none of which have been adequately substantiated—include different concentrations of adrenal hormone exposure to the testes and decreased testicular blood flow. (E. Steinberg, "Male Infertility," in *Gynelogogic Endocrimology,* J. J. Gold and J. B. Josimovich, eds., 4th ed., 1987, pp. 572–3.)

14. See a fuller discussion below, in the section regarding testicular biopsies.

15. A. T. K. Crockett, H. Takihara, and M. J. Cosentino, "The Varicocele," *Fertility and Sterility*, 41:5, 1984.

16. A. Vermeulen and M. Vandeweghe, "Improved Fertility After Varicocele Correction: Fact or Fiction?" *Fertility and Sterility*, 42:249, 1984.

17. B. J. Rogers, G. G. Mygatt, D. W. Soderdahl, and R. W. Hale, "Monitoring of Suspected Infertile Men with Varicocele by the Sperm Penetration Assay," *Fertility and Sterility*, 44:800, 1985.

18. D. Macombar and M. B. Sanders, "The Spermatozoa Count," *New England Journal of Medicine*, 200:981, 1929. An up-to-date discussion is provided by B. C. Dunphy, L. M. Neal, and I. D. Cooke, "The Clinical Value of Conventional Semen Analysis," *Fertility and Sterility*, 51:324, 1989.

19. R. J. Sherins and S. S. Howards, "Male Infertility," in *Campbell's Urology*, P. C. Walsh, *et al*, eds., 5th ed. (Philadelphia: WB Saunders, 1986), p. 645.

20. However see the discussion regarding the use of perforated condoms below, note 64.

21. The primary Talmudic source is in *Nidda* 13a (see *Magid Mishna* on *Yad HaHazaka, Issurei Bi'a* 21:18).

22. Known in Hebrew as either *hotza'at zera levattala* or more commonly as *hash-hatat zera*, generally regarded as interchangeable phrases. Feldman, *loc cit.*, p. 109, cites *Resp. Hinnukh Beit Yitzhak, E.H.*, no. 7, who proposes a plausible distinction between the two.

23. Rambam, *Yad HaHazaka, Issurei Bi'ah* 21:18 and *Tur Shulhan Arukh, Even Ha'Ezer* 23:1, based upon *Shemot* 20:13, Cf. Rambam's Mishna Commentary on *Sanhedrin* 54a.

24. *Sefer Mitzvot Ketanot* No. 292 and *Ma'adane Yom Tov* on Rosh, *Niddah* Chap. II, No: 40. Contemporary discussions: Rabbi M. Feinstein, *Resp. Iggerot Moshe, Even Ha'Ezer* III, No. 14, staunchly reiterates the biblical nature of this transgression; Rabbi E. Waldenberg, *Resp. Tzitz Eliezer* IX, 51:1.1 cites various opinions but comes to no firm conclusion.

25. *Resp. Penei Yehoshua, Even Ha'Ezer* II, no. 44 argues that the severe strictures applied by the Sages are exaggerated and were meant to underscore the repulsiveness with which they regarded Onanism.

An unusual analysis is suggested by *Hagga'ot Ezer Mikodesh* cited by Rabbi A. M. Babad, *Resp. Imre Tova*, no. 33: "The [biblical] prohibition of wasteful spillage of seed pertains only prior to the ban on polygamy promulgated by Rabbenu Gershom ben Yehuda (c. 1000) when [by having several wives] it may have been possible for *each* ejaculation to achieve fruition. Today—especially in our countries where secular laws makes [even] divorce difficult—the matter has changed and the Halakha has changed and there is no more than a Rabbinic prohibition here." R. Babad also quotes his uncle, the author of *Resp. Havatzelet*

*Hasharon* (Addenda to *Even Ha'Ezer,* vol. 1), who concluded similarly that today spillage of seed is only a Rabbinic prohibition. I am grateful to my brother-in-law, Rabbi C. Z. Pearlman of London, for directing me to these citations.

26. *Tosafot Sanhedrin* 59b. Those excluded from the mitzva of procreation would therefore be free from this restriction (Rabbenu Tam in *Tosafot, Yevamot* 12b, s.v. *shalosh*).

27. Ramban, *Niddah* 13a.

28. *"Bal tashhit"* (Devarim 20:19), undoubtedly civilization's earliest conservation legislation! Rabbi Yaakov Ettlinger in his *Resp. Binyan Tzion,* no. 137 and novella *Arukh LeNer,* on *Niddah* 13b, makes this tentative suggestion. He also suggests that this interdiction may be based upon a *halakha le Moshe m'Sinai.*

29. See *Achiezer* III, no. 24:5 based on *Devarim* 23:10 and *Avoda Zara* 20b.

30. *Bereshit* 6:12 and alluded to by Rashi on 6:11. See also *Avot D'Rav Natan* 32:1, *Zohar* I, 66:2 on *Bereshit* 7:4; Ramban and Ritva on *Niddah* 13a; Menahem Kasher in *Torah Shlema* no. 150, on *Bereshit* 6:12, comparing similar suggestions in *Shabbat* 41a.

31. *Bereshit* 38:7–10 and the Talmud's discussion thereof in *Yevamot* 34b. The passage in *Yevamot* equates the sin of Er and Onan with unnatural intercourse (*shelo k'darka*) rather than with Rashi's assumption (on *Bereshit,* loc. cit.) that the failing was coitus interruptus. See Ritva and Maharsha on *Yevamot* 34 and Ibn Ezra on *Bereshit* 38:7 who offer a variety of approaches to reconcile these differing interpretations. See the trenchant passage in *Levush, Bereshit* 38:10.

32. R. Eliezer on *Yevamot* 34b, a position with which the Sages disagree.

33. *Resp. Iggerot Moshe, Even Ha'Ezer,* no: 63, p. 154, as translated by Feldman, *Marital Relations,* p. 152.

34. *Yad HaHazakah, Hil. Issurei Bi'a,* 21:18 and so *Sefer Mitzvot Gedolot,* Neg. 126 and *Shulhan Arukh, Even Ha'Ezer* 23:1.

35. Not all authorities are always strict; some advocate coitus interruptus as the desirable method to obtain sperm for analysis: *Resp. Z'kan Aharon* vol. I, nos. 66, 67, and vol. II, no. 96, p. 18, n. 67.

36. *Nedarim* 20b. See *Bet Yosef* on *Tur, Even Ha'Ezer* 25, and *Kol Bo, Hil. Ishut,* Par. 76, p. 66a, who counsel caution to the pious.

37. *Yevamot* 34b, s.v. *"Velo."*

38. *Tur, Even Ha'Ezer* 25 and *Orah Hayyim* 240; *Yam Shel Shlomo, Yevamot,* ch. 3, par. 18, and *Haggahot HaBah* on Rosh to *Yevamot* 34b and others refer to a permissive ruling by Rosh on *Yevamot,* Ch. 3, Par 6—a text absent (censored?) from extant versions of this commentary. Similarly, Drisha on *Tur, Even Ha'Ezer* 23:1; *Resp. Maishiv Davar, Yoreh De'ah,*

no. 88; and *Resp. Iggerot Moshe, Even Ha'Ezer,* no. 63, p. 156, who also records his pleasure to hear that *Resp. Tzemah Tzedek, Even Ha'Ezer,* no. 89 supported this position.

39. For example, Rema, *Even Ha'Ezer,* 25:2: "A man may act with his wife as he wishes, having intercourse when he wants . . . [and how he wants] provided he does not ejaculate. Others are lenient and rule that he may have unnatural intercourse even if he emits sperm so long as this is not habitual. However, even though all this is [strictly speaking] permitted, 'He who sanctifies himself [by denying even] that which is permitted is called holy.' "

40. R. Yehuda HaHasid, *Sefer Hassidim,* no. 176; but Hiddah (*Petah Enayim, Nidda 13*) dismisses this as a case of unavoidable spillage and not of intentional masturbation.

41. *Yevamot* 76a.

42. *Bet Shmuel, Even Ha'Ezer,* 25:2.

43. *Levush* on *Even Ha'Ezer,* 23:5, though dyspareunia (painful intercourse) may not be an acceptable reason to suspend the restrictions (*Resp. Melamed Leho'il,* III, No. 18).

44. *Tosfot RiD* on *Yevamot* 12b.

45. In *Marital Relations,* p. 162.

46. *Resp. Hekhal Yitzhak, Even Ha'Ezer,* vol. II, no. 16.

47. *Resp. Iggerot Moshe, Even Ha'Ezer,* no. 63 and no. 64.

48. In particular, the *Zohar* on *Shemot,* 259a and 263b. Similarly strongly worded restrictive views are recorded by *Sefer Haredim,* III, Ch. 2, by R. Eliezer Azikri (1601), and in R. Isaiah Hurvitz's *Shenai Luhot HaBrit (Shlah),* I, *Sha'ar Ha'Otiyot,* 100 a, b. The latter, on p. 102b (Amsterdam ed.), writes: "Study to observe all the laws of marital relations as enumerated in the *Tur Orah Hayyim* 240 and *Even Ha'Ezer* 25. Omit nothing . . . A man should know every word by heart—except in the matter of unnatural intercourse. In that connection I have cited (the restrictive) words of *Sefer Haredim*—to him you should listen [rather than to the *Tur*]."

49. In *Bedek Habayit* on *Bet Yosef, Even Ha'Ezer* 25.

50. On *Shulhan Arukh, Even Ha'Ezer* 25:2.

51. This ancient technique was well know by Talmudic times. See for example, *Hagiga* 14b.

52. See Immanuel Jakobovits, *Jewish Medical Ethics,* rev. ed., (NY: Bloch Publ, 1975), pp. 247–250. A comprehensive review of the halakhic literature, in Hebrew, is provided by A. Steinberg in *Assia,* No. 12, pp. 5–19, 1975, with 91 In a recent issue of references. *Assia* (Vol II, no. 1, p. 21, Jan. 1991), J. Green considers, in English, the attitude of the Israeli judicial system towards artificial insemination in a married woman. See also Fred Rosner, *Modern Medicine and Jewish Law,* (NY: Yeshiva University Press, 1972), p. 89.

Several finer points warrant consideration here. For example, Jewish law proscribes conjugal relations during the *nidda* period, which is defined as the duration of the wife's menses—or at least for five days, whichever is longer—and for the next seven "clean" days. At this point relations can—nay, should—be resumed, provided the woman has "cleansed" herself by immersion in a *mikva,* a ritually prescribed "bath." Noteworthy is the caveat recorded by several authorities insisting that insemination even with the husband's sperm be confined to the non-nidda days of the wife's menstrual cycle (*Resp. Tzitz Eliezer,* Vol 9, 51:4.6, quoting Hazon Ish and others). On the other hand, Rabbi Moshe Feinstein (*Resp. Iggerot Moshe, Even Ha'Ezer* II, 18) permits this. *Resp. Ma-Harsham* (3:268), *Har Tzvi* (*Even Ha'Ezer,* no:1), by Rabbi Tzvi Pesah Frank, and *Resp. Yabia Omer* (vol. 2, *Even Ha'Ezer,* no:1) by Rabbi Obadia Yosef are inclined to permit artificial insemination after ten years of fruitless marriage. Rabbi Y. Y. Weinberg (*Resp. Seride Esh* 3:5) and others regard sperm procurement for artificial insemination as purposeful, and is therefore not considered *zera le vattala.* Assurances regarding the physician's trustworthiness are mandatory in all such matters (Rabbi Shlomo Zalman Auerbach in *Noam,* I: 157).

Other decisors hold very restrictive views on artificial insemination altogether. *Resp. Divre Malkiel* (4:107, 108), condemns the procedure even when the semen is that of the husband, partly because physician safeguards may be insufficient to insure against some *zera levattala.* Note that sperm loss must be recognized as an inevitable consequence of all forms of insemination, whether natural or artificial.

An interesting question is raised by Rabbi Eliyahu Bakshi-Doron, Chief Rabbi of Haifa, in *Assia,* 44:35–39, April 1988: May an unmarried bridegroom who requires pre-marital cancer therapy and fears that the therapy will render him infertile procure semen for freezer storage and use it later? The author concludes that this is not permitted insofar as the positive mitzva to procreate is not yet of practical application to the unmarried bridegroom. Therefore, this mitzva cannot serve as a counterweight to the negative restriction against spillage of seed. The author reports that Rabbi Yosef Eliyashiv concurred with this reasoning. This author finds this argument unconvincing: An unmarried man also has a mitzva to procreate, albeit in practice this must await his actual marriage. Compare, for example, the Rosh on *Ketubot* 17b who notes that the mitzva of *peru urevu* can be realized by procreation with a concubine and is therefore, strictly speaking, independent of marriage.

In a note, the editor of *Assia* suggests that in a situation where the bridegroom had an actual mitzva to procreate, but couldn't consummate the marriage—for example, when the bride was a *nidda*—then the husband could presumably procure semen for storage. However, in a

letter to Joel B. Wolowelsky (dated December 15, 1991), Rabbi Bakshi-
Doron disagreed, arguing that the groom of a *nidda* would also not be
prohibited to collect semen. He left open the possibility that a married
person about to undergo chemotherapy may procure semen for frozen
storage. A widow may not be impregnated with the licitly obtained
semen of her deceased husband. On the one hand, the deceased is exempt from the mitzva of procreation and hence could not claim the
usual legal protection authorizing the normal risk to the mother which
is inherent in every pregnancy. On the other hand, the woman herself
is always excused from the obligation to procreate. I am grateful to Dr.
Wolowelsky for sharing this letter with me.

Intracervical insemination, which most closely mimics coitus by placing the ejaculate "as is" into the vagina, actually may not involve much
wastage. However, this fairly simple technique is only needed for the
management of fairly unusual cases to overcome purely anatomical defects such as hypospadias or psychological difficulties which impair ejaculation.

Much more frequently, AIH is used to overcome either a low sperm
count or cervical mucus antibody mediated infertility. Here intra-uterine
insemination (IUI) must be performed. The procedure of necessity involves separating the spermatozoa from the seminal fluid, which were it
also injected into the uterus would cause painful uterine contractions
thus jeopardizing the whole procedure. Ineffective non-motile spermatozoa and seminal fluid are discarded. Inevitably some healthy spermatozoa are also lost. The situation is more complicated in in vitro
fertilization (IVF). In order to minimize the possibility of polyspermatic
fertilization, only 50,000 sperm are added to each egg-containing dish.
Even in cases of very successful harvesting of eggs, where tens of oocytes
are recovered, only about a million spermatozoa are used in the fertilization process. As the normal ejaculate has at the very least 25 million
sperm—and more often has over 100 million—IVF must involve discarding very large numbers of sperm. (I am grateful to Richard V. Grazi,
MD, for providing this technical information.)

53. See note 49. Also, *Resp. MaHarsham III*, no. 268; *Resp. Helkat Ya'a-
kov I*, no. 24; *Resp. Yabia Omer, Even Ha'Ezer*, no. 1; *Resp. Emek Halakha*,
no. 68.

54. Rabbi Moshe Feinstein devotes five responsa directly to artificial
insemination (*Resp. Iggerot Moshe*, vol. 3, *Even Ha'Ezer* I:10; I:71; II:II; vol.
7, *Even Ha'Ezer*, IV: 32.5). These are among his most controversial decisions in which he permits AID provided the sperm is obtained from a
non-Jew, arguing that while it is not as acceptable as the husband's own
sperm, a non-Jew's sperm is nevertheless preferable to an "outside" Jewish male's contribution. The child born to a Jewish mother of a non-

Jewish father is fully Jewish. A child born of a Jewish woman and a Jewish father other than the lawful husband is a *mamzer*—a bastard—which in Jewish law has important consequential marital disabilities. The issue grew into a rabbinic *cause celebré*, drawing criticism from many authorities (see *Hama'or*, Tishri-Heshvan 5725, pp. 5–9). R. Waldenberg, *Resp. Tzitz Eliezer, ibid.*, claims that R. Feinstein later withdrew from his position in a letter dated 1965, ruling negatively to an individual petitioner. See *Resp. Iggerot Moshe Even Ha'ezer* IV, 32:5 where R. Feinstein still defends the theory behind his earlier decision but emphasizing his opposition for AID using non-Jewish sperm in practice.

55. J. David Bleich, "In Vitro Fertilization: Questions of Maternal Identity and Conversion," *Tradition*, 25 (4), 82–102, Summer 1991, provides a wealth of information regarding the problems and importance of securely defined and identifiable lineage.

56. Normally, men with rabbinically-identified anatomical disfigurement of the penis are barred from wedding a genetically Jewish spouse; undamaged anatomy and function of sexual organs are prerequisites for such relationships. Elaborating, the Talmud in *Yevamot* 76a states: "If a hole which had been made in the [penile] corona itself is closed, the man is disqualified if it re-opens when semen is emitted; but if it does not [re-open, the man is deemed] fit. Rava the son of Rabbah sent to R. Joseph: Will our Master instruct us how to proceed [with a test when it is desired to ascertain whether the semen will re-open an occluded perforation]? The other replied: Warm barley bread is procured, and placed upon the man's anus. This stimulates the flow of semen and the effect can be observed. Said Abaye: Is everybody like our father Jacob . . . because [of whose saintliness] he never before [marriage] experienced the emission of semen? [An alternative technique was offered by] Abaye who said "No, colored [female] garments are dangled before him." Said Rava: Is everybody then like Barzillai the Gileadite [known for his indulgences]? In fact it is obvious that the original answer is to be maintained."

57. *Yam Shel Shlomo, Yevamot,* 8:16.

58. Quite another application of the restriction of masturbation is found in the laws of circumcision. A tense penis is recommended prior to the procedure to assure safe amputation of the foreskin and thus reduce the risk of injury to the underlying glans. This is especially true for the adult. It is permissible to achieve an erection by physical stimulation of the penis, but since this can lead to *hotza'at zera levattala,* it ought to have been banned because of the Talmud's opposition to manual masturbation as recorded in *Niddah* 13a. Rabbi Shlomo Kluger (introduction to *Sefer Kin' at Sofrim*) eliminates this apparent difficulty: in accordance with the general rule that positive commandements take

precedence over negative ones, especially when the former are Biblical and the latter Rabbinic in origin. Therefore, circumcision takes precedence over the ordinance banning masturbation. Based upon these considerations it is arguable that in spite of whatever Rabbinic restrictions may exist, masturbation would still be permitted when it is performed to facilitate reproductive capability. However, a counter-argument might point out that in the case of circumcision seminal spillage is not inevitable; in the case of infertility it is.

59. Rabbi C. O. Grodzinski, *Ahiezer* III, No. 24:4, partly based upon Rabbi Yaakov Emden, *Resp. She'elat Ya'avetz* I, No. 43; Rabbi Uziel, *Resp. Mishpetei Uziel, Even Ha'Ezer*, no. 42. *Resp. Zekan Aharon* I, no. 67 insists upon coitus interruptus rather than masturbation.

Semen analysis and procurement are discussed in detail by many authorities including: Rabbi E. Waldenberg, *Resp. Tzitz Eliezer*, vol. 7, 48:1.7, and vol. 9, 51:1; Rabbi O. Yosef, *Resp. Yabia Omer*, vol. 2, *Even HaEzer* 1:7; Rabbi M. Feinstein, *Resp. Iggerot Moshe*, vol. 3, *Even HaEzer* I:70, and II:16; vol. 5, *Even HaEzer* III:14; vol. 7, *Even HaEzer* IV:27.

A valuable review of semen destruction and contraception in general appears in the Reb Yaakov Rosenheim Jubilee Volume, New York, 1932, p. 87, by Rabbi J. Z. Horowitz of Frankfurt. He gathers the major opinions and concludes that seminal procurement for analysis intended to facilitate procreation is permissible.

60. *Otzar HaPoskim Even HaEzer*, vol. 5, p. 86a (quoting in particular *Resp. Divre Malkiel* vol. 5, No. 157); *Vaya'an Avraham*, no. 7; R. S. Engle (quoted below); etc.

61. Uncertainties include: The impediment may be in the female partner; there may in any case be no effective therapy; it may be possible for him to father children were he married to someone else; a problem with the technique of intercourse may exist.

62. In his Responsa (vol. 6., no. 75), Rabbi S. Engel recommends this radical answer when ten years of barren marriage have transpired. See Shilo, S., "Impotence as a Ground for Divorce (To the End of the Period of the Rishonim)," *The Jewish Law Annual*, 4:127–43, 1981, for an interesting historical review.

63. *Sedei Hemed "Pe'at Sadeh"* in *Ma'arekhet Ishut*, no. 13; *Resp. Ezrat Kohen, Hil. Ishut*, no. 32, by Rabbi A. Y. Kook; *Resp. Avne Nezer, Even HaEzer* 83. They advocate empiric therapeutic trials without regard to specific diagnoses. On the other hand, *Resp. Tzitz Eliezer*, vol. IX, 51:1.2, acknowledges that modern differential diagnoses may indeed have a significant impact on treatment choices. Rabbi Eliezer of Munkacz, author of *Resp. Minhat Eliezer*, in *Darkhe Teshuva, Hil. Nidda* agrees with the restrictive views, but would sanction the post-coital vaginal collection of sperm for analysis.

64. Rabbis Y. Newirth and S. Z. Auerbach are quoted by Abraham Abrahams in *Nishmat Avraham, Even HaEzer*, 23:2, p. 112, as recommending that when a condom is worn a small perforation should be made, enabling sperm to enter the female's reproductive tracts. This would obviate concerns about wastefulness of seed in that it is possible that the coital act will result in pregnancy.

65. Rabbi Y. Y. Weiss in *Resp. Minhat Yitzhok*, vol. 3, no. 108:6.

66. *Shulhan Arukh, Even HaEzer* 25:2.

67. Rabbi Waldenberg, *Resp. Tzitz Eliezer, loc cit*, takes issue with *Mahatzit Hashekel, loc. cit*, who maintains that the dispensation of *hatza'at shikhvat zera levattala* implied by *Yevamot* 76a is limited to when the investigation is needed to establish marriageability within the genetically Jewish community; R. Waldenberg argues that avoiding divorce is no less a reason for permissiveness. Evidence of spermatogenesis may be required to overcome restrictions which pertain to certain categories of infertile men. Such investigations, of course, must be made on the male in question. Rabbi Waldenberg cites *Taharas Yisrael, Orah Chayyim* 240:39, who rules that ejaculation is permitted when physicians are undertaking investigations designed to promote fertility and eventual procreation.

68. Quoted by Abraham S. Abraham in *Nishmat Avraham, Even HaEzer* 23:2, p. 111.

69. *Resp. Shevet Sofer, Even HaEzer* 1. Similar arguments are found in *Resp. Imre Esh, Yoreh De'a* 69, and *Resp. Levushe Mordekhai*, III, *Orah Chayyim* 51. A contrasting view is that of *Resp. Rav Pealim* III, *Even HaEzer* 2.

70. *Resp. Tzitz Eliezer, loc. cit.* end of 'Gate' 1.

71. Abraham S. Abraham in *Nishmat Avraham, Even HaEzer* 23:2, p. 112, reports that Rabbi S. Z. Auerbach recommends that if possible this be performed by a female doctor or nurse.

72. As recommended by *Resp. Zekan Aharon*, vol. 1, no. 66, but see next note.

73. Though other authorities would reverse this step with the previous one.

74. In accordance with *Resp. Ahiezer*, but in contrast with *Resp. Iggerot Moshe*, which would never allow self-stimulation.

75. *Resp. Zekan Aharon*, vol. 1, no. 66. He assumed the purpose of this test to be the analysis of the semen.

76. *Devarim* 23:2.

77. *Yevamot* 75b.

78. Rabbi Y. Newirth quoted by Abraham S. Abraham in *Nishmat Avraham, Even HaEzer* 23:2, p. 113.

79. Rabbi Y. Y. Weiss, *Resp. Minhat Yitzhak*, vol. 3., no. 108:7. In view of Rabbenu Tam's opinion which permits even complete excision of the

left testicle, Rabbi Weiss counsels that an elective biopsy be taken from the left side. Rabbi E. Waldenberg, *Resp. Tzitz Eliezer,* vol. 9, no. 51:1.2, agrees with him.

80. *Resp. Iggerot Moshe, Even HaEzer,* vol. 2., 3:2. Note that Rabbi Feinstein does not make his authorization contingent upon using the left side only. See also J. A. Gordon, R. D. Amelar, L. Dubin, and M. D. Tendler, "Infertility Practice and Orthodox Jewish Law," *Fertility and Sterility,* 28:480, 1975.

81. E. E. Wallach, "The Enigma of Unexplained Infertility" *Postgrad Obstetrics and Gynocology,* 5:1, 1985, alludes to some of these unexplained phenomena. In general, it emphasizes, that the shorter the duration of infertility, the better the associated prognosis.

82. *Ta'anit* 8b; *Bava Metzia* 42a. In fact several studies highlight the fact that pregnancy rates are fairly independent of treatment! See, for example, J. A. Collins, W. Wrixon, L. B. Jones, and E. H. Wilson, "Treatment-Independent Pregnancy Among Infertile Couples," *New England Journal of Medicine,* 309:1201, 1983.

83. See note 1. It should be noted that the authors report that 64% to 79% of women with infertility will conceive within nine years. Clearly, however, investigations should not be delayed until then.

84. *Resp. Minhat Yitzhak,* vol. 3, no. 108.

85. *Resp. Iggerot Moshe, Even HaEzer,* vol. 2, no. 16.

86. Hazon Ish cited by Abraham Abraham, *Nishmat Avraham, Even HaEzer* 23:2, p. 113.

87. *Resp. Tzitz Eliezer,* vol. 9, no. 51:1.2.

88. *Yevamot* 64a.

89. The Torah reading for the first day of Rosh Hashanah, taken from *Bereshit* 21, recounts the realization of Sarah's plea. Similarly, the Haftara (*Samuel* I:1 and 2) relates how Hanna was blessed with the birth of Samuel. The Talmud (*Megilla* 31a) tells us that Sarah and Hanna were both remembered on Rosh Hashanah.

# 7

# *Sperm Banking in Anticipation of Infertility*

## J. DAVID BLEICH

### I.

In some circumstances, radiation or chemotherapy in dosages sufficient to arrest certain forms of malignancy may affect the gonads
in a manner that is likely to result in sterility. Hence male patients
receiving radiation to the testes or, as is more frequently the case,
chemotherapy for conditions such as Hodgkin's disease or non-
Hodgkin's lymphoma are unlikely to be able to sire children. As
a result some men, particularly those who have not yet become
fathers, avail themselves of the option of having their semen frozen and stored in sperm banks. Utilizing a procedure that has
been available since the late 1960s, the semen is collected before
the patient undergoes treatment and his wife is later impregnated
by means of artificial insemination using the husband's previously
ejaculated sperm. Sperm can be cryobanked indefinitely. There
have been documented pregnancies resulting from semen stored
as long as fifteen years. However, some physicians report disappointing results in patients suffering from Hodgkin's disease, presumably because the quality of the sperm has been compromised
by that illness. The halakhic propriety of such procedures for unmarried men is the subject of a symposium published in *Sefer
Assia*, VII (Jerusalem, 5754), 279–303.

In the case of married men, the halakhic issues involved are
precisely those present in all instances of homologous artificial

insemination utilizing the husband's semen (AIH). Historically, the first reported employment of this technique in humans was for the purpose of overcoming the physical problem of depositing sperm in the genital tract of a woman whose husband suffered from hypospadias. That procedure was carried out at the close of the eighteenth century in approximately 1790 by the illustrious English surgeon, John Hunter, who succeeded in artificially impregnating the wife of a London linen draper.[1] Typically, AIH is recommended in situations in which the husband suffers from oligospermia, i.e., his sperm count is too low to enable him to father a child in the normal manner. AIH may also be advised when the husband is unable to maintain an erection, the husband experiences retrograde ejaculation due to neurological lesions or other causes, in instances of cervical abnormalities, anatomical abnormalities of the uterus, vaginismus, faulty spermatozoa reception of the vagina or hostility of the mucous secretions of the cervix, as well as when intravaginal coitus is impossible due to a tumor, excessive obesity, or anatomical disparity of the male and female sexual organs.[2] In such procedures, combination of ejaculates and delivery of the collected sperm directly to the uterus compensates for a low sperm count. The primary halakhic question is whether non-coital ejaculation by the husband is forbidden as a form of onanism or whether it is sanctioned in circumstances in which ejaculation is undertaken for purposes of procreation. This matter has been the subject of extensive discussion in rabbinic literature.[3]

Although a number of prominent authorities refuse to sanction the practice,[4] a majority of those who have addressed the issue permit AIH,[5] albeit with varying degrees of enthusiasm, but disagree among themselves with regard to the means of semen procurement that may legitimately be employed.[6] Among contemporary decisors, Rabbi Yosef Shalom Eliashiv as well as the late Rabbi Shlomoh Zalman Auerbach are reported as not being supportive of such procedures, particularly in instances involving unmarried men.[7] *Hazon Ish* also expressed a negative view, although it is not clear whether he decried the practice *in toto* or only when the procedure is carried out prior to the wife's immersion in a *mikveh* as a means of circumventing the fertility problem faced by some women who observe the regulations of family purity and experience a short ovulation cycle.[8]

*Tosafot, Yevamot* 12b and *Ketubot* 39a, demonstrate that normal intercourse is clearly permitted even when procreation is impossible as evidenced by the permissibility of marital relations with a minor and with an infertile woman. Intercourse with a post-menstrual woman is similarly permitted. The question is whether all non-vaginal ejaculation constitutes onanism or whether such forms of ejaculation are permitted when designed to promote procreation. The numerous authorities who permit AIH point to the talmudic discussion recorded in *Yevamot* 76a:

> Rabbi Judah stated in the name of Samuel: If [the membrum] was perforated and sealed in a manner such that it will tear when semen is emitted the man is unfit, but if [it does] not [tear] the man is regarded as fit. . . . Rava the son of Rabbah sent to Rabbi Joseph: Let our Master instruct us how to proceed [to test whether the semen will reopen the closed perforation]. Rabbi Joseph said to Rava: Warm barley bread is brought and placed upon his anus;[9] he emits semen and we observe [whether the wound has reopened]. . . . Abaye said: Colored [women's] garments are passed before him.

The talmudic discussion centers around the prohibition recorded in Deuteronomy 23:2 forbidding intercourse with a man who has sustained certain injuries to his genital organs. Included in that prohibition is a person who has sustained an unhealed perforation of the membrum. In this context healing is defined as closure of the perforation by adhesion of tissues with sufficient strength so that the perforation will not reopen upon erection and ejaculation. Whether or not such healing has indeed occurred would, of course, immediately become evident upon performance of a normal coital act. Intercourse, however, cannot be permitted unless it is known that the perforation has indeed become adequately sealed. As expressed by Rava, the result appears to be a Catch-22 situation: Marital relations cannot be permitted unless it has been demonstrated that the perforation is properly sealed. But since, ostensibly, ejaculation is permissible only in the context of intercourse such healing cannot be demonstrated. R. Joseph and Abaye both respond with advice regarding methods of achieving ejaculation without intercourse. The cogency of their replies, it is argued, is contingent upon antecedent acceptance of the thesis that only ejaculation that "wastes" the seed is prohibited as onanism but that other forms of ejaculation are permissible when undertaken in order to enable procreation to occur. Hence, since no marital relations may take place until the emission of semen occurs, such ejaculation is entirely permissible. Some scholars cite this opinion not only in support of AIH but also as the basis for sanctioning semen testing designed to facilitate treatment of male infertility, at least when there is reason to suspect that failure of the wife to conceive is due to infertility of the husband.[10]

It is clear that at least some form of non-coital seminal emission for purposes of procreation is permissible. The crucial question is whether such dispensation is limited only to the forms of emission specified in *Yevamot* 76a or whether other forms of ejaculation are permitted as well. R. Shlomoh Luria, *Yam shel Shlomoh, Yevamot* 8:15, observes that the procedures suggested by the Gemara represent indirect methods of ejaculation, i.e., they are designed to stimulate arousal that will culminate in ejaculation of semen, but do not involve a direct causal act. In general, transgression of a biblical prohibition occurs only if the act performed is the proximate cause of the prohibited effect; an act only indirectly causing such an effect (*gerama*) is generally prohibited by virtue of rabbinic decree. Rabbinic injunctions are often not universal in nature. They are enacted either as a "fence around the law" or to thwart conduct designed to frustrate the *telos* a prohibition is designed to achieve. Such rabbinic edicts frequently exclude situations in which countervailing policy considerations were regarded as paramount. Thus, it is not at all surprising to find that, in the situation addressed by *Yevamot* 76a, the Gemara sanctions sexual arousal as an indirect means of effecting seminal emission. In effect, a rabbinic prohibition is rendered nugatory in limited situations in order to facilitate marriage and thereby promote procreation. According to *Yam shel Shlomoh*, there is no evidence to contradict the presumption that the prohibition against onanism applies to all forms of biblically proscribed non-coital emission; for purposes of the biblical prohibition all acts that do not have direct procreative potential are forms of "wasting the seed."

Thus, according to *Yam shel Shlomoh*, a semen sample for diagnostic purposes may be obtained only by utilization of the methods indicated by the Gemara and by other analogous indirect methods, e.g., reading or viewing pornographic material, a method that is analogous to gazing upon colored female garments. However, at least in contemporary times, it is quite unlikely that such methods will result in a suitable seminal emission.

It may well be argued that, even according to *Yam shel Shlomoh*, direct means may be employed to obtain semen for purposes of AIH. In contradistinction to situations involving ejaculation for purposes of determining eligibility for marriage or for diagnostic purposes in which emission of semen is only indirectly related to the siring of a child, when semen is emitted for purposes of AIH the ejaculate itself is used directly for impregnation of the wife as is the case when ejaculation occurs in the context of sexual intercourse. Hence, it may be argued, the semen is not in any sense "wasted" and, accordingly, the biblical prohibition does not apply.[11]

Other authorities do not make the distinction drawn by *Yam shel Shlomoh* and permit even direct forms of semen procurement for all procreative purposes,[12] including semen testing.[13] However, R. Moses Feinstein, *Iggerot Mosheh, Even ha-Ezer*, I, no. 70, distinguishes between semen procurement through use of a condom or in the form of *coitus interruptus*[14] and masturbation. *Iggerot Mosheh* also points to the fact that the Gemara, *Yevamot* 76a, does not advise masturbation as a means of causing ejaculation to occur.[15] But instead of drawing a distinction between direct and indirect acts designed to achieve ejaculation, as did *Yam shel Shlomoh*, Rabbi Feinstein points to a statement of the Gemara, *Niddah* 13b, from which he infers that masturbation constitutes a violation distinct from, and in addition to, "wasting of the seed." In that discussion, the Gemara speaks of a prohibition regarding "licentiousness by hand" and "licentiousness by foot" and by means of talmudic exegesis, relates those acts to biblical verses describing prohibited acts. *Iggerot Mosheh* reasons that the prohibition against onanism reflects a ban against "wasting of the seed" and hence does not apply to ejaculation designed to facilitate procreation even if there exists no direct causal nexus between ejaculation and conception while the prohibition to which reference is made in *Niddah* 13b, he opines, is directed not against ejaculation *per se*, but against physical manipulation involving "licentiousness by hand" or "licentiousness by foot."[16] Since that prohibition is unrelated to the concept of "wasting" the seed *Iggerot Mosheh* concludes that it is forbidden even when undertaken for purposes of procreation.

## II.

From the foregoing it would appear that, in principle, AIH is entirely permissible and that the only area of dispute is with regard to appropriate means of semen procurement. That conclusion, however, is not entirely accurate. As has been stated, the authorities who permit this practice predicate their position upon the discussion found in *Yevamot* 76a that serves to establish that ejaculation for purposes of procreation is permitted. More precisely, that source serves to support the conclusion that emission of semen is warranted in order to establish capacity to contract a legitimate marriage in order to fulfill the biblical injunction "be fruitful and multiply" (Genesis 1:28 and 8:17). The selfsame principle would seem to render permissible semen testing necessary to determine treatment for male infertility since the goal is to enable the patient to fulfill the command "be fruitful and multiply." However, somewhat curiously, siring a child by means of AIH may not constitute fulfillment of that obligation. In order for a person to fulfill the commandment he must not only be the biological father of the child but must be recognized as the halakhic father as well. A Jewish male who consorts with a gentile woman is assuredly the biological father of the issue of that union but, since Jewish law does not recognize relationships of that nature, he is not the halakhic father. Similarly, a Hebrew servant is permitted to cohabit with a Canaanite slave but Halakhah does not recognize a paternal-filial relationship between the Hebrew servant and his offspring and, accordingly, in siring such children the Hebrew servant does not fulfill his obligation to "be fruitful and multiply."[17] The issue that must be addressed is whether Halakhah recognizes paternity only with regard to children born of sexual intercourse or whether such recognition extends also to issue born *sine concubito*. In light of the fact that AIH does not involve a coital act there are strong grounds to argue that, if intercourse is a necessary condition for establishing a halakhically recognized paternal relationship, AIH cannot be sanctioned since

the birth of a child as a result of the procedure does not constitute fulfillment of the biblical commandment.

Most authorities find a resolution of this question in a statement of R. Peretz ben Elijah of Corbeil in his *Hagahot Semak*, cited
by *Bah, Yoreh De'ah* 195, *Taz, Yoreh De'ah* 198:7, and *Bet Shmu'el,
Even ha-Ezer* 1:10, who states:

> A menstruating woman may lie upon her husband's sheets but
> should be careful not to lie on sheets upon which another man has
> slept lest she become impregnated from the semen of another.[18]
> Why is she not concerned lest she become impregnated from her
> husband's semen during her menstruation and the child be con-
> ceived of a *niddah?* He answered that since there is no forbidden
> intercourse the child is entirely legitimate even if she becomes im-
> pregnated from another, for indeed Ben Sira was legitimate. How-
> ever, from the semen of another we are particular with regard to
> determination [of paternity] lest [the child eventually marry] his
> paternal sister.

There cannot be sibling incest in the absence of a halakhically
recognized fraternal relationship. A fraternal relationship exists
only when, and because, the siblings share a common parent.
Indeed, it is tautological to say that siblings enjoy a common paternal-filial or maternal-filial relationship. In the hypothetical situation discussed by *Hagahot Semak* the brother and sister shared a
common, halakhically recognized, filial relationship even though
one was born *sine concubito*. That conclusion is accepted by *Bet
Shmu'el, loc. cit.,* R. Shimon ben Zemah Duran, *Tashbaz*, III, no.
263, and most later authorities.[19] Nevertheless, some later authorities, including R. Chaim Joseph David Azulai, *Birkei Yosef, Even ha-
Ezer* 1:14, dispute this view and maintain that a coital act is the *sine
qua non* of a halakhically recognized paternal relationship.[20] The
view of *Bet Shmu'el* and *Tashbaz* is similarly questioned by *Taz, Even
ha-Ezer* 1:8.[21]

Some scholars, including R. Joshua Baumol, *Teshuvot Emek Halakhah*, I, no. 60, R. Shlomoh Zalman Auerbach, *No'am*, I, 157,
and R. Judah Gershuni, *Kol Zofayikh* (Jerusalem, 5740), p. 367,[22]
assert that although the progenitor of a child born *sine concubito*
may not fulfill the commandment to "be fruitful and multiply"
he certainly fulfills the mandate expressed in the prophetic verse
"He created the universe not a waste, He formed it to be inhab-

ited" (Isaiah 45:18). Ejaculation for that purpose, they contend, cannot be regarded as "wasting" the seed.

## III.

Assuming that semen procurement by one means or another for purposes of insemination is permissible, is a childless man who faces imminent sterility as a result of radiation treatment or chemotherapy obligated to deposit his sperm in a sperm bank in order to impregnate his wife at a future time? For that matter, is a man who has a low sperm count obligated to avail himself of AIH in order to become a father? Rabbi Eliyahu Bakshi-Doron, the present Sephardic Chief Rabbi of Israel, *Binyan Av,* II, no. 60, correctly notes that, despite the fact that a large number of responsa have been published permitting AIH, in none of these responsa is there a hint that the procedure is obligatory. Dr. Abraham S. Abraham, *Nishmat Avraham,* IV, *Even ha-Ezer* 23:1, quotes a letter written by the late R. Shlomoh Zalman Auerbach in which the latter writes ". . . the holy Torah did not obligate a person to freeze semen." However, that cryptic statement does not explain why such measures are not obligatory in order to satisfy the obligation of procreation mandated by the commandment "be fruitful and multiply."

The Gemara, *Haggigah* 2b, describes the plight of a person whose status is "half Canaanite slave and half free," e.g., the individual was part of an estate inherited by two brothers, one of whom proceeded to execute a bill of manumission while the other did not. Such a person may neither marry a Jewess of legitimate birth nor consort with a female Canaanite slave. The part of that individual's *personam* that is a free man is prohibited from having intercourse with a slave while the part that is a slave may not cohabit with a Jewess. Accordingly, the rule is set down that the master who has a partial interest in the slave must relinquish his title and set the slave free; moreover, if he fails to do so willingly, physical duress may be brought to bear upon him in order to secure compliance.

*Tosafot, ad locum* and *Baba Batra* 13a, question the premises expressed in the dilemma posed by the Gemara. The obligation to "be fruitful and multiply" is a positive commandment; the restriction against cohabitation between freemen and slaves is the product of a negative commandment. The general rule is that when a positive commandment and a negative commandment are in conflict and one or the other must be transgressed, fulfillment of the positive commandment takes precedence (*aseh doheh lo ta'aseh*). If so, queries *Tosafot*, why is this individual not permitted to cohabit with a Jewess in fulfillment of a positive commandment even though that fulfillment entails concomitant infraction of a negative commandment? *Tosafot* responds by noting that the rule of *aseh doheh lo ta'aseh* applies only if fulfillment of the positive commandment is simultaneous with violation of the negative commandment whereas, in performance of the sexual act, transgression of the negative commandment occurs in the initial stage of penetration (*ha'ara'ah*) while fulfillment of the positive commandment does not occur until a later stage of the sexual act (*gemar bi'ah*).[23] *Tosafot*'s reasoning in applying the relevant principle is unexceptionable and hence the talmudic dilemma is entirely understandable since it is perfectly clear that fulfillment of the precept and transgression of the prohibition do not occur simultaneously. The problem is that the time lapse between transgression of the negative commandment and fulfillment of the positive commandment seems to be far greater than indicated by *Tosafot*. "Be fruitful and multiply" seems to imply propagation of the species, i.e., birth of a child. That event does not take place at the time of intercourse but only subsequent to a period of gestation. The gap is not between the earliest stage of penetration and completion of penetration—a matter of mere seconds—but between intercourse and birth of a child—a period of nine months.

It is abundantly clear that *Tosafot* regards the admonition "be fruitful and multiply" as connoting not the siring of a child, but as a commandment making the procreative act, *viz.*, intercourse, mandatory. Such intercourse is required on a regular basis until the requisite number of children has been born. A gentile who converts to Judaism together with his children is exempt from this requirement because he, in fact, has sired children. The *mitzvah* is the sexual act, but the *mitzvah* is incumbent only upon those who are yet childless.

This analysis of the nature of the *mitzvah* is logically compelling. Halakhah defines the *mitzvah* as binding only upon the male, but not upon the female. Speculative science and Hollywood fantasies aside, no male has ever experienced the pain of childbirth. It is axiomatic that God does not command the impossible. Although endocrinologists claim that, with proper hormone treatment, the phenomenon of a male carrying a fetus to term (as portrayed in the 1995 film "Junior") is theoretically possible, any attempt by a male to bear a child would pose a grave risk to the life of the putative father (or perhaps more accurately, the male mother).[24] No one need assume such risk in fulfilling any *mitzvah*. Certainly, when commanded by God, the males to whom the *mitzvah* was addressed did not understand it to require them to seek hormone treatment at the hands of endocrinologists. The *mitzvah*, then, must be defined as mandating that which is in the province of the male, *viz.*, the sexual act that has procreation as its goal.[25]

This thesis is reflected in the precise language employed by Rambam in spelling out the *mitzvah* to "be fruitful and multiply." Rambam, *Hilkhot Ishut* 15:1, states that a husband "is obligated to engage in intercourse at each designated interval until he has children for such is the positive commandment of the Torah as it is said 'be fruitful and multiply.'" The commandment requires the male to marry a woman capable of bearing children and to engage in intercourse with stipulated frequency. The essence of the commandment is the marital act; the birth of children represents the *terminus ad quem* beyond which the marital act is no longer mandated by reason of "be fruitful and multiply."[26]

Noteworthy also is the fact that in enumerating the questions put to a person on the Day of Judgment, the Gemara, *Shabbat* 31a, indicates that the first question is phrased in the words "Did you engage in procreation?" rather than "Did you sire the required number of children?" The latter question is not posed because, contrary to a literal reading of the verse, man is not commanded to sire, much less to bear, children; he is commanded to "engage in procreation," i.e., to perform the procreative act that is within his province, *viz.*, intercourse. It is thus possible, although highly improbable, for a man who suffers no reproductive abnormality to select a fertile woman as a wife, to marry at the proper age, to engage in intercourse at the stipulated intervals throughout his entire lifetime but yet not to become a father. According to this analysis, such a childless person has nevertheless discharged his obligation to "be fruitful and multiply." Accordingly, a question with regard to the birth of children would not be at all appropriate at the time of judgment; the appropriate question is that formulated by the Gemara, "Did you engage in procreation." Similarly, the Mishnah, *Yevamot* 61b, declares, "A person should not desist from procreation unless he has children." Here, too, the obligation is couched in terms of the procreative act rather than in terms of siring children.

Yet another significant halakhic conclusion flows from this thesis. Were the words of the precept to be construed as a commandment focused upon producing children, the reproductive process employed to achieve that end would be merely instrumental and would not form part of the *mitzvah*. Although sexual intercourse is the obvious means of achieving the requisite goal, the same result might conceivably be accomplished by other means. It would then follow that, since the means are not intrinsic to the commandment, a person incapable of siring a child in the usual and natural manner, would be obligated to employ artificial means, when and if available, to achieve that end. Procedures such as AIH or other forms of assisted procreation would be mandatory for otherwise infertile males.

However, since intercourse is the essence of the commandment, it is that act alone that is incumbent upon the male. A person incapable of impregnating his wife by means of natural intercourse has no obligation whatsoever to engage in any other practice designed to cause conception to occur. The result is that, although artificial means and "heroic measures" may in at least some circumstances be required in order to prolong life, they are never required in order to generate life. Of course, means such as AIH may be entirely permissible but their use is discretionary rather than mandatory.

## IV.

Rabbi Bakshi-Doron[27] permits AIH and semen banking only for an already married man. He accepts the notion that ejaculation for purposes of procreation is permissible but argues that it is permissible only for a married man who is "actually obligated" (*hayyav be-po'el*) in the performance of the *mitzvah* of procreation but not for an unmarried man whose obligation cannot yet be actually discharged. Dr. Abraham cites R. Shlomoh Zalman Auerbach as declaring, "There is no distinction at all between a married man and a bachelor for even a bachelor is obligated to marry a wife and fulfill the commandment concerning procreation. But in my opinion even a married man is not obligated [to freeze semen] for the holy Torah did not obligate a person to freeze semen. The sole matter of doubt with regard to this matter is only whether it is prohibited or permitted."

Rabbi Auerbach's view is entirely cogent. Bachelors are bound by the obligation to "be fruitful and multiply" no less so than married men. Dr. Daniel Melech, writing in *Sefer Assia*, VII, 300, compares the bachelor's obligation to that of a person who has not purchased an *etrog* for use on *Sukkot*. The latter is clearly "actually" obligated in the performance of the *mitzvah*; his obligation "actually" includes taking the necessary measures to acquire an *etrog*. A bachelor is similarly required to fulfill the *mitzvah* of procreation but only in a legitimate manner, i.e., by means of marital relations with a lawfully wedded wife, and must perform the antecedent acts necessary for that purpose.

Accordingly, the consensus of halakhic opinion is that there is no difference between married and unmarried men with regard to semen banking. At the same time, such procedures are discretionary at best; they are certainly not mandatory. The position of authorities such as Rabbi Auerbach and Rabbi Eliashiv who discourage but do not prohibit the procedure is presumably based upon well-grounded hesitation to sanction halakhically controversial methods of semen procurement for a purpose that is entirely discretionary in nature.

## NOTES

1. Magnus Hirschfeld, *Geschlechtskunde auf Grund dreisigjähriger Forschung und Erfahrung bearbeitet* (Stuttgart, 1928), II, 404; Hermann Rohleder, *Test Tube Babies: A History of the Artificial Impregnation of Human Beings* (New York, 1934), p. 40; Alan Guttmacher, "The Role of Artificial Insemination in the Treatment of Sterility," *Obstetrical and Gynecological Survey*, vol. 15, ed. by Nicholson J. Eastman (Baltimore, 1960), p. 767; and *idem*, "Artificial Insemination," *Annals of the New York Academy of Sciences*, vol. 97, art. 3 (Sept. 29, 1962), p. 623. The report is attributed to Hunter's nephew, Everett Home, "An Account of the Dissection of a

Hermaphrodite Dog, etc." *Philosophical Transactions of London*, vol. 89 (1799), p. 157.

2. Wilfred J. Finegold, *Artificial Insemination* (Springfield, 1964), p. 17; Guttmacher, *Obstetrical and Gynecological Survey*, p. 769; Barry S. Verkauf, "Artificial Insemination: Progress, Polemics, and Confusion—An Appraisal of Current Medico-Legal Status," *Houston Law Review*, vol. 3, no. 3 (Winter, 1966), pp. 280–281; and Amey Chappell, "Artificial Insemination," *Journal of the American Women's Medical Association*, vol. 14, no. 10 (October, 1959), p. 902.

3. A useful survey of that literature is presented in *Ha-Refu'ah le-Or ha-Halakhah*, ed. R. Michel Stern, I (Jerusalem, 5740), part 2, pp. 1–102.

4. *Rav Pe'alim*, III, *Even ha-Ezer*, no. 2; R. Malki'el Zevi Tennenbaum, *Teshuvot Divrei Malki'el*, IV, nos. 107–108; R. Ovadiah Hadaya, *No'am*, vol. I (5718), pp. 130–137, reprinted in *idem, Teshuvot Yaskil Avdi*, V, *Even ha-Ezer*, no. 10; R. Ya'akov Breisch, *Teshuvot Helkat Ya'akov*, I, no. 24; R. Shlomoh Epstein, *Teshuvah Shlemah*, II, *Even ha-Ezer*, no. 4; R. Ben-Zion Uziel, *Mishpetei Uzi'el*, *Even ha-Ezer*, no. 19; and others.

5. R. Shalom Mordecai Schwadron, *Teshuvot Maharsham*, III, no. 268; R. Simchah Bunim Sofer, *Teshuvot Shevet Sofer*, *Even ha-Ezer*, no. 1; R. Chaim Ozer Grodzinski, *Teshuvot Ahi'ezer*, III, no. 24; R. Abraham Bornstein of Sochachev, *Avnei Nezer*, *Even ha-Ezer*, no. 63; R. Aaron Walkin, *Teshuvot Zekan Aharon*, I, nos. 66–67 and II, no. 97; R. Zevi Pesach Frank, *Teshuvot Har Zevi*, *Even ha-Ezer*, no. 1; R. Moses Feinstein, *Iggerot Mosheh*, *Even ha-Ezer*, I, nos. 70–71, II, nos. 16 and 18 and III, no. 14; R. Ovadiah Yosef, *Teshuvot Yabi'a Omer*, II, *Even ha-Ezer*, no. 1; R. Joshua Baumol, *Teshuvot Emek Halakhah*, I, no. 68; R. Ya'akov Yitzchak Weisz, *Teshuvot Minhat Yitzhak*, I, no. 10, III, no. 47 and IV, no. 5; R. Shlomoh Zalman Auerbach, *No'am*, I (5718), 145–166; R. Eliezer Waldenberg, *Tzitz Eli'ezer*, III, no. 27 and IX, no. 51, *sha'ar* 4, chap. 6; R. Yisra'el Zev Mintzberg, *No'am*, I, 129; and others.

6. Retrieval of semen from the vagina of the wife after coitus presents no halakhic problem; see *Teshuvot R. Akiva Eger*, no. 72; *Iggerot Mosheh, Even ha-Ezer* I, no. 70 and II, no. 16; and R. Joel Teitelbaum, *Teshuvot Divrei Yo'el*, II, *Even ha-Ezer*, no. 107, sec. 6. Testicular puncture and aspiration of spermatozoa, sometimes recommended for men whose epididymes or vasa deferentia are occluded, is also acceptable; see *Teshuvot Zekan Aharon*, I, nos. 66–67; *Teshuvot Minhat Yitzhak*, III, no. 108; *Tzitz Eli'ezer*, IX, no. 51, *sha'ar* 1, chap. 2; and *Iggerot Mosheh, Even ha-Ezer*, II, no. 3.

7. See Abraham S. Abraham, *Nishmat Avraham*, IV, *Even ha-Ezer* 23:1. Rabbi Eliashiv's view is reported by R. Eliyahu Bakshi-Doron, *Binyan Av*, II, no. 60.

8. See letter of *Hazon Ish* published in R. Kalman Kahana, *Taharat*

*Bat Yisra'el,* 3rd ed. (Jerusalem, 5723), p. 11 and in *idem, Taharat Bat Yisra'el* Daughter of Israel (Jerusalem, 5730), pp. 135–136.

9. This method of stimulation is probably an approximation of rectal massage of the prostate gland and seminal vesicles with pressure on the ampulla of the vas deferens described in medical literature as a means of obtaining semen for artificial insemination. See G.P.R. Tallin, "Artificial Insemination," *Canadian Bar Review,* vol. 34, no. 1 (January, 1956), p. 7.

10. An even more permissive view is expressed by R. Jacob Emden, *She'ilat Ya'avez,* I, no. 43. *She'ilat Ya'avez* understands the talmudic phraseology prohibiting "purposeless emission of seed" (*le-vatalah*) quite literally and hence sanctions destruction of the male seed for any legitimate purpose, e.g., in order to overcome "grave pain." R. Jacob Emden's view is rejected by most authorities as an isolated opinion. Cf., however, *Tzitz Eli'ezer,* XIII, no. 102 and the sharp rejoinder of *Iggerot Mosheh, Hoshen Mishpat,* II, no. 69, sec. 4.

11. It seems to this writer that this is the thrust of the point made by *Teshuvot Zekan Aharon,* I, no. 97, s.v. *ve-'al dvar ha-safek ha-sheni.*

12. *Zekan Aharon,* I, no. 67, and *Teshuvot Divrei Yo'el,* II, *Even ha-Ezer,* no. 107, sec. 6, suggest that seminal emission is permitted by the Gemara, *Yevamot* 76a, solely in the case of a person who would otherwise never be able to marry and hence is likely to experience non-procreative emission of semen on an ongoing basis.

13. See, for example, *Bet Shmu'el, Even ha-Ezer* 25:2, who cites *Yevamot* 76a in connection with coital bleeding which, if from the wife, renders ongoing marital relations forbidden but, if from the husband, is halakhically innocuous. *Bet Shmu'el* tentatively permits non-coital ejaculation in order to examine the ejaculate for the presence of blood but fails to specify that only indirect stimulation is permissible.

14. *Iggerot Mosheh, Even ha-Ezer,* I, nos. 70 and 71, II, no. 16, and III, no. 14, regards use of condoms and *coitus interruptus* as equally acceptable. R. Chaim Ozer Grodzinski, *Teshuvot Ahi'ezer,* III, no. 24, sec. 5, permits use of a condom but not *coitus interruptus. Iggerot Mosheh* also appears to prefer that method in deference to the views of *Ahi'ezer.* However, *Teshuvot Zekan Aharon,* I, no. 66 and II, no. 97, and *Tzitz Eli'ezer,* IX, no. 51, *sha'ar* 1, chap. 2, regard *coitus interruptus* as the preferred method. That conclusion would also flow from the position of *Teshuvot Yismah Levav, Even ha-Ezer,* no. 7; *Teshuvot Erez Zevi,* no. 45; and *Teshuvot She'erit Yitzhak,* no. 21; see also R. Moshe Sternbuch, *Teshuvot ve-Hanhagot,* I, no. 361. Cf., *Teshuvot Yabi'a Omer,* III, *Even ha-Ezer,* no. 7; R. Moshe Turetsky, *Teshuvot Yashiv Mosheh,* p. 169; R. Joseph Rosen, *Teshuvot Tzofnat Pa'aneah,* I, no. 115 and III, no. 161; R. Schmaryah Menasheh Adler, *Mareh Kohen, Mahadura Telita'ah,* nos. 48 and 49; and *Ozer ha-Poskim,* IX, 20:1, sec. 7.

15. *Coitus interruptus* is, of course, not an option in situations in which intercourse cannot be sanctioned since in all instances in which intercourse is prohibited even minimal penetration is prohibited as well.

16. The prohibition, however, is directed only against "licentiousness" of this nature that leads to emission of semen. For that reason, it appears to this writer that there would be no objection to masturbation for purposes of AIH by a person who suffers from retrograde ejaculation. In such cases spermatozoa are recovered from urine collected subsequent to orgasm. From a halakhic perspective, such recovery of sperm would appear to be no different from testicular aspiration.

17. R. Shlomoh Zalman Auerbach, *No'am*, I, 157, argues that since such liaisons are permissible, halakhically recognized paternity cannot be a necessary condition for permissible emission of seed. In point of fact, this argument is readily rebutted. Natural intercourse does not constitute "waste of the seed" and is always permitted as evidenced by the absence of a restriction against consorting with a minor, an infertile or post-menopausal woman. Only non-coital ejaculation requires the warrant of procreative potential.

18. In 1905 a German court was asked to consider the case of a woman who claimed that, without her husband's knowledge, she had scooped up fresh semen ejaculated by him on the bedclothes and introduced it into her genital tract causing a pregnancy that resulted in the birth of a baby girl. A trial court in Coblenz ruled that this artificial fecundation was a legal act. See Rohleder, *Test Tube Babies*, pp. 184–85. That decision was upheld in 1907 by an appeals court in Cologne. Shortly afterwards, in a second and remarkably similar case, a woman claimed to have discovered freshly ejaculated semen, probably the result of a nocturnal emission, which she inserted in her vagina. Despite (questionable) medical testimony denying that pregnancy could have resulted from that act, the appeals court in Cologne affirmed the legitimacy of the child. Later, the German Supreme Court took a similar position. See Rohleder, pp. 186 and 197–199. See also Alfred Koerner, "Medicolegal Considerations in Artificial Insemination," *Louisiana Law Review*, vol. 8, no. 3 (March, 1948), p. 492; Finegold, *Artificial Insemination*, pp. 67–70; and Anthony F. LoGatte, "Artificial Insemination: Legal Aspects," *Catholic Lawyer*, vol. 1, no. 1 (January, 1968), p. 174.

19. See, for example, *Mishneh la-Melekh, Hilkhot Ishut* 15:4 R. Jonathan Eibeschutz, *Bnei Ahuvah, Hilkhot Ishut* 15; *Teshuvot Bet Ya'akov*, no. 124; *Teshuvot Mishpatim Yesharim*, no. 396; *Turei Even, Haggigah* 26a; *Arukh la-Ner, Yevamot* 10a; *Teshuvot Divrei Malki'el*, IV, no. 107; *Teshuvot Yaskil Avdi*, V, no. 10; *Tzitz Eli'ezer*, XX, no. 51, *sha'ar* 4, chap. 3; and *Teshuvot Minhat Yitzhak*, I, no. 50.

20. This is also the position of *Teshuvot Bar Leva'i, Even ha-Ezer*, no. 1

and *Mishpetei Uzi'el, Even ha-Ezer,* no. 19; cf., R. Menachem Kasher, *No'am,* I, 125–128; and *idem, Torah Shelemah,* XVII, 242.

21. A number of authorities maintain that, although a paternal-filial relationship may arise *sine concubito,* birth of a child under such circumstances does not constitute fulfillment of the commandment. See, for example, *She'ilat Ya'avez,* II, no. 97; R. Chaim Joseph David Azulai, *Birkei Yosef, Even ha-Ezer* 1:14; *Maharam Shik al Taryag Mitzvot,* no. 1; *Teshuvot Yaskil Avdi, Even ha-Ezer,* no. 15, sec. 8; *Bigdei Yesha,* no. 123; and *Bigdei Shesh, Even ha-Ezer,* no. 1, sec. 11.

22. Rabbi Gershuni's article first appeared in *Or ha-Mizrah,* (Tishri 5739), pp. 15–22.

23. For an elucidation of the conflicting opinions regarding the precise meaning of these terms see *Encyclopedia Talmudit,* vol. III, 2nd ed. (Jerusalem, 5715), pp. 98–99.

24. For a non-technical discussion of the feasibility of such pregnancy see Dick Teresi and Kathleen McAuliffe, "Male Pregnancy," *Omni,* vol. 8, no. 3 (December, 1985), pp. 51–56 and 118, and Dick Teresi, *New York Times Magaziine,* November 27, 1994, pp. 54–55. As reported in *Omni* in experiments conducted upon animals, male mice and at least one male baboon have carried fetuses. There are some two dozen reported cases of women who became pregnant subsequent to undergoing hysterectomies. In 1979, an Auckland, New Zealand woman underwent a hysterectomy in the course of which an errant fertilized ovum lodged in her abdomen and that pregnancy resulted in the birth of a healthy baby girl.

25. It should, however, be noted that this thesis is rejected by *Minhat Hinnukh,* no. 1 and presumably by the authorities cited *supra,* note . See, however, *Teshuvot Har Zevi, Even ha-Ezer,* no. 1; *Teshuvot Zekan Aharon,* II no. 97; *Iggerot Mosheh, Even ha-Ezer,* II, no. 18; R. Elchanan Wasserman, *Kovetz He'arot,* no. 69, secs. 26–27; and R. Moshe Sternbuch, *Olam ha-Torah,* no. 2 (Tevet-Shevat 5736), pp. 16–23; cf., *Teshuvot Divrei Yo'el,* II, *Even ha-Ezer,* no. 107, sec. 6.

26. Thus, even a non-Jew who has fathered children is not bound by this commandment subsequent to conversion. See R. Joseph Rosen, *Teshuvot Tzofnat Pa'aneah,* no. 185.

27. Rabbi Bakshi-Doron's responsum first appeared in *Assia,* vol. II, no. 4 (Nisan 5748), pp. 34–39 and is published in his *Binyan Av,* II, no. 60.

# 8

# Halakhic Approaches to the Resolution of Disputes Concerning the Disposition of Preembryos

## Yitzchok A. Breitowitz

The development of new reproductive technologies over the past 15 years or so has offered great hope to many infertile couples. Along with the blessings they bring, however, these technologies are also a source of major ethical dilemmas.[1] For the Jew whose every decision is guided by *devar Hashem*, it is Halakha to which he or she must turn. The specific topic of this article concerns the preembryo, a particular configuration of human cells that did not exist in externalized form until the advent of in-vitro fertilization (IVF) in the late-1970's.

In-vitro fertilization may exist in various forms, but at its simplest, it involves extracting immature eggs (oocytes) from a woman's ovaries, placing those eggs in a petri dish supplied with nutrients, obtaining sperm from a donor, fertilizing the egg in the dish, and transplanting the fertilized ovum into the woman's uterus (usually at the 48–72 hour developmental stage). If all goes well, the embryo will implant and a pregnancy will ensue and be

Rabbi Breitowitz is Associate Professor of Law at the University of Maryland and rabbi of the Woodside Synagogue in Silver Spring.

This is an abridged form of a longer work-in-progress that will address the issues of preembryos in a more comprehensive manner. The author wants to express his appreciation to Dr. Joel B. Wolowelsky for his assistance in unearthing hard-to-find source material.

detectable within 10–14 days after the transfer. Since the procedure was first introduced in 1978, over 25,000 IVF babies have been born. The average take-home baby rate is 17%; 19% for women under 39, 6.6% for older women. "Preembryo" is the term often used for a fertilized ovum that has not yet been transferred into a uterus.[2]

Although in the natural course of ovulation, a woman's ovaries release only one egg at a time, the modern IVF procedure extracts multiple oocytes to raise the probability of successful fertilization.[3] As a consequence, several eggs may be fertilized. Multiple eggs may be transferred for implantation, cryopreserved (frozen) for future use in another reproductive cycle, donated to other infertile couples, used for experimentation and research, destroyed, allowed to thaw, or just kept in storage, which will effectively result in their destruction with the passage of time. At least under American law, all of these options are legal possibilities, though the locus of dispositional authority in the event of disagreement has not been definitely identified.

The existence of literally thousands of preembryos in freezers raises difficult problems. What happens if both or any one of the gamete (egg or sperm) donors die? What if they get divorced? Are frozen embryos "children," subject to a custody determination, or marital property? Do preembryos have inheritance rights? In light of the Jewish restrictions on abortion, must all preembryos be implanted? May they be donated? In the event of a donation (whether permissible or not), whom does Halakha regard as the parents? Must thawed preembryos be buried? Are they considered "human life" for purposes of *hillul Shabbat*, etc.? What about *yibum*? A number of these issues have been discussed extensively; some have not.

Space limitations do not permit a full consideration of all these problems. This article will focus on only one, albeit one that has received considerable attention in the United States, Israel (in both the religious and secular courts), and Australia: who has ultimate decisional authority over preembryos if the husband and wife are divorced, deadlocked, or dead?[4] As a background to a fuller understanding of this issue, however, it may be helpful to briefly summarize some of the general halakhic principles concerning IVF technology.

## I. General Considerations on the Use of IVF Technology

The halakhic literature on assisted reproductive technologies is quite large and cannot be fully surveyed here. Much of it concerns artificial insemination, where either husband or donor sperm is inserted vaginally or into the uterus.[5] Many of the halakhic concerns with AIH (Artificial Insemination with Husband's Sperm), particularly those involving the methods by which sperm is procured, apply equally to in vitro fertilization.[6]

Subject to careful supervision of the physician, waiting periods, and exploration of alternatives, AIH is generally regarded as a halakhically permissible procedure through which paternity can be established and the mitzvah of *peru u-revu* or at least *lashevet* can be fulfilled.[7] By and large, most *posekim* have assimilated IVF to AIH and have permitted its utilization subject to the same limitations.[8] A notable exception is Rabbi Eliezer Waldenberg, who maintains that IVF is an impermissible procedure and that even *ex post facto*, one does not fulfill the mitzvah of *peru u-revu*.[9] He argues that IVF is more problematic than AIH in a number of distinct respects: (1) unlike AIH, where all sperm is deposited into the vagina or uterus, IVF transfers only the fertilized ova, with the rest of the sperm discarded, thus violating the edict against *hashhatat zera* (wanton destruction of male seed).[10] (2) One does not fulfill the mitzvah of procreation where fertilization occurs outside of the womb. This independently creates a violation of *hashhatat zera*.[11] (3) There is neither a paternal nor even a *maternal*[12] relationship with an IVF-offspring. Rabbi Moshe Sternbuch[13] also denies paternal identity in cases of IVF, and consequently, prohibits the practice as violative of *hashhatat zera*. R. Yehuda Gershuni[14] agrees with Rabbis Sternbuch and Waldenberg that there is no paternal bond between a sperm donor and an externalized embryo even if later brought to term, but he nonetheless permits the procedure; since IVF does in fact result in the creation of a physical human being, albeit one that is not halakhically related to the genetic parents, it is a fulfillment of the prophetic statement, "He did not create the world to be void, but He formed it so that it would be settled" [*lashevet yetsara*] (*Isaiah* 45:18). R. Gershuni argues that even the mere fulfillment of *lashevet* is enough to prevent the emission of the seed from being *levatala*.

As noted, Rabbis Waldenberg, Sternbuch, and Gershuni are decidedly in the minority. Virtually all contemporary *posekim* have concluded, first, that the egg and sperm providers do have a parental relationship with an IVF-generated offspring; second, that the procedure, if undertaken for procreation by an otherwise infertile couple,[15] does not violate the prohibitions against *hashhatat zera*; third, that one may fulfill, through any resulting offspring, either the mitzvah of *peru u-revu*, or, at the very least, the "lesser" mitzvah of *lashevet*.[16] These will be the assumptions on which this article is predicated.

## II. What Can Be Decided: Options for the Disposition of Preembryos

A married couple who participate in an IVF program will have a number of options regarding the disposition of fertilized ova: (1) implanting all or some of the preembryos, (2) destroying or at least not implanting them, (3) experimentation, (4) donating them to an infertile couple, or possibly to an unmarried woman desirous of being a mother, or (5) using a gestational surrogate who agrees to carry the embryo/fetus to term and then return the baby to the couple whose egg and sperm have been united. Under the laws of most states, all of these options are legitimate, although some are subject to varying degrees of governmental regulation.[17]

This article will not address the halakhic permissibility of these options other than to note that some choices are less problematic than others.[18] At one extreme, most contemporary *posekim* (who have written on the subject) have allowed the destruction or at least the passive discarding of "unwanted" preembryos, ruling that the strictures against abortion apply only to embryos or fetuses within a woman's womb and not to preembryos existing outside of it.[19] Experimentation on preembryos not destined for implantation would appear to be permitted as well. By contrast, embryo donation to infertile couples—whether Jewish or non-Jewish—or to a single woman, raises numerous halakhic and ethical complexities and has not to date received widespread halakhic sanction.[20] (Indeed, in a worst-case scenario—embryo donation to a married Jewish couple—such donation may even constitute the commission of halakhic adultery and result in the birth of

*mamzerim.*[21]) The Chief Rabbinate of Israel recently gave its quali-
fied approval to the use of a gestational surrogate who meets certain conditions,[22] but whether the Rabbinate's ruling will be
accepted by other *posekim* and what effect it will have on the
growth of surrogacy within the Torah-observant community remain to be seen.[23]

While this article limits its focus to the problems of deadlock
and disagreement between the parties, it must be emphasized
that the issue of *who* decides becomes relevant only if the decision
under question is within the range of alternatives that Halakha
legitimates. It makes little difference *who* has the right to make
dispositional decisions if Halakha does not permit a decision to
be made. This itself suggests that, in a halakhic system, the problem of deadlock assumes somewhat less significance than it does
in a secular society where the right to make decisions concerning
reproduction is well-nigh absolute. Nevertheless, Halakha clearly
permits some, if not all, choices to be made and it is therefore
necessary to identify who gets to make them.


### III.  Who Decides: Davis v. Davis and the Nahmani Case

In *Davis v. Davis,*[24] a Tennessee couple experiencing infertility employed in vitro fertilization to produce a number of fertilized ova
which were cryopreserved for future implantation. The couple
eventually were divorced, and the husband no longer desired to
have children from his former spouse. Concerned that this could
have been her last chance for a pregnancy, Mrs. Davis petitioned
the trial court to award her "custody" of the frozen preembryos.
The trial court, ruling that "human life begins from conception,"
treated the embryos as "children," saw the issue as one involving
custody and, as such, to be resolved by reference to the "best
interests of the children." Since it was undoubtedly in the children's (embryos') best interest to be born[25] (at least in the absence of genetic defect or the like), the judge awarded custody
to Mrs. Davis. The judge's ruling was reversed by the Tennessee
Appellate Court and later its Supreme Court. (To date, the case
has not gone further.) Treating preembryos as human life, stated
the Tennessee Supreme Court, would be inconsistent with the
constitutional principles governing abortion, which generally per-

mit termination of a pregnancy.[26] However, the potential of these preembryos to be implanted and come to fruition as fully developed human beings necessitates that they be regarded as more than mere property. The Tennessee Supreme Court concluded that the constitutionally protected rights of privacy, which include both the right to procreate and not to procreate, indicate that ultimate dispositional authority should reside with the gamete providers, for they are the ones who will or will not become parents. If they both agree, their wishes should be respected by hospitals, IVF clinics, and courts.[27] If they are presently in disagreement, the courts should follow the terms of any prior agreements the parties may have executed. In the event that no such agreement exists (and indeed this was the case in *Davis*), a balancing of the respective benefits and burdens of each of the parties must be undertaken. The court concluded that normally, the party *not* wanting implantation should prevail. The burdens and responsibilities of unwanted parenthood are considered to be greater than the burden on a person who desires to be a parent and who is temporarily denied that right. The person who wants to be a parent has alternatives that may be pursued with other partners, adoption, etc., while the person "shackled with involuntary parenthood" has no way of escaping at least the moral obligation of a parenthood relationship. The court therefore sustained Mr. Davis's veto.

The analysis in *Davis* has received widespread approval in both the legal and medical communities.[28]

An Israeli secular court, however, originally went the other way.[29] An Israeli couple had been infertile for a number of years. The woman had a hysterectomy and could not carry a child. They had agreed to an IVF program which, after fertilization, would transfer the zygotes to a surrogate. Because of marital discord, the husband no longer desired that the frozen embryos be transferred. The District Court of Haifa, taking account of the pain and suffering of the woman in undergoing the laparascopic extraction of eggs, her inability to carry children on her own, her biological clock, and the potential of male abuse, ruled that an agreement to participate in an IVF program *was* an agreement to allow implantation and that that decision was irrevocable (at least on the part of the man) as soon as the eggs have been extracted. Admittedly, the *Nahmani* case, unlike *Davis*, involved a couple that were still married. Indeed, the Haifa court specifically noted that, had the Nahmanis been formally divorced, the result would have been different. Yet it is equally clear that, insofar as the *Davis* case is concerned, the marital status of the parties is irrelevant. The basic approach of *Davis* is that participation in an IVF program carries no obligation to complete it. The basic approach of the trial judge in *Nahmani* cuts the opposite way.[30] How would Halakha approach the resolution of these disputes?[31]

## IV. A Halakhic Approach To The Resolution of Preembryo Disputes

If Halakha does not permit disposal of embryos, then no one has the right to decide their disposal. Assuming, however, as do most *posekim,* that destruction of preembryos is permitted,[32] the question becomes one of decisional authority: whose desire governs in case of a deadlock?

It is important to note that the halakhic question of deadlock will generally run in one direction only: where the wife or former wife desires implantation, while the (former) husband does not. Where the wife desires to terminate the IVF protocol but the husband wants to continue, it is highly unlikely that the husband could demand that an unwilling woman be impregnated, if for no other reason than that pregnancy and childbirth are life-threatening conditions.[33]

With a bit of imagination, however, one could conjure up circumstances under which the (former) husband's desire to continue the process *might* be given credence even over the wife's objections. What if the husband desires to use a gestational surrogate within the guidelines authorized by the Chief Rabbinate? Could the wife veto that decision? Or what if husband and wife are now divorced, but the husband wants the preembryos generated from the first marriage transferred and implanted to a new spouse? Assuming that this might be intrinsically acceptable,[34] could the first wife stop it from going forward?

There are a number of general approaches that one may draw upon to answer these questions, but none of them are fully satisfactory. I have not been able to formulate a definitive approach,

but would like to offer five models that may furnish a framework
for analyzing these difficult issues.

Before proceeding to these models, however, one further assumption must be articulated. For reasons of space, this paper will
assume, but not prove, the existence of both a maternal and a
paternal relationship towards the preembryo, *i.e.*, that it has both
a halakhic father and mother, or conversely, that neither party
bears such a relationship.[35] In short, one party is no more or less
a parent than the other. I recognize that this assumption may
be questioned, and some may regard a differential definition of
parenthood as a key in determining who has final decisional authority. A Talmudic passage in *Yevamot* is often cited to demonstrate that although paternity arises upon conception, maternal
bonds are not generated until birth.[36] Standing alone, this passage might lead to the conclusion that the female egg contributor
should have no say in the disposition of the preembryo simply
because, in the eyes of Halakha, she is not yet a mother. A perusal
of other passages indicates, however, that such a dichotomy is not
compelling.[37] Indeed, proof could be brought from *Sanhedrin* 69a
that no *paternal* bond can exist until the conclusion of the first
trimester,[38] and a comment of R. Akiva Eiger seems to apply the
same standard to the maternal bond as well.[39] This would indicate
that *neither* party has parental rights in a preembryo, a stage well
below first trimester development. Conversely, one could look at
the law of *demei veladot* (see *Exodus* 21:22), awarding financial
compensation for the death of prenatal life to the father, and
(according to Rambam), where the father has died, to the
mother, and conclude that *both* parties have full parental rights
prior to birth.[40] To make matters even more confusing, mention
should also be made of a recent view, based on a *pesak* of R. Shaul
Yisraeli, that would deny the existence of *any* parental bond until
there is embryo transfer and uterine implantation.[41] Rather than
maternity arising from birth and paternity from conception (as
implied from Rashi's comments in *Yevamot*), and in lieu of a uni-
fied "first trimester" test (as suggested by *Sanhedrin* 69a and R.
Akiva Eiger), a single standard based on implantation would define the moment at which both maternity and paternity arise.[42]
This too would lead to the conclusion that no one "parent"
would have greater presumptive authority than the other, for vis-
a-vis the preembryo which is not yet *in utero*, neither has halakhic

parental status. (This interpretation of R. Yisraeli's view, however, is problematic in a number of respects and requires further analysis.[43])

In short, the question of decisional authority in the event of deadlock cannot necessarily be resolved by asking which of the two parties is halakhically regarded as a parent; if the answer is "both" or "neither," alternative bases for priority would have to be identified.[44] I will now endeavor to suggest what those bases might be.

*Model #1:* Halakhic Lacuna. Assuming that both or neither have parental status, it is possible that there is no one that Halakha vests with definitive decision-making authority. Except in the case of an *eved kena'ani*, a human being cannot be owned by another human being. Indeed, not only do parents not own their children, one does not even own one's own body. Thus, as Rabbi Shlomo Yosef Zevin pointed out in a classic halakhic study of the *Merchant of Venice*,[45] Antonio's contract with Shylock to forfeit a pound of flesh in the event of default is halakhically unenforceable not merely because it is *forbidden* to wound oneself, but because one's body is not property that can be subject to disposition.[46] For the same reason, although one can, by explicit waiver, forego rights to compensation in the event of personal injury, one cannot authorize the commission of such injury *ab initio*.[47] The concept heard so much in the abortion debate or the "right to die" movement—that one has the absolute right to control one's body—is patently false in Halakha.

A preembryo can be characterized in a variety of ways. But whether we regard it as the human cells of the gamete providers or the beginnings of a separate human entity (and a distinct genome), it is not a "property interest" that can be controlled or disposed of. *"Ein damim le-ben horin."*[48]

Let me emphasize that I am most decidedly *not* speaking about *issur ve-heter.* Certainly, some of the philosophical considerations stated above could, in fact, be the basis for prohibiting disposal and requiring implantation. Yet my point here goes beyond that: even if we assume that the externalization of the embryo from the body means that there is in fact no affirmative obligation of *hatzala,* no obligation of *kevura,* and no *issur hana'a,* and that therefore a range of options may exist, neither the gamete providers nor anyone else is vested with presumptive decision-making au-

thority, since human tissue—and certainly, potential human beings—are not capable of being "owned."[49] In essence, even if
Halakha permits choices to be made, it says nothing about who
gets to make them, which in effect provides free reign for private
agreement or regulation by the state.[50]

*Model # 2*: Paternal Authority. There is one Biblical source that
may on some level suggest paternal "ownership" of children
prior to birth in spite of the fact that once born, they are no
longer property. This is the Halakha of *demei veladot*, which awards
financial compensation for the wrongful death of the fetuses to
the father, not mother.[51] (Although the Torah speaks of the husband, the Talmud in *Baba Kama* 43a makes clear that such compensation is payable even where impregnation occurred out of
wedlock. The Jerusalem Talmud adds the qualification that the
relationship be one in which marriage is at least possible *ex post
facto*, excluding, for example, pregnancies arising from incest or
adultery).[52] If we posit that the husband's entitlement to *demei
veladot* rests on some sort of prenatal property right in the embryo
or fetus, then perhaps the husband (or at least father) should
have the final say.

Even if this line of reasoning were to be accepted, its application would be limited. If, for example, the man wanted the preembryos to be implanted but the woman refused, it is obvious
that for reasons of *sakkana*, she has the right to decline.[53] If, however, the woman desires implantation but the man wants to back
out, as was the case in *Davis*, arguably the man's veto should be
controlling. Moreover, to the extent that Halakha may permit preembryo donation for experimentation, perhaps the husband
should have the authority to decide whether and how. Finally,
perhaps the father should have the right to transfer the preembryos to his new wife or employ a gestational surrogate.[54]

Using *demei veladot* as a predicate, however, is highly questionable on a number of fronts. First, as a matter of formal Halakha,
it is not at all clear that there is *demei veladot* for damage to a
preembryo or even for a pregnancy of less than forty days' duration.[55] Second, if there is a property right belonging to the father,
it can exist only where there is a paternal relation. According to
some opinions, there is no paternal relation to IVF-produced embryos, and thus no "father" to assert this property right.[56]

Let us assume, however, that in accordance with the majority of *posekim*, a paternal bond does exist from the moment of fertilization. The question then becomes, does the entitlement to *demei veladot* presuppose some type of prenatal ownership or property in the fetus, or is it a stand-alone privilege of compensation not derivable from, or related to, any interest in property?

One might suggest that this is a subject of dispute between Rambam and Ra'avad.[57] The Halakha is clear that if a pregnant woman was injured, as a result the fetus was killed, and the father died subsequent to the death of the fetus, the right to collect *demei veladot* passes to his heirs just as any other debt would. What is the law, however, if the father dies first and then the fetus is killed? According to Rambam, the *demei veladot* are not payable to the husband and instead belong to the mother. Ra'avad disagrees and awards *demei veladot* to the heirs of the father even where he predeceases the fetus. While there are various approaches in understanding the reason and the source of this *mahloket*, one explanation may be based on these two ways of understanding *demei veladot*. According to Ra'avad, the entitlement to *demei veladot* is based on a preexisting (albeit limited) ownership or property right in the body of the fetus itself. The father is compensated because in a limited but literal sense, "his property" was damaged. Accordingly, when he dies, that "property interest" passes to the heirs, who will similarly be entitled to compensation if "their" property gets destroyed. Rambam, on the other hand, regards the entitlement to *demei veladot* as a free-standing personal right of the father, bearing no relationship to a property interest in the fetus; indeed, there *is* no property interest in the fetus. Hence, if the father predeceases the fetus, there is nothing for his heirs to inherit. (Why the mother gets *demei veladot* instead of no one is a question left for another time.[58]) Thus, even if the *demei veladot* analogy is relevant, at most it is valid only according to Ra'avad, not Rambam.

R. Shaul Yisraeli has offered an alternative explanation for Rambam's view.[59] He points out that Rambam omits the rule that even an unmarried father collects *demei veladot*. While *Minhat Hinukh* assumes that Rambam agrees with the law despite his failure to codify it,[60] R. Yisraeli asserts that according to Rambam, if the man was unmarried to the mother or was divorced before the *havala*, the *demei veladot* would go to the woman. Fundamentally, the fetus is regarded as the mother's property, subject only to paramount rights of her husband. When the marriage terminates, by death *or* divorce, the right to *demei veladot* reverts to her. According to this understanding, Rambam too may concede the concept of "property rights," but vests the right in the woman, subject to her husband's paramount rights deriving from *ishut*.[61] Ra'avad vests the right directly in the father; marital status would thus be irrelevant.

R. Yisraeli further asserts that whether the father would get *demei veladot* in an IVF pregnancy followed by implantation[62] would depend on this analysis. According to Ra'avad, *demei veladot* would still go to the husband; according to Rambam, they would go to the woman, since her marital status does not obligate her to conceive and bear children via IVF.

What is significant, and indeed counterintuitive, is that according to Ra'avad, not only would the father have dispositional authority (whether married or not), but the right to exercise such authority would pass to his heirs, *i.e.*, the preembryo's brothers would have a right to veto its implantation over the desires of their mother. According to Rambam, however, there are a range of possible outcomes: either the fetus/preembryo is not "property" at all, in which case no one is vested with definitive decisional authority (the first approach), or the fetus is fundamentally the mother's property, subject to the husband's paramount right of compensation (R. Yisraeli's approach). In that case, it is clear that at least in the event of death or divorce, the decision would be the mother's, and possibly this would be so even if the husband were alive and married, since his paramount rights may be limited to compensation alone.[63]

Using *demei veladot* as a paradigm for dispositional authority is admittedly a highly questionable approach.

*Model #3*: "Given" to Woman as a Gift. When sperm is procured for use in an IVF program in order to try to achieve fertilization and implantation, one can argue that in fact, the clinic acquires it for the benefit of the woman; halakhically, it becomes her property. According to this analysis, not only could she demand implantation of an embryo, but even impregnation with sperm. Indeed, in a letter approved by R. Yisraeli, it was ruled that in the event of the husband's death, the woman on whose behalf the sperm was procured has the right to have it utilized.[64] (Ironically, however, R. Yisraeli himself takes a contrary position in a case of divorce or even of marital discord.[65])

To say that it is exclusively the woman's property seems to ignore the fact that the decision to bear children cannot be regarded as exclusively a "gift" to the woman. There is no particular reason to characterize the clinic's procurement of sperm as a *zekhiya* on behalf of the woman, at least in an exclusive sense. There are obviously two parties involved, and the notion of *kinyan* does not establish a preference of one party over the other.

*Model #4*: Paradigm of Child Custody. Halakha is replete with rules governing decision-making when parents are deadlocked.[66] In the event of divorce, Halakha provides various rules of custody subject to the overarching goal of protecting the best interests of the child. Obviously, some of the child custody rules make no sense in the preembryo context (for example, there is no "boy" or "girl" to consider), and in light of the fact that maternity may not yet have been established,[67] there may not be two parents entitled to equal say. Consequently, this may either lead to the father, being the only parent, having the controlling voice, or to the *bet din* making its own determination as to what the best interests of the child are. Presumably, this determination will normally lead to a decision in favor of implantation,[68] but in some cases, *e.g.*, serious genetic disease, may permit discretion to be exercised the other way. (Of course, if best interests truly becomes relevant, could the *bet din* intervene against the wishes of both gamete providers? Could they do so in the case of an already-born child?)

*Model #5*: Joint Venture.[69] Perhaps this would be the most sensible way of analyzing an IVF "transaction." Recognizing that no one "owns" a human being *per se*, Halakha may nevertheless regard an agreement to participate in an assisted reproductive program as essentially a joint venture, with each spouse contributing a component to achieve a desired result. By analogy to mercantile ventures, partnerships are created when the respective contributions of the partners are commingled into an indistinguishable mass.[70] Once a partnership is created, each partner is normally bound to keep his assets committed to the affairs of the partnership until the partnership's goals are accomplished or its term expires.

The partnership analogy does not definitively resolve all dispositional questions, but does furnish useful guidelines. According to *Shulhan Arukh H.M.* 171:1, a partner is entitled to demand a division of partnership assets at any time, but only if the partnership assets are capable of physical division. In the case of fields, gardens, buildings, etc., this requires that the asset be large enough to enable each partner to retain something useful and productive. If the entity is not large enough, the partner who wants to leave must give the other the option to buy out his interest or to let him buy it out (*gud* or *agud*). In effect, one partner cannot unilaterally take away the benefits of the partnership by compelling a forfeiture. A fertilized egg is analogous to a *sade she-ein ba din haluka*—an entity not subject to physical division—in which case a partner does not have the right to take back his contribution. Moreover, because of the non-economic nature of that contribution, neither would the partner have the right to demand compensation or buy the other party out.[71] The analogy to business partnerships would thus suggest a result contrary to *Davis*: that in the absence of express agreement, the husband would not as a matter of course be able to withdraw his consent. Note, however, that contrary to the decision of the Haifa District Court, this inability of the husband to withdraw does not arise from the moment of the agreement nor from the extraction of the sperm and egg, but only from their mixture in the petri dish. No binding partnership is formed until the respective contributions are commingled. There would certainly be no limitation on revocation merely because sperm was deposited. Thus, frozen embryos would be treated quite differently than frozen sperm.[72]

Taking the partnership analogy further, there may be a number of instances where revocation may be proper. Under Anglo-American law, contractual obligations may be voided if there has been the failure of a basic assumption upon which the contract was predicated.[73] This is true not only if such failure existed at the time of the agreement (in which case the contract at the time of its inception was a nullity), but also if circumstances changed subsequently. Halakha similarly recognizes avoidance based on changed circumstances.

The Mishna[74] states that if one hires workers to transport musical instruments for a wedding or funeral and they wrongfully retract, the aggrieved party may hire other workers and charge the contract breakers with the difference. (This is similar to the familiar expectation damage recovery under Anglo-American law.[75])

The workers are liable for the extra costs they compelled the owner to incur. Nevertheless, if the reason they retract is because of a significant change of circumstances, such as illness or death of a family member, even though performance was not rendered physically impossible, the workers incur no liability, since it was never their intention to assume a binding commitment in the event of such a contingency.[76] In effect, the nonoccurrence of such a contingency should be regarded as an *implied* term in the agreement.

R. Yisraeli convincingly argues that when husband and wife consent to an IVF program and establish their "joint venture" (which halakhically they are not obligated to do), their agreement is normally predicated on one of a number of common assumptions: (1) that they will dwell together as husband and wife, (2) that the child will be raised in a two-family household, or (3) at the very least, that the relationship between the parties will be such that each will desire that the other be the parent of their child. If the parties subsequently divorce, the common assumptions behind the agreement have failed, and thus, the unwilling partner is permitted to terminate his obligations under the partnership even in the case of a *sade she-ein ba din haluka.* This is analogous to the common law defenses of impossibility, commercial impracticality, and frustration of purpose.

In sum, the following conclusions emerge:

(1) In the event of an unforeseen marital breakup, the husband or the wife should have the right to stop the process from going forward, as the *Davis* court held.

(2) Marital discord short of divorce may perhaps be treated differently (thus, the Israeli case may be different than the one in Tennessee).

(3) The argument of changed circumstances and implied conditions or limitations should be valid only if the subsequent event was unforeseeable and unexpected, thereby qualifying as an *oness* (unanticipated contingency not within the contemplation of the parties). Where the parties at the time of the contract are clearly aware of a significant possibility that the contingency may occur and fail to provide for its occurrence, the implication would be that the commitment is absolute. One can imagine that in many cases of IVF, the parties are already in a state of discord and are attempting IVF as a last-ditch effort to save a marriage in trouble.

While this practice may be quite unwise, it would effectively preclude the use of *oness* as a means of blocking the procedure from going forward.[77]

(4) Where the claim of *oness* is not available either because of its foreseeability or because the agreement expressly provides that the process will continue, the (former) wife's right to demand implantation would exist only until her remarriage, since after that point, implantation would raise halakhic concerns of adultery or *mamzerut*.[78] Nor would she then have the right to demand the use of a gestational surrogate over her (former) husband's veto (even within the guidelines of the Chief Rabbinate[79]), since that is an alternative that goes beyond the scope of the original partnership undertaking.

(5) The husband should always have the right to block the use of his sperm prior to fertilization since no "partnership" has yet been formed by commingling.[80]

(6) The partnership/joint venture model would validate, and indeed encourage, express advance directives.

(7) In all cases (even when *oness* is not applicable), the woman may refuse to go forward with implantation for considerations of *sakkana.*

(8) In no case could the (former) husband demand over his first wife's objections that preembryos be implanted in a new wife or in a gestational surrogate, since both alternatives go beyond the scope of the original partnership agreement. In the event that the first wife has no objection, however, or if a prior agreement so provides, it is possible that either procedure may be halakhically permissible even if the first wife has already remarried.

## V. The Application of Partnership Law Upon Death

*Davis* and *Nahmani* dealt with deadlock because of divorce or marital discord. Neither case addressed the issue of death: what if the husband has died? Would the widow have the right to have the embryos implanted? Most ethicists have assumed a right of survivorship, meaning that whichever gamete provider survives has the authority to determine disposition.[81] How would Halakha deal with death?

Using the partnership paradigm, *i.e.*, viewing the combination of egg and sperm as the formation of a joint venture to achieve procreation, does not afford a clear resolution. Rambam rules in *Hilkhot Sheluhin veShutafin* 5:11 that a partnership terminates upon the death of one of the partners even when the partnership was explicitly established for a fixed term that has not yet expired. He cites this in the name of the *Geonim*, and according to *Kesef Mishne*, this is also the view of Rosh, Ramban, Rashba, and Ritva in the name of "his teacher." On its face, this expressly rules out the notion that the surviving party has any "right of survivorship." But what is supposed to happen?

The reason Rambam gives for his ruling is that immediately upon death, the heirs are the owners of the decedent's share in the partnership and may thus force a dissolution. This reasoning may not be applicable to preembryos, which, particularly according to Rambam, are arguably not "property" susceptible to inheritance.[82] As such, the woman's right to pursue the objectives of the joint venture, *i.e.*, attempt a pregnancy, should remain intact at least until her remarriage.[83] (Once she remarries, however, implantation may raise problems similar to embryo donation in general.[84]) Conversely, since there is no longer a partnership, she should be equally free to decline implantation (which in any case could not be forced on her because of *sakkana*) and have the embryos thawed or destroyed regardless of any agreement to the contrary or the wishes of the heirs.

Once we proceed beyond those two choices, matters become less clear, at least from the perspective of *hilkhot shutafut* (partnership law): could the woman decide to donate the embryos to an infertile couple (assuming such a choice in the abstract is halakhically permitted)?[85] Could she employ a gestational surrogate (single, *etc.*) within the guidelines of the Chief Rabbinate? What if the mother has died and the father wants to implant the preembryo into the womb of his *new* wife or to use a gestational surrogate?[86]

In the absence of an agreement authorizing these alternatives, neither embryo donation (even if permitted), surrogacy, nor implantation in another spouse can be regarded as an objective of the joint venture, and are thus inconsistent with the objectives and purposes for which the respective contributions were made. Given the fact that the "partner" is dead, however, and the fact that his heirs apparently have no proprietary interest in the preembryos, what halakhic principle disables the woman or the man from such unilateral action? Who would the *tove'a* (claimant) be?

Property and partnership concepts make no sense when applied to a noninheritable joint venture with one of the partners dead. What might be relevant, however, is the religious and moral duty of *mitsvah le-kayeim divrei ha-met*—"There is an obligation to fulfill the wishes of the decedent."[87] As such, if a person donated a portion of his body for a specific purpose (although in terms of "ownership," the sperm was not truly his), there is a religious obligation to respect those wishes and not use the property in a manner inconsistent with those wishes. There are many authorities who would limit this mitzvah only to cases where an *intervivos* escrow was established (*hushlash mi-tehila le-kakh*) and not where there is merely a verbal declaration.[88] Nevertheless, it is obvious that participating in the IVF program and the handing over of the sperm or the egg to the clinic constitutes the very type of escrow that the principle requires. Thus, it would be morally improper for the wife to donate either the embryo or frozen sperm to a third party even if, in the abstract, such donation might be permitted.[89] This is supported by R. Yisraeli's ruling.[90] For similar reasons, surrogacy could not be employed unless the father would have consented had he been alive.

It should be noted that the application of *mitzvah le-kayeim divrei ha-met* to egg, sperm, or embryos is not entirely obvious. First, it is possible that the principle applies only to the disposition of assets acquired by inheritance. Thus, while the mitzvah may morally bind a son to respect his father's wishes concerning money received from the father, it would not extend to money the son earned on his own. If, as we assume, neither sperm nor preembryos constitute "property," perhaps *mitzvah le-kayeim divrei ha-met* is inapplicable. Second, to the extent that *mitzvah le-kayeim divrei ha-met* rests on considerations of *kibud av ve-eim*, it could arguably be a binding directive only on lineal offspring, imposing no responsibility on a suriviving spouse. At least with respect to the second contention, however, the halakhic sources clearly support the extension of the mitzvah to all third parties, not only children.[91]

Admittedly, *mitzvah le-kayeim divrei ha-met* may be somewhat of a slim reed. Even where it applies, at most it is a religious and moral obligation, but not one that is halakhically enforceable (though in 20th-Century America, where no religious obligations are enforceable, this may be a theoretical distinction without a practical difference). Nevertheless, at least as a moral directive, the principle of *mitzvah le-kayeim divrei ha-met* would apply not only to bind the wife to the husband's wishes in the event of his death, *i.e.*, precluding her use of the embryos or sperm in a manner inconsistent with his express or implied wishes, but would apply equally to binding the husband to the wishes of the wife, *e.g.*, preventing him from donating the embryos for implantation into another woman, either a surrogate or a second wife, unless it can be ascertained that this would be his first wife's desire. While it is true that a husband inherits his wife's "property interests," the embryos are fundamentally not property. Even if they were, the religious duty of *mitzvah le-kayeim* remains intact as it does for all heirs. Indeed, this religious directive would govern even if both parents died.[92]

*Application of These Principles to Frozen Sperm:* The only difference between frozen sperm and preembryos is that donating sperm does not yet effect a joint venture by virtue of commingling. As such, even in the absence of a divorce, the husband would be able to terminate his involvement.[93] The principles of *mitzvah le-kayeim divrei ha-met*, however, would appear to be identical. Thus, if, for example, it was the husband's wish that his sperm be used to fertilize his wife's ovum after his death, his heirs would be morally bound not to object, notwithstanding the potential diminution of their inheritance. (The wife, however, could always decline pregnancy on the grounds of *sakkana*.)

*Limitations on Dispositional Authority:* A final point is obvious but deserves reiteration. Any rule requiring deference to the wishes of the *met* is conditional on those wishes not conflicting with Halakha generally. To the extent that Halakha prohibits donations of sperm, egg, or embryos to third parties because of considerations of adultery, *mamzerut*, unknown parentage, or the like,[94] those choices will not be validated because of *mitzvah le-kayeim divrei ha-met*. As a practical matter, then, according to the views that prohibit embryo donations, *mitzvah le-kayeim divrei ha-met* cannot be used to permit them[95] even if the decedent expressly indicated such a preference; the principle can be invoked, however, to permit a surviving spouse to receive the sperm or embryo even over the objection of the heirs.

174 JEWISH LAW AND THE NEW REPRODUCTIVE TECHNOLOGIES

## NOTES

1. The most comprehensive discussion of these dilemmas from a secular perspective appears in a document entitled *Ethical Considerations of Assisted Reproductive Technologies*, prepared by the American Fertility Society, an organization of physicians who specialize in treating infertility. The document is periodically updated, with the most recent version issued in November 1994. Another important source is a report issued under the auspices of the National Institutes of Health, *Final Report of the Human Embryo Research Panel* (September 22, 1994). A recent book that summarizes basic medical, ethical, and halakhic considerations in fertility treatment is Dr. Richard Grazi (ed.), *Be Fruitful and Multiply* (Genesis Jerusalem Press, 1994).

2. Technically, immediately after fertilization, the fertilized ovum is known as a zygote. The zygote becomes a true preembryo only after cleavage, which occurs shortly after fertilization. The preembryonic stage lasts until implantation into the uterine wall, which commonly takes place within 10–14 days after fertilization. (Obviously, in the case of an IVF frozen embryo, implantation can occur only after transfer to a uterus, which may occur years later.) Upon implantation, the embryonic stage begins. This stage lasts for around eight weeks, by which time there is at least rudimentary development of differentiated organs. After that point, the organism is termed a "fetus." See *Ethical Considerations* (cited in note 1) (Nov. 1994), 29S–31S. This usage is not consistently followed, and the terms "embryo" and "preembryo" are often used interchangeably.

3. The best chance of achieving an IVF pregnancy involves the transfer of 2–4 embryos. Fewer than two greatly reduces the chance of pregnancy. More than four increases the risk of multiple gestation, which may pose dangers to mother and fetus. In order to obtain the optimal number of embryos, eight or more eggs are routinely retrieved, and recovery of more than 20 is increasingly common. See Wood, *et al,* "Factors Influencing Pregnancy Rates Following In-vitro Fertilization and Embryo Transfer," 43 *Journal of Fertility and Sterility* 295 (1985), for some of the recent references pertaining to this subject.

4. Although the relevant literature will be cited extensively in the course of the discussion, it may be useful to mention at the outset some of the recent references pertaining to this subject. The only halakhic responsum that I have seen that directly deals with the question of decisional authority, albeit partially, is an article by Rabbi Shaul Yisraeli (z.t.l.), *"She'eilat haBa'alut al Beitsit Mufarit Lifnei Hashtala beRehem haEim,"* appearing as an appendix to volume 4 of the *Entsyclopedia Hilkhatit Refu'it*, pp. 37–44 (A. Steinberg, ed.).

R. Yisraeli also authored an earlier article discussing paternity in the event of postmortem insemination, "*Avhut beHazra'a she-lo keDarka,*" 33 *Torah sheBe'al Pe,* pp. 41–46 (5752), which is pertinent in cases of the husband's death. See text at notes 41–43. Finally, Dr. Joel B. Wolowelsky was kind enough to make available to me two very interesting letters issued by Machon Eretz Chemdah, an Israeli *kollel* and "think tank" devoted to contemporary Halakha and headed by R. Yisraeli, in response to a number of questions submitted to the Machon by Dr. Wolowelsky concerning frozen sperm and preembryos. The first letter, dated 9 *Tevet* 5754, was written by Rabbis Ehrenreich and Carmel but bears R. Yisraeli's signature of approval. The second letter of 22 *Tevet,* issued as a brief follow-up clarification, was signed by Rabbi Carmel alone. The contents and conclusions of these documents will be discussed at notes 41–43 and 80.

Mention should also be made of a recent decision of the Rabbinical Court of Haifa discussed at note 30.

5. Artificial insemination with husband's sperm (AIH) may be a helpful procedure for men who have low sperm counts, since it allows the combination of several ejaculates and may also be indicated when a woman's fertile period around ovulation precedes the date she can go to the *mikva.* See generally Dr. A. Steinberg, "Artificial Insemination in the Light of *Halakha,*" *Sefer Assia* 128–141 (1982) and Rabbi A. Cohen, "Artificial Insemination," 13 *Journal of Halakha and Contemporary Society* 43 (Spring 1987).

6. The issues raised by AIH included: (1) whether or not the husband has a paternal relationship to the child; (2) whether or not a child conceived through AIH is a fulfillment of the Torah commandment of *peru u-revu* or at least the prophetic edict of *lashevet;* (3) whether the methods that were employed for the procurement of semen violated the edicts against *hashhatat zera* and what alternatives could minimize the prohibition; and (4) fear concerning substitution or mixing with donor semen.

7. See, for example, *Teshuvot Maharsham* III, no. 268; *Minhat Yitzhak* I, no. 51; Rabbi Shlomo Zalman Auerbach, I *Noam* at 157 (5718); *Seridei Eish* III, no. 5; *Tzitz Eliezer* IX, no. 51; *Yabia Omer* II, E.H. no. 1. See also the excellent summary in *Nishmat Avraham E.H.* 1:5. [*Lashevet* is the shorthand expression for the prophetic exhortation, "*Lo tohu bera'a la-shevet yetsara*" ("He did not create the world to be desolate, but rather inhabited"—*Isaiah* 45:18), an exhortation that may be binding even on those not obligated in *peru u-revu, e.g.,* women, and that may be fulfilled even in ways that *peru u-revu* cannot be. See *Tosafot, Hagiga* 2a and *Baba Batra* 13a, s.v. *kofin; Minhat Hinukh,* end of Mitzvah One; and note 16.]

8. See Rabbi Ovadia Yosef, I *Tehumin* at 287; Rabbi Avigdor Neben-

zal, 34 *Assia* (Tishrei 5743); Rabbi Shmuel Wozner, *Shevet haLevi* V, no. 47 (although one may not desecrate Shabbat to save the preembryo because of the low probability of its ever coming to term).

9. *Tzitz Eliezer* XV, no. 45.

10. The prohibition against the wanton destruction of male "seed" is based on *Nida* 13a and is codified in *Shulhan Arukh, Even HaEzer* 23:1. See also *Genesis* 38:7 and Rashi's comments.

11. There is a variation of IVF termed Gamete Inter-Fallopian Transfer (GIFT), where the egg and sperm are mixed together in the petri dish but are then placed in the fallopian tube, where fertilization takes place. It would be interesting to know what Rabbi Waldenberg would rule concerning GIFT, since fertilization does indeed take place *kederekh kol ha-aretz.*

12. Even where the egg donor carries the baby to term and is thus both the genetic and birth mother.

13. *BiShvilei haRefu'a*, no. 8 (*Kislev* 5747), p. 33.

14. *Kol Tzofayikh*, pp. 361–367.

15. Whether AIH or IVF may be undertaken by a couple who already have the minimum son and daughter but desire to have more is a matter of dispute. Compare the views of Rabbi Auerbach (even where he has a son and daughter, a man may be permitted to obtain sperm in order to fulfill the imperative of *lashevet* or where his wife is in significant psychological distress in not having more children) cited in *Nishmat Avraham E.H.* 23:1 (however with the qualifying term *"yitakhen"*—it *may* be possible) with the contrary view of Rabbi Eliyahu Bakshi-Doron, the present Sephardic Chief Rabbi of Israel (then Rav of Haifa), who ruled that the ban on *hashhatat zera* can be lifted only for the Torah commandment of *peru u-revu* and not for the lesser mitzvah of *lashevet*. Letter to Dr. Joel B. Wolowelsky, Dec. 15, 1991. Rabbi Moshe Feinstein also seemingly subscribes to this restrictive view. See *Iggrot Moshe E.H.* IV, no. 73. Note, however, that both Rabbi Feinstein and Rabbi Bakshi-Doron are addressing the use of sperm procurement for *testing*, not actual *procreative* use. The latter may be considerably more lenient. Note, too, that any halakhic distinction between *peru u-revu* or *lashevet* must assume that one fulfills *peru u-revu* through AIH or IVF. This too is a matter of controversy. See next note.

16. It appears to be unresolved whether one can fulfill the Torah command of *peru u-revu* through either AIH or IVF. Rabbi Auerbach in his *Noam* article states that the matter is not clear. The *Arukh leNer* to *Yevamot* 10a explicitly rules that one does not fulfill *peru u-revu* in the absence of a sexual act. On the other hand, Rabbi Bakshi-Doron apparently assumes that *peru u-revu* is fulfilled, since he permits the procedure only to achieve this purpose. See also *Minhat Hinukh*, Mitzvah One, who

notes that the mitzvah of *peru u-revu* is not marital intercourse *per se* but the actual having of children; the act which generates those children is nothing more than a *hekhsher mitzvah* (a necessary preliminary). Under this analysis, it should be a matter of indifference whether children are created through intercourse, AIH, or IVF; *peru u-revu* should be fulfilled irrespective of the method employed.

The foregoing assumes a *paternal* bond. If one adopts the views of Rabbis Waldenberg, Sternbuch, and Gershuni, that sperm contributors do not have paternity in IVF cases, it is clear that there is no mitzvah of *peru u-revu,* though, as noted, Rabbi Gershuni even here would concede the mitzvah of *lashevet.*

17. See Robertson, "Reproductive Technology and Reproductive Rights: In the Beginning—The Legal Status of Early Embryos," 76 *Virginia Law Review* 437 (April 1990) and Eggen, "The Orwellian Nightmare Reconsidered: A Proposed Regulatory Framework for the Advanced Reproductive Technologies," 25 *Georgia Law Review* 625 (1991).

18. I hope to address these halakhic issues in my longer work-in-progress. See footnote on page 1 of this article.

19. See Rabbi Mordechai Eliyahu (the former *Rishon leTziyyon*), "Discarding Fertilized Eggs and Fetal Reduction," 11 *Tehumin* (1991); Rabbi Chaim David HaLevi (Ashkenazic Chief Rabbi of Tel Aviv), "On Fetal Reduction," *Assia* 47–48 (12:3–4) (1990); Rabbi Moshe Sternbuch, *BiShvilei haRefu'a,* no. 8 (Kislev 5747), p. 29. This also appears to be the implicit assumption of Rabbi Shaul Yisraeli in an essay published as an Appendix to *Entsyclopedia Hilkhatit Refu'it,* vol. 4. See text at notes 69–80.

20. Some of these complexities—which may also apply to sperm and egg donations as well as the use of a surrogate—are spelled out in Rabbi J. David Bleich, "In Vitro Fertilization: Questions of Maternal Identity and Conversion," *Tradition* 25(4), Summer 1991, p. 82; Rabbi Ezra Bick, "Ovum Donations: A Rabbinic Conceptual Model of Maternity," *Tradition* 28(1), Fall 1993, p. 28; and Rabbi Bleich's rejoinder at "Maternal Identity Revisited," *Tradition* 28(2), Winter 1994, p. 52. See also Volume 5 of *Tehumin* (5744), which contains major discussions of this issue by Rabbis Zalman Nechemiah Goldberg, Avraham Kilav, and Zerach Warhaftig and *Nishmat Avraham* (App. Vol.) *E.H.* 22:2 at p. 186.

21. Whether or not children born to married women from third party sperm donors were *mamzerim* was the subject of a long-standing debate. Compare, *e.g., Iggrot Moshe E.H.* I, no. 71 (child is not a *mamzer*) with the well-known contrary position of the Satmar Rav in *HaMaor* 15(9):3–13 (1954). A number of *posekim* have stated that a child born from Jewish donor semen is a *safek mamzer.* See Rabbi Auerbach in I *Noam; Tzitz Eliezer* IX, no. 51. See also the extensive review in Rabbi Alfred Cohen's article

cited in note 5. The point here is that whatever problems exist with the use of third party *sperm* should apply equally to the use of third party *embryos*. I will address this point at greater length in my forthcoming work. See footnote on page one of this article.

22. As reported in *HaAretz* (February 14, 1995). Among the necessary conditions: (1) the surrogate be single and not bear a relationship to the sperm contributor that would be halakhically incestuous, *e.g.*, a sister or even a sister-in-law; and (2) records be kept detailing the identities of both the surrogate and the egg donor (the mother who will raise the child) so that the child will not marry relatives of either.

23. See generally *Nishmat Avraham* (App. Vol.) *E.H.* 5(2) who records a number of negative views concerning the use of surrogates.

24. 842 S.W.2d 588 (Tenn. 1992).

25. But *cf. Eruvin* 13b: *noah lo le-adam she-lo nivra yoter mi-she-nivra* ("It is better for a person to have never been created"), and explanation of Maharsha.

26. See *Roe v. Wade*, 410 U.S. 113 (1973) (ruling by Supreme Court that women have an absolute constitutional right to terminate pregnancies before the first trimester). The Tennessee Court understood *Roe* to mean that a person has a constitutional right *not* to be a parent and as such, prospective fathers, as well as mothers, may invoke its protections. There is, however, an alternative understanding of *Roe*. Professor John A. Robertson of the University of Texas Law School, a leading expert in this area, has argued that *Roe* merely protects the bodily integrity of a woman in not being forced to carry an unwanted pregnancy, but does not preclude other state inventions to protect fetal or embryonic life once it is outside of a woman's womb. Robertson, cited in note 17, 453 n.46. The court's ruling that it would effectively be unconstitutional to compel a *father* to be a parent against his will clearly rejects Professor Robertson's reading. Note, however, that *Davis* is only the opinion of a state supreme court and is not binding in other jurisdictions.

27. The concept that the gamete providers have ultimate decisional authority over the disposition of preembryos (whether or not that is a constitutional necessity) has been recognized by other cases as well. See *York v. Jones*, 717 F.Supp. 421 (E.D. Va. 1989).

28. See Robertson article cited in note 17 (approving the "balance of equities" test but noting that where a woman has no alternative opportunities to reproduce, it may be fairer to award preembryos to the party for whom they represent the last chance.). The *Davis* approach is consistent at least in part with the guidelines of the American Fertility Society and the American College of Obstetrics and Gynecology, which validate the use of advance agreements, but do not address the default rules, *i.e.*, what happens when no such agreement was executed.

29. See *Nahmani v. Nahmani*, District Court of Haifa, Case No. 599/ 92 (1992), reversed by High Court of Justice, Case No. 55877/93 (28 Adar II, 5755; March 30, 1995).

30. Significantly, however, the decision of the Haifa District Court was reversed by the Israeli High Court of Justice (its Supreme Court), which cited *Davis* with approval. Similarly, in a parallel action brought by Mr. Nahmani in the rabbinical courts, the *Bet Din* of Haifa ruled that the IVF process should be discontinued, though much of their analysis rested on their condemnation of gestational surrogacy.

31. The following discussion of *Nahmani* is limited to the issue of decisional authority and will not address the use of a "surrogate womb."

32. See note 19.

33. See *Shulhan Arukh, Orah Hayyim* 330:1. Indeed, a woman could not be forced to agree to implantation under secular law either, because of her rights under *Roe v. Wade*. See text at note 26.

34. This type of "embryo donation" does not raise the adultery and *mamzerut* issues that arise when the embryo is donated to a different couple. This too will be addressed in my forthcoming work.

35. It is important not to confuse the point in the text with two other points that were made earlier. First, the majority of *posekim* accord full maternity and paternity rights to parents of IVF-babies once the child is born. See text at note 15–16. Second, where the genetic egg donor is not the same person who carried and delivered the baby, there is halakhic uncertainty as to whom the mother is, though a majority of authorities would regard the birth mother as having maternal status. See articles cited in note 20. The question now being addressed, however, is not who the mother is *when* the child is born, but whether there is any mother or father at all *before* the child is born. Is there a halakhically-cognizable parental bond that exists prior to a child's being born, and which person has it? When does a parent become a parent? As noted in the text, this issue becomes relevant on the issue of decision-making authority only if maternity and paternity have different definitions. To the degree both or neither are parents, such definitions furnish no guidance in cases of deadlock.

36. *Yevamot* 97b. The Gemara states that if a non-Jewish woman converted while pregnant, the children that are born after she became Jewish (*horatam she-lo bi-kdusha ve-leidatam bi-kdusha*) are regarded as half-siblings from the same mother but are not regarded as sharing a common father. As Rashi explains, since the paternal bond is generated at the moment of conception, the conversion of the mother, which constitutes a valid conversion of the children, erases all prior familial relationships based on the principle of *ger she-nit-gayer ke-katan she-nolad dami*, "a convert is a newly-born entity." Once the conversion is effective, how-

ever, a new *maternal* bond is forged by virtue of birth. On its face, this text supports a split definition of parenthood. See also *Megilla* 13a, *Rashi s.v. be-sha'a.*

37. The most that the Gemara establishes is that even if a preexisting bond can be erased by conversion, a new maternal bond can be established by birth. The fact that viable birth is a sufficient condition for maternity does not prove it is a *necessary* one. It is entirely possible that, in the absence of conversion, a full maternal bond can exist even during pregnancy and even with respect to preembryos.

38. See next note.

39. See comments to *Yore De'a* 87. According to the Mishna in *Hullin*, milk that is obtained from an animal after its death is not subject to the prohibition of being consumed with meat. This is based on the fact that the Torah prohibits only the milk of an animal that has the capacity to be an *aim* ("mother"). What about milk that is obtained from a live animal that is a *tereifa*? Rabbi Akiva Eiger tentatively suggests that although a *tereifa* is incapable of giving birth, it is capable of carrying a pregnancy at least through the first trimester, and at that point would indeed be considered an *aim* just as, according to *Sanhedrin* 69a, the father would be deemed an *av*. Thus, R. Akiva Eiger equates "maternity" and "paternity."

[To fully understand the import of his comments, the relevant passage in *Sanhedrin* must be cited. *Sanhedrin* 69a states that a child cannot become a *ben sorer u-more* after the age of 13 years and three months. Since the child is described as a *ben*, this excludes someone who already has the capacity to be an *av*. A boy is generally incapable of impregnating a woman until he reaches the age of majority at 13. If he would impregnate a woman, the fetus would not be discernable until the end of the first trimester. The Talmud therefore concludes that the earliest moment at which a child acquires the capacity to be an *av* is not at the age of 13, when impregnation and conception could take place, but only three months later, when the pregnancy would be physically recognizable. Thus, contrary to the implication of the *sugya* in *Yevamot*, that paternity arises upon conception, *Sanhedrin* 69a delays paternity to a much later stage.

R. Akiva Eiger's use of *Sanhedrin* 69a to establish an identical definition of *maternity* again departs from the implication of the Gemara in *Yevamot*, but in the opposite direction. While *Yevamot* seems to say (but see note 37) that the maternal bond arises no earlier than birth, R. Akiva Eiger understands that it too arises no later (and no earlier) than the end of the first trimester.]

40. See text following note 51 for a fuller discussion.

41. The use of the phrase "based on" is deliberate. Rabbi Yisraeli

himself never explicitly recorded such an opinion, but his views have been so interpreted by the directors of Machon Eretz Chemdah, a *kollel* that was under his leadership. In an article written in 5752, R. Yisraeli concluded that a child conceived from sperm after the death of the sperm donor bore no relationship to the donor and would not be entitled to share in the donor's estate, since conception did not take place in the donor's lifetime. See *Torah sheBa'al Pe*, vol. 33, pp. 41–46 (5752). A follow-up letter signed by Rabbi Carmel, the director of Machon Eretz Chemdah, contained the following language: "The conclusion that there is no relationship between a sperm donor and his sperm once he dies, applies equally to an egg that was fertilized in a test tube during the husband's lifetime." Letter, Machon Eretz Chemdah to Dr. Joel B. Wolowelsky (22 *Tevet* 5754) (my translation). While this subsequent "clarification" was signed only by Rabbi Carmel and not Rabbi Yisraeli, Rabbi Carmel has reported that the clarification was sent with Rabbi Yisraeli's approval and represents his halakhic position as well. Letter, Machon Eretz Chemdah to Dr. Joel B. Wolowelsky (25 *Elul* 5755).

42. Thus, the implication of the law of *demei veladot*, that both father and mother have parental rights prior to birth—at least according to Rambam, who awards mother *demei veladot* if father died—applies only to an embryo or fetus that is carried *in utero* and not to an externalized preembryo. See also note 55–56.

43. The problems are two-fold. First, Rabbi Yisraeli's own conclusion that there is no paternity when conception takes place after the death of the sperm donor is based on a ruling of *Noda biYehuda* I, *E.H.* no. 69, that a child that is born as a result of post-mortem fertilization (*kelitat hazera*) is not considered a child of the decedent and would not exempt its mother from *yibum* or *halitsa*. That very *teshuva* specifically states that in all other respects, including inheritance, incest with relatives *etc.*, a full paternal relationship does exist. As R. Yisraeli noted, he was applying the *Noda biYehuda's pesak* further than the *Noda biYehuda* himself was willing to go. Second, the conclusion of Machon Eretz Chemdah extending this already-extended *pesak* to the preembryo appears incorrect. The absence of paternity in the *Noda biYehuda's* case was based on the lack of *kelitat ha-zera me-hayyim*. *Kelitat ha-zera*, which Hazal say may occur up to 72 hours after intercourse, appears to refer to "fertilization" or "conception," not "implantation," which could occur up to two weeks later. See note 2. In the case of preembryos, there has been a *kelitat ha-zera* and as such, both the *Noda biYehuda* and R. Yisraeli would recognize a parental bond.

In support of the Machon, it might be stated that to the extent the Halakha permits the indiscriminate destruction of preembryonic life, see note 19, that factor alone suggests that it is not a human being susceptible of forming bonds with a "father" or "mother." It is questionable, however, whether the laws governing abortion are directly relevant in determining parentage.

44. The fact that decisional authority over frozen embryos need not be correlated to parental status is further borne out by the rulings of Rabbi Shaul Yisraeli. Although he would deny any paternal status until implantation (according to the understanding of Machon Eretz Chemdah), he was nevertheless willing to give father veto rights based on the law of partnership. See text further at notes 69–80 (Model #5).

45. See Rabbi Shlomo Yosef Zevin, "*Mishpat Shylock leOr haHalakha,*" *LeOr Halakha*, pp. 310–338. [But *cf.* comments of Rabbi Shaul Yisraeli in *HaTorah veHamedina*, Vol. 4–6, p. 106.]

46. See *Shulhan Arukh haRav, H.M., Nizkei haGuf veNefesh* 4.

47. See *Baba Kama* 92a, as explained by the reference in the preceding footnote.

48. See *Baba Kama* 84a: *ben horin mi it lei demei* ("Does a free man have a market value?").

49. Whether a person can "own" human cells has posed problems in American law as well. See, *e.g., Moore v. Regents*, 51 Cal. 3d120, 739 P.2d 479 (Cal. 1990).

50. See *Shakh, H.M.* 73:39 (*dina de-malkhuta dina* legitimates secular governmental regulation only when *Din Torah* furnishes no applicable rule). *Cf.* comments of Hazon Ish, quoted in *Hitorerut*, pp. 41–42 (1988), who denied the possibility of such a lacuna.

51. See *Exodus* 21:22 and text at note 40. This Halakha was previously cited merely to establish the existence of paternal and maternal bonds. I am now suggesting that it can also be utilized to establish a hierarchial priority in decision-making.

52. The *Yerushalmi* is quoted in *Tosafot, s.v. Afilu, B.K.* 43a.

53. See text at note 33.

54. See text at notes 22 and 34.

55. Even if a paternal relationship towards preembryo exists, there are two other reasons why *demei veladot* liability could not be imposed. First, embryos, implanted or not, that are less than 40 days old, have the status of *mayim be-alma*; this alone may preclude any tort liability for their wrongful destruction. Second, the amount awarded as *demei veladot* is calculated not on the basis of damage to the fetus, but on the basis of damage to the woman's person. The perpetrator pays the difference in value between a woman bearing child and a woman without child. See *Rambam, Hilkhot Hovel uMazik* 4:2. While this measure could indeed suggest liability for the destruction of an *implanted* embryo even if it less than 40 days old, it would preclude liability for destruction of an externalized preembryo, since there is no damage to the woman's market

value. See also *Minhat Hinukh,* no. 49 (whether Noahides have *demei veladot* liability) and next note.

56. There are three distinct reasons why paternity, and hence liability for *demei veladot,* may not exist. First, according to Rabbi Waldenberg, there is never a paternal relationship to an IVF-generated offspring even if it is implanted and brought to term. See text at note 9. Second, according to Rabbi Akiva Eiger, one does not acquire the status of *av* until the completion of the first trimester, and the preembryo has not yet reached that state. See text at note 39. Third, according to one understanding of the *Noda biYehuda,* no paternity can exist prior to uterine implantation. See text at note 42–43. (This understanding, however, is probably incorrect).

57. See *Hilkhot Hovel uMazik* 4:1–4 and comment of Ra'avad to *Halakha* 2.

58. See, for example, *Levush Mordekhai B.K.* no. 26 and *Marheshet* II, no. 38(4) for representative explanations of this point.

59. See Appendix to *Entsyclopedia Hilkhatit Refu'it,* vol. 4, pp. 29–35.

60. *Minhat Hinukh,* no. 49.

61. An analogy, albeit one drawn from rabbinic law, is the husband's right for the duration of the marriage to any income generated from property the wife inherited or brought into the marriage (*peirot nikhsei melog*). See *Ketubot* 79a.

62. For the two reasons stated in footnote 55, there would be no *demei veladot* at the preembryo stage.

63. This, of course, assumes the existence of a *maternal* relationship towards the preembryo. As noted before, *Yevamot* 97b is often cited to demonstrate that no maternal relationship exists until birth. See note 36. Such an interpretation, however, appears flatly inconsistent with Rambam's view, which awards *demei veladot* to the mother in the event of the husband's death, an award that is sustainable only if she is in fact the mother. In any case, the Gemara in *Yevamot* may be understood in alternative ways. See note 37.

64. The 5754 letter is cited in footnote 4.

65. See Appendix to *Entsyclopedia Hilkhatit Refu'it,* vol. 4, pp. 37–44.

66. A good survey of these rules appears in Broyde, "Child Custody in Jewish Law: A Pure Law Approach," *Jewish Law Ass'n Studies* VII (1994) and Herring, "Child Custody," II *Jewish Ethics and Halakha for Our Times* 177 (1989).

67. See text at note 36.

68. But see *Eruvin* 13b cited in note 25. *Cf. Sota* 20a (life with prolonged pain preferable to death).

69. This approach is articulated in R. Yisraeli's article, Appendix to *Entsyclopedia Hilkhatit Refu'it,* vol. 4, pp. 37–44.

70. See *Shulhan Arukh Hoshen Mishpat* 176:2.

71. See also *Gittin* 31a and *Shulhan Arukh H.M.* 176:14 (if a partnership was formed for the sale of wine and the established market days arrive, one partner may not stop the other partner from carrying out the purposes of the partnership. The fertilization of an ovum and the woman's readiness to receive it constitute the equivalent of the *yom ha-shuk*—the market days).

72. Note, too, that the inability to withdraw would fall only on the husband; the wife could always refuse to participate on grounds of *sakkana* and indeed, this would probably be the case even if there were an express agreement to the contrary. Moreover, at least in the absence of an express agreement, the woman could at most demand implantation; she could not insist on embryo donation or surrogacy, since those alternatives are beyond the scope of the original undertaking.

73. See, for example, §2–615 of the Uniform Commercial Code applicable to contracts for the sale of goods.

74. *Baba Metzia* 75b–76a.

75. See Farnsworth, *Contracts* (2nd Ed.), pp. 871–875.

76. See *Shulhan Arukh H.M.* 333:5.

77. The distinction between unforeseen circumstances and those that were reasonably foreseeable emerges from *H.M.* 334, particularly paragraphs 1 and 4. If one hired a worker to irrigate a field from a specific water source and that water source unexpectedly dried up in the middle of the day, where the event was equally unforeseeable to both parties, the obligation of the owner to pay is discharged. Although not expressly stipulated, the continued existence of the water supply is taken as an implied condition of the agreement. If, on the other hand, both parties are aware of the risk but elect to contract anyway, the commitment to pay is treated as absolute.

78. See note 21. This is true only if the first husband has paternity over IVF-generated offspring, which is the view of most *posekim* and the assumption of this article. According to Rabbi Waldenberg, who would deny paternity, there could, of course, be no *mamzerut* or adultery. See text at notes 81–92 with respect to problems arising after death.

79. See text at notes 22–23.

80. In the letter of 9 *Tevet* 5754 from Machon Eretz Chemdah cited above at note 4, Rabbi Yisraeli concluded that in the absence of changed circumstances, the husband must allow his wife access not only to the preembryos, but even to his sperm. The result in this letter appears inconsistent with the joint venture approach articulated in his article.

81. See, *e.g.*, Robinson cited above at note 17.

82. See text at note 57 (Rambam's opinion regarding *demei veladot*—if father died before fetus was killed, heirs do not get *demei veladot*). More-

over, even according to Ra'avad, who awards *demei veladot* to the heirs, their inheritance rights in the fetus may be limited to compensation and not extend to any presumptive veto.

83. My hesitancy on this point is based on a concern that it would normally be contrary to Jewish ethical norms to facilitate a woman's bearing children out-of-wedlock. Nevertheless, while this consideration may preclude either sperm or preembryo donations to single women, it should have no application to a widow who desires to carry the preembryo created by her own egg and husband's sperm.

84. See text at notes 21–23. As therein noted, this article does not purport to discuss whether embryo donation is permitted or not. To the extent, however, that embryo donation is prohibited because it constitutes adultery and generates *mamzerut* by causing a Jewish married woman to bear a child from a man other than her husband, this concern applies with equal force to implantation within the womb of the egg donor herself once she marries another man. Whether in fact such donation causes *mamzerut* and if it does, whether this is the case even after the death of the sperm contributor, is discussed in my upcoming work.

85. This of course is itself a major question that needs to be resolved. See note 21 and note 84.

86. Interestingly enough, apart from the partnership concerns elucidated in the text, there appears to be no halakhic impediment to implantation in Wife #2. Because she is married to the father, there is obviously no issue of adultery, *mamzerut*, or unknown paternity. The only halakhic concern would be the need for the child to be aware of his genetic mother for purposes of incest, but since both the father and the birth mother have that information, this problem would be obviated by simply telling the child.

87. See, *e.g. Gittin* 15a; *Baba Batra* 151a.

88. See *Shulhan Arukh H.M.* 252.

89. As noted, for the most part, this may be prohibited anyway, but see note 84 (after husband's death, embryo donation may not raise *mamzerut* problems).

90. This is true notwithstanding Rabbi Yisraeli's ruling that a sperm contributor bears no paternal relation to a child born from postmortem insemination or implantation of an embryo. His wishes must still be respected. While R. Yisraeli does not indicate why, I would suggest that *mitzvah le-kayeim divrei ha-met* may apply.

91. It is clear, for example, that *mitzvah le-kayeim divrei ha-met* binds the escrow agent. See *Rama,* end of *H.M.* 252.

92. This was the situation in the well-known *Rios* case. Dr. and Mrs. Rios, a Los Angeles couple, had three frozen embryos in an IVF clinic in Melbourne, Australia. They both died in a plane crash, leaving an

estate of several million dollars. This case triggered a world-wide discussion regarding the need for advance directives addressing these various contingencies. In May 1985, a California Superior Court found that the embryos were not legal heirs of Dr. Rios' estate, since the sperm was procured from a donor, and in 1987, they were made available for adoption. See New York Times 12/5/89, §L at 35, Col. 1.

93. *Query*: would that mean that the obtaining of sperm was therefore *le-vatala?*

94. See text at notes 21–23.

95. The exception would be Rabbi Yisraeli, who apparently would allow postmortem donation of sperm on the grounds that the donor bears no paternal bond to the resulting offspring but only if the husband so provided in his will or otherwise. See text notes 41–43 and at note 90 and my forthcoming work.